WHO'S WHO of AFRICAN GOLF

Copyright © 2024 by Barry John Cohen

The right of Barry John Cohen to be identified as the Author of the Work has been asserted in accordance with the Copyright Act 98 of 1978.

All rights reserved. No portion of this book may be reproduced, stored in a retrieval system, or transmitted in any form or by any means, electronic, mechanical, photocopying, recording, or otherwise without the prior permission of the copyright owner.

First Edition November 2024 in paperback

Project by New Voices Publishing Services

guiding authors to self-publish

www.newvoices.co.za

ISBN: 978-1-0370-1067-5

WHO'S WHO of AFRICAN GOLF

Barry John Cohen

BOOKS BY THE SAME AUTHOR

"Blazing the Trail" is a captivating sport collector's volume that delves into the rich and inspiring history of black golfers and their significant role in overcoming discrimination in the world of golf. The book chronicles the struggles and triumphs of these trailblazing athletes as they broke down the barriers of apartheid and systemic racism, paving the way for future generations. Through a compelling narrative, it highlights key figures, milestones, and the enduring legacy of black golf, showcasing their courage, resilience, and the profound impact they had on both the sport and society.

"Let Me Play" tells the powerful and inspiring story of Papwa Sewgolum, a self-taught golfer who rose from humble beginnings to challenge the dominance of the golfing elite. Despite the odds, Sewgolum won three Dutch Opens and two Natal Opens, famously defeating Gary Player in the process. However, his remarkable success came at a cost. As a man of Indian descent in apartheid-era South Africa, he was banned from competing in white-only tournaments, and his passport was revoked, cutting short a career that could have soared even higher. Sewgolum's story is one of talent, determination, and the cruel hand of racial injustice.

"Let The Storm Burst" is an exhilarating tale set in 1895, following a group of intrepid trekkers as they journey by wagon through the rugged bushveld, bound for the goldfields. Along the way, they encounter romance, thrilling adventures, and intrigue, with a hidden plot to overthrow the Boer Republic at the heart of the story. Set against the backdrop of South Africa's tumultuous history, this gripping narrative weaves together personal ambition, betrayal, and the clash between settlers and the republic, offering readers a captivating blend of historical drama and human resilience.

"The Boys from Bulawayo" is a gripping legal drama that follows two former Rhodesians who step in to help a desperate mother fleeing with her twins from sexual abuse. For four years, they hide the family, shielding the children from further harm. However, their actions lead to their arrest, and the Australian Federal Police take a hard stance, pushing the legal system to its limits. At the heart of the story is a tense courtroom battle, where a Family Court order collides with the fundamental rights of the children. This compelling narrative challenges notions of justice, morality, and the sacrifices made to protect the vulnerable.

"The Cedric Kushner Story" is an inspiring account of a man who defied the odds to achieve greatness. Arriving in the USA with just $400, Cedric Kushner, a New York Hall of Fame Boxing inductee, shattered conventions by following his passion for promoting musicians, bands, and boxers at the highest levels. Despite facing skepticism from those who judged potential by school reports, Kushner forged his own path, proving that success lies in discovering one's true passion. This biography celebrates his remarkable journey, highlighting the importance of resilience, vision, and the belief that everyone has something they excel at – if only they find it. Cedric was the embodiment of that philosophy.

"Papwa" Against All Odds tells the extraordinary story of Papwa Sewgolum, a self-taught golfing prodigy discovered at the age of 27. Despite his late start, Papwa rose to international fame, winning the Dutch Open three times, placing second in the South African Open, and twice claiming victory at the Natal Open, famously defeating Gary Player. His success made him a symbol of defiance against apartheid, as his achievements highlighted the racial injustices of the time. In response, the South African government banned him from playing in white tournaments and revoked his passport, preventing him from competing abroad. Papwa's journey is a tale of talent, courage, and the crushing weight of systemic oppression.

"Journey of a Muizenberg Boy" is a reflective and deeply personal narrative about discovering one's true passion amid the noise of self-doubt and societal expectations. It chronicles the author's experience of initially ignoring their calling, instead choosing to follow the crowd. Along the way, they had to summon courage, disregard the naysayers, endure painful lessons, and ultimately embrace their authentic self. This is a story of resilience, self-acceptance, and the realization that while not everyone shares your values, it's possible to rise above disappointments and pursue your dreams. It's a powerful reminder that we all have something we're uniquely good at, if only we dare to listen to our inner voice.

"When We Were Champions" is a captivating sport collector's volume that sheds light on the untold stories of black and white golfers across Africa. Spanning from Egypt to South Africa, this collection chronicles their remarkable achievements, contributions, and the impact they had on the sport, often hidden from mainstream recognition. For the first time, their fascinating and diverse journeys are brought to life, documenting their records, struggles, and triumphs in the face of adversity. This volume serves as a tribute to the forgotten champions of African golf, offering a unique perspective on the sport's rich and diverse history.

INTRODUCTION

This book project is an effort to recognise the legacy of African golfers, especially those whose achievements may have been overlooked or undocumented. The intention to include not only South African golfers but also players from lesser-documented regions such as Morocco, Egypt, Sierre Leone, Uganda, Tanganyika, Zambia, Mozambique, Namibia, Kenya, and others is an ambitious and necessary step in balancing the global narrative of golf history.

A few key points worth noting:

1. Historical Coverage: Starting from the late 1880s, with Lt. Gen. Sir Henry D'Oyley Torrens, the Cape Colony Governor-General, as the starting point, and stretching to modern major champions like Immelman, Schwartzel, Oosthuizen, and Buhai, the timeline offers a broad scope that will give readers a sense of the evolution of African golf over more than a century.

2. Diverse Representation: The inclusion of a variety of African nations and regions is vital. Players from countries such as Uganda, Egypt, Morocco, and Sierre Leone, who may be unknown to the vast

majority of readers, add depth and dimension to the project. By showcasing these golfers, the book aims to bridges the gap between local accomplishments and global recognition.

3. Tiered Tours: Highlighting the existence of tiered tours such as the Safari Tour, MENA Tour, Zimbabwe Winter Tour, and the Sunshine Tour, especially in the context of past racial discrimination and the former TPA Tour, adds an important socio-political element to the narrative.

4. Focus on Major Championships: The emphasis on success in the four majors – the Masters, U.S. Open, The Open Championship, and the PGA Championship – as well as the LPGA Majors and key amateur events, acknowledges the global stage on which the best African players have proven themselves. The decision to weigh performance in these championships over regional or lesser-known victories ensures a balanced evaluation of careers.

5. Recognition of Women and Black Golfers: Compiling a list of the top 20 men golfers, the top 10 women golfers and top 10 Black golfers across Africa is unique. It acknowledges not only gender but racial representation in a sport that historically has been exclusive. By including these categories, the aim is for the book to offer a comprehensive look at African golf's diversity.

This book serves as both a history lesson and a source of inspiration, bringing to light stories of perseverance, skill, and success from a continent with a deep, yet often under-acknowledged, connection to the sport of golf. It will likely become a valuable resource for future generations of golfers and historians alike.

CONTENTS

A

Abery, Warren	15
Ackerman, Raymond	15
Adamson, Mandy	17
Ahlers, Jaco	18
Angel, Judy	18
Aitken, Thomas	19
Alexander, Casandra	19
Allem, Fulton	20
Amm, Cedric	21

B

Baiocchi, Hugh	21
Baker, Robert South Africa	22
Baker, Vin	22
Basson, Christiaan	23
Bekker, Oliver	23
Bezuidenhout, Christiaan	24
Bland, John	25
Blumberg, George	26
Blumberg, Isabel (Kay)	27
Bodmer, Maurice	27
Boodhun, Ramnath 'Bambata'	28
Bossert, Andre	29
Boshoff, Attie	29
Botes, Desvonde	30
Bothma, Michiel	30
Boyd, Jimmy	30
Bregman, Stacy	31
Bremner, Merrick	31
Brews, Harry	32
Brews, George 'Jock'	32
Brews, Sid	33
Bright, Ruby (Armstrong)	34
Brinton, May	35
Britz, Tienie	35
Bruce, Jenny	35
Bruiners, Heinrich	36
Bruyns, Dennis	36
Buhai, Ashleigh (Simon)	37
Buhrmann, Hendrik	38
Burd, Jeanette (Wahl)	39
Burmester, Dean	40

C

Cayeux, Marc	41
Charamba, Tongoona 'TC'	42
Chen, Connie	42
Chitengwa, Lewis	44
Chowglay, Ismail "Boy"	45
Clark, Tim "Penguin"	47
Clarke, Neville	48
Clemence, Mary	48
Coetzee, George	49
Cohen, Barry	50
Cole, Bobby "King"	51
Coleman, George	52

Collis, Helen	53
Conyers-Kirby, H (Walter) 'Mussolini'	54

D

Da Silva, Adilson Jose	56
De Jager, Louis	57
De Jonge, Brendon	57
Dias, Mrs Mc Prata	59
Dickson, Vernon	59
Ditsebe, Ronald	60
Dlamini, Joe 'Mkhulu'	60
Dlamini, Nobuhle	61
Dodds, Trevor	62
Downs, Madge	63
Drysdale, John	64
Dunne, Phil,	65
Du Plessis, Hennie	65
Du Toit, Comrie	66

E

Easton, Bryce	67
Easton, Rita (Levetan)	68
Elkin, Bert H.	69
Elkin, Major Ken	70
Els, Theodore Ernest 'Ernie'	70

F

Fall, R.G.	73
Ferris, Mrs E Grindley	73
Fichardt, Darren	74
Finlayson, Ken	75
Fisher Jnr, Trevor	75
Follet-Smith, Benjamin	76
Fotheringham, George Lyall	76
Fourie, John	77
Franklin, Barry	78
Friedlander, Paul	79
Frittelli, Dylan	79
Frost, David Laurence	80

G

Gaille, Esther	82
Gammon, Muss	82
Garcia, Nicole	83
Geddes, Doug	84
Gibb, Maud (Titterton)	84
Glennie, Ronnie	86
Godbold, A.B.	86
Goosen, Retief	87
Gordon-Stewart, H.	89
Gough, Jamie	90
Govender, Henry	91
Grace, Branden John	92
Gray, Alan	93
Green, Reggie	94
Grimsdell, Robert 'Bob'	94
Groenewald, Vaughn	95
Guthrie, Sandy	95

H

Haig, Anton	96
Harding, Justin	96
Harvey, George	97
Hassanein, Hassan	98
Hast, Rae	99
Hawkes, Jeff	100

Hayes, Dale	100
Hayes, John	102
Hayes, Otway	102
Henning, Allan "Doc"	103
Henning, Brian "Bruno"	104
Henning, Graham	105
Henning, Harold "The Horse"	106
Henning, Nick	108
Hess, Rodney	108
Higginson, John	109
Higgo, Garrick	110
Hlapo, Simon 'Cox'	110
Hobday, Justin	112
Hobday, Simon	112
Hockey, Angela (Burwell)	113
Holland, Val	114
Horak, Vivian	115
Horne, Keith	116
Hooper, R.W.	116
Hugo, Jean	117
Hutchings, Ian	117
Hutchinson, Denis	118

I

Immelman, Mark	119
Immelman, Trevor	120
Inggs, Hugh	121
Ingram, Colin Wray	121

J

James, Derek	122
Jangle, Fred	122
Janks, Mickey	123
Jephcott, Edith	123
Johnson-Sedibe, Edward	124
Johnstone, Tony	125
Jonas, Philip	127
Jooste, Mrs K	128

K

Kamte, James	129
Kaplan, Richard	130
Karmis, Peter	131
Keartland, Basil	131
Kemp, Derek	132
Keyter, Bruce	132
Kingsley, C.W.M.	133
Kingston, James	134
Kruyswijk, Jacques	135
Kruger, James Barry 'JBE'	135

L

Lassen, Werner	136
Lawrence, Thriston	137
Leadbetter, David	137
Lebbie, James	139
Leeds, Mrs	140
Leemhuis, Michael	140
Leen, Mauritz	141
Le Grange, Cobie	142
Le Roux, Jannie	143
Levenson, Gavan "Sticks"	144
Lewthwaite, Lejan	145
Liddle, Brett	145
Lincoln, Bobby	146
Little, Sally "Sunday Sal"	146

Locke, Arthur D'arcy "Bobby" 148
Lombard, Zander 151
Louw, Peter 152
Lowry, Mrs (Owen) 153

M
Manie, William 154
Manyama, Theophilus 'Theo' 155
Maqubela, Alfred 156
Marjane, Ahmed 157
Maritz, Laurette 'Lolly' 158
Marshall, Robbie 160
Mashego, Mokgeteng John 160
Matkovich, Peter 161
Mcguigan, Doug 163
Mclardy, Andrew 163
Mcnulty, Mark 'Sparkles' 164
Mercer, Jacquie (Smith) 165
Midgley, Cecil 167
Mogoerane, Richard 'Boikie' 168
Moore, Eric 169
Moore, Tich 169
Moses, Leticia & Amelia 171
Motati, David 172
Muller, Grant 174
Mulroy, Garth David 174
Muridzo-Chitengwa, Lewis 175
Muridzo, Rhodah 177
Murray, Dr C.M. 177
Muthiya, Madalitso 178

N
Naidoo, "Star" 179

Nelson, Louis 180
Norris, Shaun 181

O
Olander, Clarence 183
Okello, Jacob 184
Onita, Sadi 185
Oosthuizen, Andries 186
Oosthuizen, Louis 188

P
Pace, Lee-Anne 189
Pappas, Brendan 191
Pappas, Dean 191
Pappas, Sean 192
Parham, Fiona (Waters) 192
Peltz, Betty (Bentel) 193
Player, Gary James 193
Porteus, Haydn 198
Prentice, Jimmy 198
Price, Nick 200
Proudfoot, Doug 201

R
Reto, Paula 203
Rice, Andrew 204
Ritchie, Juan Carlo 'J.C.' 205
Ritson, Phillip 205
Roestoff, Ashley Trevor 207
Rolfe, A 207
Roos, Jake 207
Rowe, Lyle 208
Rupert, Johann 208

S

Sabbatini, Rory	209
Sauerman, Peter	210
Schieteket, Neil	211
Schutte, Warren	211
Schwartzel, Charl	212
Sewgolum, Sewsunker 'Papwa'	213
Shean, Kelli 'Kellogs'	215
Sheard, Alison	215
Smit, Monique	217
Sole, Mel	218
Solomon, Harry	219
Stent, William C.	219
Sterne, Richard	220
Stewart, Arthur	222
Stone, Brandon	223
Strydom, Ockert 'Ockie'	224
Suddards, David	224
Suddards, Kevin	225
Sundelson, Neville "Rock"	226
Swanepoel, Chris	227
Swartz, S	227
Symons, Dave	228

T

Tait, Lt. Freddie Guthrie	229
Taylor, Reg	230
Tebbutt, Gillian (Whitfield)	230
Terblanche, Des South Africa	231
Thomas, Frank	231
Tindall, Jean South Africa	233
Tomlinson, Gaby	233
Torrens, Lt. General Sir Henry D'Oyley	234
Treloar, Ken	235
Tshabalala, Vincent	237
Turner, Brian	238

V

Van Aswegen, Tyrone	239
Van Den Berg, Ulrich	240
Van Der Walt, Tjaart	240
Van Rensburg, Nico	241
Van Rooyen, Erik	242
Van Tonder, Daniel	243
Van Vuuren, Steve	244
Van Zyl, Jaco	245
Vaughan, Bradford	246
Vernon, Mrs A.E. (Ormsby)	246
Verwey, Bobby	247
Verwey, Jock	249
Vincent, Kieran	249
Vincent, Scott Nicholas	249
Vincent, Dr Vane	250
Von Ruben, Tandi (Mccullum)	251

W

Walker, Arthur "King"	251
Waltman, Retief	252
Warrington, Wendy	253
Watermeyer, Christian	254
Watermeyer, H.E. Jack	255
Waters, Laurie	255
Watson, Denis	256
Webber, Teddy	258

Wessels, Roger Mark	260	Africa's Greatest Golfers	281
Westbrook, Terry	260	Africa's Greatest Women Golfers	282
Westner, Wayne	261	Africa's Greatest 'Black' Golfers	282
Wharton-Hood, Dorian	262	African World Rankings	283
Wiltshire, Mark	263	African Major Winners	283
White, Bob	265	Africa Senior Major Winners	284
Whitelaw, Clinton John	265		
Wilkes, Brian	265		
Wilkes, Trevor	266		
Williams, Anne	267		
Williams, Bob	268		
Williams, Chris	269		
Wulff, Graham	270		
Wynne, Bernard	272		

Z

Zerman, Manny 272

Young guns to watch ....

Jarvis, Casey	273
Lamprecht, Christo	274
Nienaber, Wilco	276
Jovan Rebula	276
Potgieter, Aldrich	277
Van Velzen, Ryan	278
Williams, Robin	278

AFRICA'S GREATEST GOLFERS

A

ABERY, WARREN (1977) SOUTH AFRICA

Warren Abery had a distinguished career in professional golf following his win at the South African Amateur Championship in 1995. After turning professional in 1997, Abery made a significant impact on the Sunshine Tour, achieving eight victories and finishing as a runner-up in three tournaments after playoff losses. His notable wins include the 2005 Telkom PGA Championship and two Nashua Masters titles in 2006 and 2010.

ACKERMAN, RAYMOND (1931–2023) SOUTH AFRICA

2015 Raymond Ackerman, Pat van Heerden, President FW de Klerk, Barry Cohen

Raymond Ackerman's impact on golf and his role in dismantling racial barriers in South Africa are both significant and inspiring. He inherited Clovelly Country Club, which had a constitution prohibiting discrimination based on race, religion, or creed. Despite this, apartheid policies effectively barred people of color from joining or playing at the club.

In January 1976, Ackerman proposed to open Clovelly to all races during apartheid. Prime Minister B.J. Vorster agreed to this plan, contingent on 87% of the members consenting. In a remarkable turn of events, 94% of the members approved the proposal, making Clovelly the first golf club in apartheid South Africa to welcome members of all races. This groundbreaking decision set a significant precedent, prompting F.W. de Klerk, the new Minister of Sport and future Prime Minister who would later release Nelson Mandela, to permit all sports clubs to determine their own membership policies. By 1977, this led to the inclusion of all races in sports clubs across the country.

In addition to his work at Clovelly, Ackerman founded the Raymond Ackerman Golf Academy to support disadvantaged children from impoverished communities. The academy focuses on providing assistance with schoolwork, life skills, and golf training, while also supporting students in their pursuit of further education. In recognition of his selfless contributions to the advancement of golf and his dedication to promoting inclusivity, Ackerman received the Harry Brews Award from the Southern Africa Golf Hall of Fame in 2014.

Ackerman's legacy stands as a testament to his commitment to equality and his passion for enhancing the lives of young people through the sport of golf.

ADAMSON, MANDY (1972–2022) SOUTH AFRICA

Mandy Adamson's golf career is distinguished by a blend of notable amateur achievements and a successful professional trajectory. As an amateur, she made a significant impact by winning the South African Amateur Championships three times and reaching the semi-finals of the British Ladies Amateur in 1994. Additionally, she represented South Africa twice in the Espirito Santo Trophy, showcasing her talent on an international stage.

Turning professional, Adamson competed on the Ladies European Tour from 1994 to 2004, where she established herself as a formidable player. Her accomplishments on the tour include winning the South African Women's Open three times and securing victories in the South African Women's Masters twice. Her exceptional performance in 2002 earned her the Order of Merit title, highlighting her dominance in the sport during that period.

After retiring from competitive golf, Adamson transitioned into coaching, where she has earned respect for her contributions to the development of the game. Her career reflects a significant impact on both amateur and professional golf, as well as a dedication to fostering future talent in the sport.

AHLERS, JACO (1982) SOUTH AFRICA

Jaco Ahlers has built a noteworthy career primarily on the Sunshine Tour, where he has amassed a total of 13 tournament victories. His key wins include the Vodacom Business Origins of Golf Tour at Erinvale in 2009, the Lion of Africa Cape Town Open in 2014, and the Investec Cup in 2015. In 2016, Ahlers showcased his resilience by winning the KCM Zambia Open, the Sun Wild Coast Sun Challenge, and the Vodacom Origins of Golf at Euphoria, all in sudden-death playoffs. Other significant victories include the Dimension Data Pro-Am in 2018, the King's Cup and Vodacom Origins at Selborne in 2019, and the Players Championship in 2022. His most recent achievement came in 2023 with a win at the Tour Championship.

In addition to his Sunshine Tour successes, Ahlers has made a mark on the Asian Tour with a victory at the Taiwan Masters and has had two runner-up finishes in playoff events. His career reflects a consistent high-level performance on the Sunshine Tour and a competitive presence internationally, underscoring his skill and determination in the sport.

ANGEL, JUDY (1945–2016) SOUTH AFRICA

Judy Angel's remarkable golf career is distinguished by her achievements both in South Africa and internationally. As an amateur, she proudly represented South Africa as a Springbok in 1966, 1969, 1971, and 1973. She also competed in the British Team Trophy in 1970 and contributed to South Africa's third-place finish in the prestigious World Women's Team Championship. Angel's amateur career was filled with notable victories, including winning the South African Ladies Championships in 1966 and 1972. She also captured the South African Stroke Play Championship in 1972, having finished as runner-up in both 1969 and 1971, and became a three-time champion of the South African Women's Open Championships.

After immigrating to the United States in 1980, Angel joined the LPGA Tour, where she continued her winning ways, accumulating over 32 titles throughout her career, both as an amateur and professional. Her contributions to the game extended beyond her playing days, as she became a beloved figure in the golf world for her role in advancing the sport, particularly as a coach.

In 2017, Judy Angel's contributions and legacy were honored with a special award from the Southern Africa Golf Hall of Fame. Her impressive competitive record and lasting impact on the game solidify her place as one of South Africa's most celebrated golfers.

AITKEN, THOMAS (1983) SOUTH AFRICA

Thomas Aiken's golf career is marked by numerous achievements both as an amateur and a professional. He first made his mark in 2001 when he was named South African Amateur of the Year, showcasing his potential early on. Turning professional in 2004, Aiken quickly found success on the Sunshine Tour's Winter Swing, winning three times in his early years. His dominance on the tour continued, and in 2005, he topped the Winter Swing money list with two additional victories. His success culminated in 2013 when he topped the Sunshine Tour Order of Merit.

On the European Tour, Aiken also made a name for himself. In 2011, he won the prestigious Open de España, and two years later, he secured victory at the Avantha Masters in 2013. Throughout his career, Aiken amassed 11 professional titles and reached his highest world ranking of 73. His skill and consistency across different tours solidify his reputation as a talented and accomplished golfer.

ALEXANDER, CASANDRA (HALL) (1999) SOUTH AFRICA

Casandra Alexander has made a significant impact in the world of golf with notable achievements both as an amateur and professional. In 2018, she gained attention by winning the South African Stroke Play Championship, marking the beginning of her ascent in the sport. As a professional, Alexander's success continued with a victory in the Ladies Event at the Investec Royal Swazi Open in 2020, followed by a win at the Joburg Ladies Open in 2021. She also triumphed in the 2020 Saudi

Ladies Team International, teaming up with Emily Kristine Pedersen and Michele Thomson to secure the title.

In 2021, she capped off an impressive season by finishing second in the Order of Merit, further solidifying her reputation as a rising star on the Ladies European Tour. With a total of five titles to her name, Casandra Alexander has established herself as a formidable player, achieving success both individually and in team events.

ALLEM, FULTON (1957) SOUTH AFRICA, USA

Fulton Peter Allem's illustrious golf career is highlighted by 19 professional victories and notable achievements across multiple tours. His rise to prominence began on the Sunshine Tour, where between 1985 and 1991, he collected a series of significant titles. Among his early wins were the Million Dollar Challenge in 1985 and 1988, the Minolta Match Play Championship in 1986 and 1989, and three SA PGA Championships in 1986, 1987, and 1990. Allem also came close to victory in the SA Open, winning it in 1984 and finishing second in 1987. His consistency earned him second place in the South African Order of Merit in both 1986 and 1987, and he represented his country in the 1984 Presidents Cup.

Allem's success on the Sunshine Tour paved the way for his entry onto the PGA Tour. In 1987, he finished second at the NEC World Series of Golf, which led to him joining the tour. His first PGA Tour victory came in 1991 at the Independent Insurance Agent Open. He followed this up with a stellar 1993 season, securing two more victories at the Southwestern Bell Colonial and the NEC World Series of Golf, finishing ninth on the money list that year.

In the later stages of his career, Allem transitioned to the Champions Tour, where he remained competitive, recording three runner-up finishes between 2008 and 2009 in his first two full seasons. Allem's career is a testament to his enduring talent, with success spanning multiple tours and decades.

AMM, CEDRIC (1940) SOUTH AFRICA

Cedric Amm's golf career is characterized by early success and strong performances that earned him recognition from some of the sport's leading figures, including Gary Player. In 1964, Amm claimed his first major victory by winning the Natal Open, a triumph that set the stage for an impressive run of achievements. The following year, in 1965, he finished second in the South African Masters and secured a win at the Flame Lily Tournament in Rhodesia. His international success was highlighted by a runner-up finish at the Caltex Tournament in New Zealand and the Forest Products Tournament, as well as a third-place finish at the New Zealand Wills Masters.

Amm's career reached its pinnacle in 1966 when he won the South African Masters and earned the honor of representing the Rest of the World in a team event against the British Isles and Commonwealth. Despite his promising start, Amm's career began to decline in the late 1960s, ultimately leading to his retirement from professional golf. His legacy is defined by his early triumphs, strong showings in international tournaments, and the respect he garnered from the golfing community.

B

BAIOCCHI, HUGH (1947) SOUTH AFRICA

Hugh John Baiocchi's illustrious golf career has earned him a well-deserved induction into the Southern Africa Golf Hall of Fame. As an amateur, Baiocchi quickly made his mark by winning the Brazilian Amateur Championship in 1968 and the South African Amateur Championship in 1970. He also secured the Hurberto Almeido Trophy that same year and represented South Africa as a Springbok player, with seven caps, including appearances in the prestigious Eisenhower Trophy in 1968 and 1970.

Turning professional, Baiocchi found success on the European Tour, where he won six titles and consistently performed at a high level, finishing in the top ten of the Order of Merit on several occasions. He placed 3rd in 1973, 6th in 1975, and 2nd in 1977, solidifying his reputation as a world-class competitor. On the Southern Africa Tour, he collected 11 victories, including notable wins such as the 1978 South African Open, where he narrowly defeated Gavan Levenson, and the 1980 PGA Championship, where he edged out Mark McNulty and Gary Player. He topped the Order of Merit in 1978/79 and was a runner-up five times throughout his career.

Baiocchi's international success included victories at the Swiss Open in 1973 and 1979, as well as the Dutch Open in 1975. He also represented South Africa and the Rest of the World in various team competitions, including the Double Diamond International and the World Cup, contributing to his team's Datsun International win in 1976.

In his senior career on the Champions Tour, Baiocchi won three times and finished runner-up twice, narrowly missing out to Bruce Crampton and Bruce Summerhays. Beyond playing, Baiocchi has also made his mark in golf course design, most notably with the Legend Course at Constance Belle Mare Plage Resort, leaving a lasting legacy in the world of golf.

BAKER, ROBERT SOUTH AFRICA

Robert Baker is a highly respected golf coach based in the USA, known for working with some of the world's top players. He has served as a coach or consultant to several number-one world-ranked golfers, including Ernie Els, Greg Norman, Seve Ballesteros, Nick Price, and Nick Faldo.

BAKER, VIN (DIED 1990) SOUTH AFRICA

Vincent E. R. Baker's golf career was marked by significant achievements, particularly on the European and South African Tours. One of his most memorable victories came in 1973 when he won the Benson & Hedges Festival of Golf with a stunning final-round 64, securing a two-stroke win over Dale Hayes. That same year, Baker showcased his competitive edge with a runner-up finish at the Scandinavian Enterprise Open, followed by another in 1978 at the Italian Open.

On the South African Tour, Baker's most notable win came in 1974 at the ICL Transvaal Open, where he triumphed in a sudden-death playoff against Andries Oosthuizen. He also had a string of runner-up finishes, including the 1973 South African Open and South African PGA Championship, and the 1975 South African Masters.

Baker represented the Rest of the World in the 1972 Double Diamond International, further highlighting his standing in international golf. Tragically, his life was cut short in July 1990 when he was stabbed to death during a carjacking incident near Durban, a devastating end to a career filled with promise and achievement.

BASSON, CHRISTIAAN (1982) SOUTH AFRICA

Christiaan Basson represented South Africa as an amateur in the 2006 Eisenhower Trophy. He turned professional in 2007 and joined the Sunshine Tour, where he secured his first victory at the Coca-Cola Charity Championship in 2009. Basson claimed his second win at the Investec Royal Swazi Open in 2012. To date, he has won a total of 4 professional tournaments.

BEKKER, OLIVER (1984) SOUTH AFRICA

Oliver Bekker has also carved out an impressive career, with nine professional wins to his name, including eight on the Sunshine Tour. In recognition of his exceptional performances, Bekker was named the Sunshine Tour Players' Player of the Year for the 2017-18 season. His strong play continued into 2021, where he finished as runner-up in the South African Open Championship in December. By May 2022, Bekker had broken into the top 100 of the Official World Golf Ranking, further solidifying his reputation on the global stage. In June 2022, he competed in the inaugural LIV Golf Invitational Series event, showcasing his adaptability to new formats and tours.

BEZUIDENHOUT, CHRISTIAAN (1994) SOUTH AFRICA

Christiaan Bezuidenhout is a prominent South African professional golfer, celebrated for his resilience and skill, as well as his three European Tour victories. Born on May 18, 1994, Bezuidenhout overcame personal challenges, including anxiety and a stutter caused by accidental poisoning as a child, which led to a suspension in 2014 after testing positive for beta blockers. However, his passion for the sport remained unwavering, and he turned professional in 2015. quickly finding success on the Big Easy Tour and securing his Sunshine Tour card by winning the Q School. He finished runner-up in the 2016 BMW SA Open, co-sanctioned by the European Tour. In 2016 and 2017, he claimed wins on the Sunshine Tour and was named the 2016–17 Sunshine Tour Rookie of the Year.

In 2019, Bezuidenhout broke through with his first European Tour win at the Estrella Damm N.A. Andalucía Masters, propelling him into the world top 100 and securing a place in The Open Championship. He also posted notable performances, including third place in the BMW PGA Championship.

In 2020, he added two more European Tour victories, winning the Alfred Dunhill Championship and the South African Open in consecutive weeks. These wins elevated his status in the golfing world, and he continued to contend in high-profile events, including a runner-up finish at the 2022 John Deere Classic and a tie for second at the 2024 American Express.

Bezuidenhout has also represented the International team at the 2022 and 2024 Presidents Cup. His calm demeanor under pressure and consistent performance have made him one of South Africa's most successful golfers on the international stage. In 2021, he reached a career world ranking high of 33.

BLAND, JOHN (1945–2023) SOUTH AFRICA

John Louis Bland became a prominent figure in golf, known for his consistent performances and remarkable achievements. After turning professional in 1969, Bland quickly made his mark by winning the Transvaal Open in 1970, the first of many triumphs in a career that spanned decades. His ability to thrive under pressure was one of his defining qualities, with 1977 standing out as a particularly notable year. During this time, Bland won the South African PGA Championship, defeating the legendary Gary Player, while also claiming victories at the Victoria Falls Classic and the Champion of Champions tournament. These wins further established his reputation as one of South Africa's most formidable golfers.

The 1980s were another period of dominance for Bland, particularly on the Sunshine Tour and the European Tour. One of his most memorable moments came in 1983, when he edged out Bernhard Langer by one stroke to win the Benson & Hedges International Open, solidifying his place among the top competitors in the world. Bland continued his European success in 1986, where he defeated Seve Ballesteros by four strokes to win the Suze Open, showcasing his ability to compete against some of the game's biggest names.

On the Sunshine Tour, Bland was a consistent force, winning the Order of Merit in 1978, 1988, 1990, and 1991. He was also named South Africa's Player of the Year in 1981, a recognition of his sustained excellence over the years. Among his many accolades, Bland recorded a historic round of 59 at the ERPM Golf Club in 1977, a score that remains one of the highlights of his illustrious career. Representing South Africa in the World Cup in 1977, Bland was a frequent competitor in international events, bringing his talents to the global stage.

Bland's European Tour record was equally impressive, finishing in the top 20 on the Order of Merit six times. His travels took him around the world, where he amassed a total of 36 professional titles, a testament to his enduring talent. After turning 50 in 1995, Bland transitioned to the Senior PGA Tour in the United States, where he continued to find success. His standout season came in 1996, when he won four tournaments, including the Bruno's Memorial Classic and the Transamerica, finishing third on the money list. His senior career also extended to the European Senior Tour, where he added three more victories, including a win at the Bad Ragaz PGA Seniors Open in 2009.

Throughout his career, John Bland competed against some of the greatest golfers in history, from Gary Player to Seve Ballesteros and Nick Price. His calm demeanor, resilience, and competitive spirit earned him respect on every tour he played. Bland's legacy is not only defined by his impressive victories but also by his sportsmanship, as he left a lasting impact on the world of golf.

BLUMBERG, GEORGE SOUTH AFRICA

George Blumberg played a critical role in the development of professional golf, both locally and internationally.

In the early days of professional golf, both locally and internationally, it was exceptionally challenging for young talent to establish themselves. Golf was not yet the glamorous TV spectacle it is today, and the support of someone like George Blumberg was crucial for rising stars in the local scene. Blumberg's backing was instrumental for players such as Gary Player, Sally Little, and Bobby Cole, among others, who would have struggled to afford international competition without his assistance. Blumberg's contribution went beyond mere financial support; he offered invaluable life lessons and became a mentor to many. He and his wife, Brenda, served as 'on tour' parents, providing guidance and support to young players.

George was a familiar figure on the golf course, often seen with his shooting stick behind the green, signaling that one of his protégés was making progress. His influence extended beyond South Africa, as many players were able to showcase their skills on European and other international tours thanks to his support. George Blumberg also played a pivotal role in the formation of IMG, convincing Mark McCormack to establish the agency. Additionally, he served as an Executive Member of the South African PGA from 1978 to 1979 and was the Honourary President of the South African PGA from 1979.

Blumberg's contributions were instrumental in shaping the careers of many golfers and advancing the sport's development globally.

BLUMBERG, ISABEL (KAY) UNION SOUTH AFRICA

A dominant ladies' champion in the late 1950s, she won the South African Ladies Amateur Championship twice, in 1956 and 1957, and represented South Africa as a Springbok in 1957. Her other notable victories include the Transvaal Ladies Amateur in 1955 and 1957, the Natal Ladies Amateur in 1955, the British Team Trophy in 1959, and the Israel Ladies Amateur in 1966. She also achieved second place in the Australian Ladies Amateur and the NSW Ladies Championship, both in 1966, and in the Sydney Ladies Championship in 1969.

BODMER, MAURICE UNION SOUTH AFRICA

Maurice Bodmer was a prominent figure in South African golf, serving as the professional at Clovelly Country Club for an impressive 45 years, from 1935 to 1980. His golfing career was marked by his rivalry and partnership with the legendary Bobby Locke. As an amateur, Bodmer came close to glory in 1937 when he finished as the runner-up to Locke in the South African Open. A year earlier, he also finished second in the

South African Amateur, losing to Clarence Olander. Despite these near-misses, Bodmer's talent was evident, and his connection to Locke would later define parts of his life.

Bodmer and Locke formed a formidable partnership, even teaming up for an exhibition match at Clovelly. Together, they faced two golfing giants, Sam Snead and Norman von Nida, and secured an impressive victory, winning 2 & 1. Bodmer's personal and professional life, however, was touched by tragedy. His brother, also a well-known golfer, was killed in World War II, leaving a deep mark on Bodmer's life.

In 1960, a tragic and controversial event occurred that would test Bodmer's loyalty to his old friend, Bobby Locke. After a party in Fish Hoek, Locke, under the influence of alcohol, was involved in a serious car accident. As he waited at a railway crossing, Locke misjudged the situation and pulled out in front of an oncoming train. The crash left him with severe injuries, including the virtual loss of sight in one eye. To protect Locke's reputation, a story was concocted that placed Bodmer behind the wheel during the accident. Though this fabrication saved Locke from public scandal, it added a bittersweet chapter to the story of their friendship.

Bodmer's life in golf was a mix of triumphs, tragedies, and unspoken sacrifices, forever tied to his love for the game and his loyalty to those around him.

BOODHUN, RAMNATH 'BAMBATA' (DIED 1934) UNION SOUTH AFRICA – DISCRIMINATED

Ramnath 'Bambata' Boodhun contributions and legacy cannot be understated. He was known as the "father of South African Black golf", a pioneer. He worked under George Fotheringham, a former SA Open champion at the Durban Country Club, and became an accomplished club-maker over 20 years learning to make and repair clubs.

Insofar as his golfing Skills he was known for exceptional shot-making, particularly with mashie and putting, and impressive driving distance despite his light weight of just over 45 kg. In 1929 he became the champion Indian golfer from Natal and the first black golfer to compete in the British Open in Scotland.

As a founding member, he helped establish the Durban Indian Club, the first black golf club in South Africa, alongside his brother, R.L. Boodhun, who served as secretary, and served as a committee member.

Despite racial barriers and colonial South Africa's restrictions on participation in white Open tournaments, Boodhun's pioneering efforts raised awareness of black golfing talent. His contributions inspired the creation of several golf clubs across South Africa, and in 1935, he was honoured with the annual "Bambata Cup" trophy for caddies by the Royal Durban Golf Club. His pioneering efforts in golf under apartheid-era restrictions and his contributions to the development of golf for black South Africans are highly regarded.

BOSSERT, ANDRE (1963) SOUTH AFRICA, SWITZERLAND

André Robert Bossert, originally from Johannesburg, is a Swiss professional golfer with a distinguished career that includes ten wins. His notable achievements feature a victory at the 1995 Air France Cannes Open. Bossert has also made his mark on the Challenge Tour with wins at the 1990 Neuchâtel Open and the 1992 Kenya Open, while he has secured a title on the European Senior Tour.

As an amateur, Bossert represented Switzerland in prestigious events such as the 1988 Eisenhower Trophy and the World Cup from 1990 to 1996 and 2002. He also participated in the 1991 Dunhill Cup.

BOSHOFF, ATTIE RHODESIA, FEDERATION

Attie Boshoff was a highly successful amateur golfer whose career spanned multiple decades, leaving a lasting mark on the sport through his numerous victories. His triumphs began as early as 1944 when he won the Matabeleland Amateur, a title he would claim three more times in 1952, 1955, and 1960. Boshoff's dominance continued throughout the

1950s, with victories at the Central African Amateur in 1950 and 1956, and at the Rhodesia Amateur in 1950 and 1957. He was also a consistent contender in this event, finishing second in 1953, 1959, and 1962.

In addition to these achievements, Boshoff showcased his skill by winning the Federation Amateur in 1949 and the Mashonaland Amateur in 1946. His strong performance in the Mashonaland Open was particularly notable, where he secured victories four times between 1952 and 1956. Boshoff's record of success across a wide range of amateur tournaments established him as one of the most accomplished golfers of his time.

BOTES, DESVONDE (1974) SOUTH AFRICA

Desvonde Pierre Botes had a notable career in golf with significant achievements: South African Amateur Championship in 1991 at age 16. He turned Professional: 1992

His first Professional Victory: 1993 Mercedes Benz Golf Challenge on the Southern Africa Tour. Other notable wins: 1999 South African Masters; 1996 Zambia Open. In all he has won a total of 14 professional victories Botes' early success as an amateur and continued achievements as a professional highlight his significant impact on the Southern Africa Tour.

BOTHMA, MICHIEL (1973) SOUTH AFRICA

Michiel Frederick Bothma is a prominent golfer on the Southern Africa Sunshine Tour with a solid record of achievements, with a total of 12 victories. Notable Wins include the 2002 and 2010 Telkom PGA Championship. His success in these prestigious tournaments underscores his prominent role in South African golf.

BOYD, JIMMY UNION SOUTH AFRICA

Jimmy Boyd was a dominant figure in South African amateur golf during the post-war era, recognized for his powerful play and numerous achievements. His career highlights include winning the South African Amateur Championships twice, in 1946 and 1958, with runner-up finishes in 1949 and 1951. He claimed victory in the 1953 South African Open, adding to his third-place finish in 1950. Boyd also secured four

Transvaal titles, one Natal victory, and victories in the 1949 Rhodesian and Natal Amateurs, alongside winning three Freddie Tait Trophies.

He earned seven Springbok caps between 1954 and 1963, representing South Africa in international competitions such as the 1959 Commonwealth Eisenhower Trophy. Boyd's length off the tee and strong match play performance were key aspects of his game, with his victory in the 1953 SA Open standing out as a major amateur achievement. In 2010, Boyd was inducted into the Southern Africa Golf Hall of Fame, cementing his legacy as one of the leading figures in South African golf history.

BREGMAN, STACY (1986) SOUTH AFRICA

Stacy Lee Bregman, the 2018 Sunshine Ladies Tour Order of Merit winner, is also a player on the Ladies European Tour (LET). Her achievements include three runner-up finishes on the LET and being part of the winning team at the 2021 Aramco Team Series – Sotogrande. Bregman has won six titles on the Sunshine Ladies Tour and, as an amateur, claimed the Espirito Santo Trophy.

In her amateur career, she was a semi-finalist in the South African Amateur in 2005 and 2006 and reached the final 16 in the 2006 British Ladies Amateur Championship. As a professional, Bregman has secured seven titles, including the 2013 South African Women's Open and the 2018 Lacoste Ladies Open de France.

BREMNER, MERRICK (1986) SOUTH AFRICA

Merrick Bremner, a distinguished South African golfer, has built a notable career with a total of 13 professional wins, reflecting his skill and consistency across various tours. On the Sunshine Tour, Bremner has secured eight victories, including one notable playoff loss, demonstrating his competitive edge and proficiency on home soil. In addition to his Sunshine Tour success, Bremner has also made significant strides on the IGT Pro Tour, where he has won five events, further solidifying his reputation as a formidable player.

Internationally, Bremner has made his mark on the European Tour, with his best finish being a tie for third place at the 2014 D+D Real Czech

Masters. His impressive performances both locally and abroad highlight his strong playing ability and versatility across different golf tours.

BREWS, HARRY (DIED 2011) UNION SOUTH AFRICA

Harry Brews, the son of legendary South African golfer Sid Brews, played a pivotal role in preserving the region's golf heritage. With remarkable foresight, he advocated for the retention of Southern Africa's golf history at a time when neither amateur nor professional golf bodies showed much interest in its preservation. Harry co-founded and co-financed the Southern Africa Golf Hall of Fame and Museum, ensuring that the region's rich golfing legacy would be remembered for future generations.

In addition to his contributions to golf history, Harry was an accomplished golfer himself. He became the first Southern African golfer to win an international event, claiming the prestigious International University 'Boyd Quaich' trophy in 1949. His brother, Roger Brews, also had a successful golf career, winning the South African Amateur Championship in 1952. The Brews family significantly contributed to South African golf both on and off the course.

BREWS, GEORGE 'JOCK' UNION SOUTH AFRICA

Jock Brews was a celebrated South African golfer and esteemed club maker whose career left a lasting impact on the sport. As a prominent figure in golf, Brews held several notable positions, including serving as the President of the South African & Rhodesia PGA from 1946 to 1947 and being a respected Kensington Professional for 20 years. He was honoured as the 4th Honorary Life Member of the South African PGA, a testament to his dedication and contributions to the game.

Brews' impressive record includes 14 professional victories. He won the South African Open four times, in 1921, 1923, 1926, and 1928, and finished as the runner-up on multiple occasions in 1913, 1922,

1924, 1925, and 1930. His success extended to the SA PGA Match-Play Championship, where he claimed victory in 1924 and 1925, and again finished as a runner-up in 1928 and 1931. On the Transvaal Open circuit, Brews won in 1913, 1921, 1923, and 1930, with several second-place finishes in 1922, 1924, 1926, 1934, and 1938. He also captured the Natal Open title in 1925 and 1927 and finished second in 1938.

Inducted into the Southern Africa Golf Hall of Fame, Jock Brews' career was marked by dominance on the course and significant contributions to the sport, reflecting his exceptional talent and enduring legacy in golf.

BREWS, SID (1899–1972) UNION SOUTH AFRICA

Sydney Francis Brews was a key figure in South African golf, renowned for his achievements and contributions to the sport: Brews one of South Africa's greatest golfers, and spent 30 years as the club pro at Houghton Golf Club in Johannesburg.

He helped found the Transvaal PGA which grew into SA PGA, and later became the PGA President. He played for England 1934 (vs. Scotland), and was the 1st Honourary SA PGA Life Member.

Professional wins 37, of which he dominated South African golf including twenty-nine were South African wins including eight South African Opens 1925, 1927, 1930, 1931, 1933, 1934, 1936, 1949, and 1952 (he had to be persuaded to participate in 1949, and 1952 when almost 54, and remains the oldest SA Open winner), runner-up three times 1928, 1938, ….; and six each in the South African PGA 1926, 1928, 1933, 1934, 1936, 1952, runner-up 1938, 1946, 1952; and the South African Match Play. He also won the Transvaal Open eight times 1924, 1930-1936 and the Natal Open four times 1926, 1927, 1929, 1937.

He still found time to make the long trip back to England and play some tournaments in Europe, where he enjoyed considerable success outside of South Africa. In 1922 he won the Gloucestershire and Somerset Alliance Professional Championship, the Gloucestershire and Somerset Open; and the Belgium Open in 1929

In 1934, probably his finest year, he finished runner-up in the British Open to Henry Cotton, and won both the French Open and Dutch Open championships. He would retain both of those titles in 1935, and represented England again in the England-Scotland Professional Match of 1935.

He had a naturally high ball flight and liked to play a fade. He was notable as a very fast player – quickly playing all shots but particularly quick to pull the trigger on putts.

He also designed golf courses in South Africa, including the Firethorn Course at Randpark Golf Club near Johannesburg. Many of Brews' designs were in conjunction with Gary Player, with whom Brews formed the first golf course design and construction company in South Africa: Gary Player, Sid Brews & Associates.

Sydney Francis Brews' legacy in golf is marked by his extensive successes on the course and his impact on golf course design and development in South Africa.

BRIGHT, RUBY (ARMSTRONG) CAPE COLONY, UNION SOUTH AFRICA

For longevity, Ruby Bright is celebrated for her impressive achievements in golf. She won the South African Ladies Championship in 1908, 1910, 1911, and 1923, and finished as runner-up in 1914 and 1930, with third-place finishes in 1912 and 1920. Bright was also the runner-up in the British Ladies Championship in 1929 and won the Notts County Ladies Championship in 1935 and 1939, with second-place finishes in 1929 and 1936. She was inducted into the Southern Africa Golf Hall of Fame in 2013.

BRINTON, MAY CAPE COLONY, UNION SOUTH AFRICA

May Brinton was a pioneering figure in South African golf. She was the first winner of the South African Ladies Championship in 1907 and won again in 1911 and 1912. She finished as runner-up in 1910 and 1911 and came in third in 1909. Brinton also claimed victories at the Transvaal Ladies Championship in 1921 and 1924. As an administrator, she served as Captain of the Royal Cape Golf Club from 1904 to 1907, contributing 25 years of active service, which led to the creation of the May Brinton Trophy in her honor. Additionally, she represented Ireland in 1922.

BRITZ, TIENIE (1945) SOUTH AFRICA

Chain smoking Tienie Britz is a notable South African golfer with a distinguished career who won 8 professional events, including the South African PGA Championship twice in 1971 and led the South African Tour Order of Merit in 1971/72.

He also played extensively on the European Tour and the European Seniors Tour. His best finish on the European Tour's Order of Merit was 19th place in 1977. That year he also won his only event on the tour at the German Open, having had to first pre-qualify.

He represented South Africa three times in the 1972, 1975, 1980 World Cup: in Australia with Gary Player, in Thailand with John Bland, and in Columbia with Bobby Verwey. Since 1986, Britz has been the head teaching professional at Broome Park Golf Club in England.

Tienie Britz's career highlights include his victories on the South African and European Tours, his successful World Cup appearances, and his long-term role as a teaching professional.

BRUCE, JENNY SOUTH AFRICA

Jenny Bruce was a standout amateur golfer and a Springbok representative in 1974, 1975, 1977, and accumulated nine victories in total during her amateur career. She received the Sports Merit Award in 1974 for her achievements. Her amateur victories include the South African Amateur Championship in 1973, 1975, and 1977, with runner-up finishes in 1976 and 1978. She was also second in the 1973 Stroke Play Championship.

Other notable victories include: Northern Transvaal Championship in 1972; Transvaal Championship in 1973 and 1978; Mozambique Championship in 1973; Natal Championship in 1973; British Team Trophy in 1973; Champion of Champions in 1973 and 1978, and second in 1976; South Transvaal Championship in 1975 and second in 1978; Transvaal Stroke Play Championship in 1975 and 1977, with second place in 1979; and Northern Free State Championship in 1975.

BRUINERS, HEINRICH SOUTH AFRICA

Heinrich Bruiners is showcasing impressive achievements that highlight his growing prominence in the sport. His career began to gain traction with a victory at the Vodacom Origins of Golf in 2013, marking his entry onto the professional scene. Bruiners continued to build on his success with notable wins at the co-sanctioned European Tour Joburg Open in both 2021 and 2022. These victories cemented his status as a formidable player on the international stage. In 2024, he further solidified his reputation by claiming victory at the Players Championship, a significant milestone in his career. Bruiners' achievements reflect his talent and potential, establishing him as a prominent figure in both local and international golf.

BRUYNS, DENNIS (1951–2023) SOUTH AFRICA

Dennis Bruyns, a PGA Master Professional and Honorary Life Member, was a cornerstone of South African golf, contributing over 45 years to the sport as a Master Professional and past CEO of the PGA of South Africa. Known affectionately as the "Rules Guru," Dennis was a highly respected authority on the Rules of Golf, and his expertise in course setup, rulings, and scoring made him an integral figure in South Africa's golfing landscape.

Dennis played a pivotal role in shaping the PGA of South Africa, leading the organization for nine years. Under his leadership, the PGA saw remarkable growth, and Dennis was widely regarded as a man of great vision and influence. His dedication to education was evident through his work as a lecturer at the Golf Management Campus, where he shared his knowledge with future generations of golf professionals.

In addition to his work with the PGA, Dennis was also a founding editor of Compleat Golfer magazine, partnering with Dale Hayes to establish it as a leading publication. He maintained a long-standing involvement with the Sunshine Tour, where he served as executive director, further solidifying his legacy within the sport.

An exceptional junior golfer, Dennis broke the course record at Windsor Park Golf Club in Durban with a round of 65 at just 15 years old. His natural talent led him to compete internationally at prestigious events like the Orange Bowl Junior in Miami. Although he briefly pursued a professional playing career, his lasting contributions came through his leadership and passion for the rules and future of the game.

Dennis's balanced philosophy on pin placements emphasized fairness and skill, ensuring that every player had to use the full range of clubs throughout a tournament. His deep understanding of golf's intricacies and unwavering commitment to the sport made him one of the most influential figures in South African golf history.

BUHAI, ASHLEIGH (SIMON) (1989) SOUTH AFRICA

Ashleigh Buhai stands out as a prominent figure in women's golf, having achieved remarkable success both as an amateur and a professional. Her career has been distinguished by groundbreaking accomplishments and consistent excellence. Buhai's journey began with an extraordinary amateur career in South Africa, where she set multiple records and became the youngest player to receive full African colours at just 14. She also played No.1 for South Africa in the Commonwealth Tournament, won the Ladies South African Amateur Stroke Play and Match Play double, and became the first player in 101 years to win the South African Open title three times.

Turning professional, Buhai quickly made a mark on the South African Women Professional circuit. In 2004, she won the Acer Women's South

African Open, becoming the only amateur to do so, and continued to demonstrate her talent by securing a professional women's golf tour event each year since, including another win at the Acer Women's South African Open in 2007. Her impressive performance also saw her finish as the top points scorer of the Ladies African Tour that year.

Buhai's professional achievements include her historic victory at the Catalonia Ladies Masters in 2007, where she became the youngest ever winner on the Ladies European Tour at 18 years and 37 days. Her success continued with notable wins such as the 2022 Women's Open, making her the only South African woman since Sally Little to win a major championship in women's golf. She further solidified her reputation by successfully defending her title at the ISPS Handa Women's Australian Open in 2023 and winning the ShopRite LPGA Classic.

With a total of 22 professional victories, including 12 on the Sunshine Ladies Tour, and a world ranking of 23 in 2023, Buhai's career reflects her consistent excellence and significant contributions to the sport. She remains one of the hottest talents in professional golf, with her achievements underscoring her exceptional skill and impact on the game.

BUHRMANN, HENDRIK (1963) SOUTH AFRICA

Hendrik Theodor Smit Buhrmann is a seasoned golfer with a successful career highlighted by eight tournament victories on the Southern African Sunshine Tour. He has been a member of the Asian Tour since 1995 and after a string of four second-place finishes stretching back a decade, he finally secured his first win on that tour after eleven-years at the 2006 Aamby Valley Asian Masters ahead of Simon Hurd after a series of near misses. His team appearances include the 1995 World Cup and the Alfred Dunhill Challenge.

BURD, JEANETTE (WAHL) SOUTH AFRICA

2011 Golf Hall of Fame inductees Jeanette Burd and Hugh Baiocchi, with Sally Little, Hilmari Viljoen, Dorian Wharton-Hood

Jeanette Burd is celebrated as one of South Africa's pioneering lady golf professionals, distinguished by her impressive playing career and contributions to the sport as a teacher. Her achievements on the golf course are a testament to her exceptional talent and dedication.

Burd earned Springbok colours in 1959 and was recognized as Natal Sportsman of the Year in 1967. She was consistently ranked among South Africa's top three lady golfers during the 1960s. Her contributions to amateur golf were significant, with notable performances on the South Africa World Amateur Ladies Team in 1964, 1968, and 1970, and captaining the team in 1969. Her Springbok appearances spanned multiple years, including 1959, 1963, 1964, 1968, 1969, and 1971. In 1971, she set an extraordinary record by shooting a 63 in official competition, the lowest recorded score by a lady golfer worldwide at that time.

Inducted into the Southern Africa Golf Hall of Fame in 2011, Burd's legacy extends beyond her playing career. She was one of South Africa's first professional women golfers and made significant contributions as a golf teacher. Her name was also stamped on golf clubs made by Slazenger, marking her influence in the equipment side of the sport.

Burd's excellent playing record includes multiple victories in the South African Ladies Amateur 1964, 1967, 1969, 1970 and South African Ladies Match Play 1964, 1967, 1970. She also excelled in Natal Ladies Match Play 1957, 1961, 1962, 1966, 1967, 1968, 1970, 1971 and Natal Ladies Stroke Play 1961, 1963, 1966, 1967, 1968, 1971. Additionally, she played a significant role in the British Team Trophy, winning in 1959, 1964, and 1965, and finishing second in 1970.

Jeanette Burd's remarkable career highlights her as a trailblazer in women's golf, celebrated for her achievements both on and off the course.

BURMESTER, DEAN (1989) SOUTH AFRICA, ZIMBABWE

Dean Burmester's golf career is a testament to his exceptional talent and perseverance. His journey began with a breakthrough victory at the Golden Pilsener Zimbabwe Open in 2015, setting the stage for an impressive rise in professional golf. By 2017, he made a significant mark on the European Tour, claiming his maiden victory at the Tshwane Open, a moment that solidified his place among golf's elite.

The years that followed saw Burmester's star continue to rise. In 2021, he achieved another milestone with his second European Tour win at the Tenerife Open, where a remarkable final round of 62 showcased his skill and determination. That year, he also added a victory at the PGA Championship on the Sunshine Tour, further demonstrating his ability to perform under pressure with a final round of 65.

Burmester's ascent didn't stop there. In 2022, he transitioned from the Korn Ferry Tour to the PGA Tour, with a notable 4th place finish at the Sanderson Farms Championship marking his debut on the bigger stage. His success continued into 2023 with victories at both the DP Tour co-sanctioned Joburg Open, where he closed with a final round of 64, and the Investec South African Open Championship, finishing with a round of 68.

April 2024 marked a new chapter in his career as Burmester secured his first title on the LIV Golf League. Playing for Louis Oosthuizen's Stinger team, he clinched victory at the LIV Golf Miami event, winning in a dramatic playoff against Sergio Garcia with a decisive three-footer.

With a total of 16 professional wins and a highest World Ranking of 55, Dean Burmester has firmly established himself as a prominent figure in global golf, his career a narrative of growth, skill, and relentless pursuit of excellence.

C

CAYEUX, MARC (1978) ZIMBABWE

Marc Elton Cayeux's career is a compelling story of success and resilience in the world of golf. A prominent golfer from Zimbabwe, Cayeux made his mark by representing his country in the 1996 Eisenhower Trophy, a significant early achievement that highlighted his potential on the international stage.

Throughout his career, Cayeux secured 12 professional victories, demonstrating his exceptional talent and determination. Nine of these wins came on the Sunshine Tour, where he became a respected figure in the golfing community. One of the standout moments in his career occurred in 2008 when he won the Nashua Masters, a victory that not only showcased his skill but also allowed him to regain his position on the European Tour.

However, Cayeux's career was abruptly affected by a tragic event in September 2010. He was involved in a severe automobile accident that resulted in significant injuries to himself and was fatal for the other driver. This incident cast a shadow over his promising career, highlighting the unpredictability and fragility of life.

Despite the challenges and the tragic turn of events, Marc Elton Cayeux's contributions to golf, particularly on the Sunshine Tour, are fondly remembered. His career remains a testament to his talent and the impact he made in the world of golf before his untimely setback.

CHARAMBA, TONGOONA 'TC' (1982) ZIMBABWE

Tongoona Charamba is a notable Zimbabwean golfer who had a distinguished amateur career before turning professional. Charamba rewrote the history books by becoming only the third black player to win on the Sunshine Winter Tour since 1991 holding off Jean Hugo and Hennie Otto with a 40-foot birdie putt on the 16th and a 12-foot putt on the 18th.

During his amateur years, he secured 12 wins, including victories in the Zimbabwe Amateur Matchplay and Strokeplay Championships in 2002.

Charamba also dominated the Zimbabwe Order of Merit from 2000 to 2002 and proudly represented Zimbabwe in the prestigious Eisenhower Trophy. After turning professional in 2003, Charamba continued to build on his success with two victories on the Sunshine Tour, along with two second-place finishes.

CHEN, CONNIE (1992) SOUTH AFRICA

Connie Chen's remarkable journey in professional golf is a testament to her dedication and passion for the sport. Beginning at just fifteen, Chen represented South Africa internationally at the 2008 Junior Open Championship, signaling the start of a promising amateur career. Her impressive performances continued in high-profile tournaments like

the Annika Invitational, The British Girls Championship, and The Duke of York Invitational in 2009 and 2010. The pinnacle of her amateur achievements came in 2010, where she secured over ten victories, represented South Africa at the Espirito Santo Trophy (finishing third), and earned the prestigious Compleat Golfer South African Woman Golfer of the Year award.

At 18, Chen transitioned into professional golf, qualifying for the 2011 Ladies European Tour (LET) season. Her talent was evident, particularly at the 2013 Omega Dubai Ladies Masters, where she memorably scored a hole-in-one and won a car. However, her crowning moment came in 2014 when she claimed her first LET title at the Open de España Femenino in Tenerife, Spain, finishing 12 under par and defeating Carlota Ciganda by two strokes.

Chen's journey didn't end with competitive success. In 2018, she became a full member of the PGA UK&I, blending her playing career with coaching. She earned recognition as one of Golf Digest's Top 75 Best International Teachers in 2020 and continued playing on the Chinese LPGA Tour while coaching golfers globally. Recently, her coaching excellence was acknowledged again when she was named to Golf Digest's Best Young Teachers in America for 2025-2026.

Connie Chen's evolution from a top-tier player to an internationally respected coach highlights her dedication, skill, and enduring influence on the world of golf.

CHITENGWA, LEWIS (1975–2001) ZIMBABWE

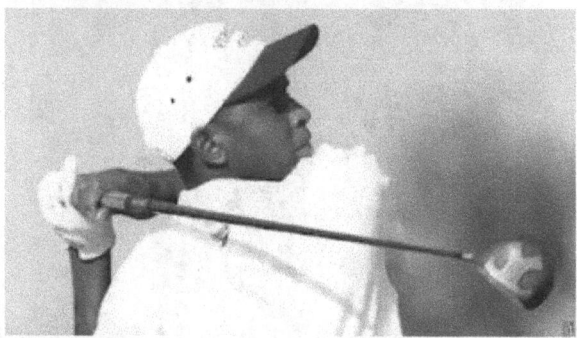

"There's no telling how good he could have been" – Gary Player.

Lewis Chitengwa's journey from Zimbabwe to becoming an internationally recognized golfer is a powerful testament to breaking barriers and inspiring others. His career is marked by groundbreaking achievements, both on and off the course.

Chitengwa first gained attention in 1992 when he defeated Tiger Woods by three shots at the Orange Bowl Junior tournament, a victory that immediately captured the interest of college coaches across America. He later became a two-time All-American at the University of Virginia (1995, 1996) and earned All-ACC honours in 1995, where he was named the league's Rookie of the Year.

In 1993, Chitengwa made history as the first Black golfer to win the South African Amateur Championship, defeating Rory Sabbatini in a country still grappling with apartheid. His victory was a symbolic moment, akin to Jackie Robinson's barrier-breaking success in baseball and Jesse Owens' triumphs at the Olympics.

Chitengwa's promising professional career saw him competing on the Buy.Com Tour as the first Black Zimbabwean to do so, and he consistently performed well on the Canadian Tour, where he was ranked 13th. His achievements include top finishes at the South Carolina Challenge and the Shell Payless Open, as well as notable victories like the 1996 USA Furman Intercollegiate and the 1997 USA Seminole Classic.

Tragically, Chitengwa's life was cut short in 2001 when he contracted meningitis during a tournament in Edmonton, robbing the world of a golfing prodigy. His legacy, however, lives on. In 2015, he was posthumously inducted into the Southern Africa Golf Hall of Fame. The Lewis Chitengwa Memorial Golf Tournament on the Canadian PGA Tour continues to honor his memory, inspiring future generations to follow in his footsteps.

Chitengwa's story is a reminder of the power of perseverance, the importance of breaking down barriers, and the enduring impact one individual can have on a sport and a community.

CHOWGLAY, ISMAIL "BOY" (1933–1992) UNION SOUTH AFRICA – APARTHEID

A Golfing Legend in the Shadow of Apartheid, Ismail 'Boy' Chowglay was one of South Africa's most gifted golfers, yet his name is not as widely celebrated as it should be due to the oppressive apartheid regime that kept him from competing alongside white golfers. Born with a natural talent that rivaled the likes of Sewsunker 'Papwa' Sewgolum, Ismail's career was a testament to resilience and excellence in the face of extreme adversity.

By 1962, Chowglay had already established himself as a dominant force on the South African Non-European Tour, winning the prestigious SA Non-European Open that year. Many believed that his talent had surpassed even that of Papwa Sewgolum, who famously won the Natal Open against white competitors in 1963, breaking racial barriers. Despite his early success, apartheid laws prevented Ismail from competing on the main South African professional tour, denying him the opportunity to showcase his full potential.

For a decade, he was largely restricted to the segregated non-European circuit. It wasn't until 1972, after years of struggle, that Ismail reclaimed the SA Non-European Open title while continuing to win the Western Province championship, a title he had held for years. He used a unique back-to-front grip that defied conventional golfing techniques, yet his control over the ball was second to none. Known for hitting his 3-wood up to 250 meters, he rarely used a driver, opting instead for his trusty club and an instinctive feel for the game. He preferred not to use tees, often fashioning his own from turf or sand, which only added to his reputation as a golfer who played on feel and skill alone.

Often carrying fewer than the standard 14, his back-to-front grip allowed him to shape shots with precision, controlling the trajectory and placement of the ball with ease.

Despite apartheid's limitations, Ismail amassed an impressive tally of 17 professional tournament victories. His provincial dominance was unmatched, winning 15 provincial titles, including eight Western Province Non-European titles, two Transvaal titles, two Eastern Province titles, and the Natal Non-European title in 1976. His crowning achievements on the national stage were his two SA Non-European Open titles, in 1962 and 1972, though he had several other near victories, including second place finishes in 1955 and 1967.

In 1970, Ismail's talents were finally taken abroad, where he further proved his mettle on the international stage. Competing in Europe, he finished 6th at the German Open and 6th at the 1972 French Open, while also making the cut at The Open Championship, placing a respectable 56th. These results demonstrated that, had he been given the same opportunities as his white counterparts, Ismail could have competed among the best golfers in the world.

Even as apartheid policies forced him to work as the caddy master at Clovelly Country Club, Ismail continued to inspire the next generation of golfers. He would 'illegally' coach juniors, passing on his skills and wisdom to those who sought to learn from one of South Africa's unsung heroes. His love for the game never waned, and in 1983, at the age of 51, Ismail won Transvaal title, defying the odds once more. Although apartheid robbed him of the chance to compete on equal terms, his skill and accomplishments ensured that his name would forever be etched in the annals of South African golf history.

CLARK, TIM "PENGUIN" (1975) SOUTH AFRICA

Timothy Henry Clark's career stands as a remarkable testament to skill, determination, and overcoming personal challenges in the world of golf. Hailing from South Africa, Clark's journey is both inspiring and notable for his resilience and impressive achievements.

Clark's amateur career was distinguished by several significant milestones. In 1994, he earned Springbok colours, a prestigious honour following a runner-up finish in the South African Amateur at Royal Cape. He further cemented his reputation in 1997 by being named ACC Player of the Year and winning the U.S. Amateur Public Links Championship, triumphing among 6,209 entries.

Turning professional in 1998, Clark made an immediate impact. His success on the Nike Tour in 2000, where he secured two tournament victories, earned him a spot on the PGA Tour for 2001. Clark's professional career flourished as he accumulated 14 victories on the PGA Tour, including a career-defining win at the 2010 Players Championship. His impressive run on the PGA Tour also included eight runner-up finishes.

Clark's achievements extended beyond the PGA Tour. He won three titles on the European Tour and claimed victory in the Australian Open in 2008, outlasting Mathew Goggin in a dramatic playoff. On the Sunshine Tour, he won the Order of Merit for the 2001/02 season, and in 2014, he added the RBC Canadian Open to his list of accolades, defeating Jim Furck.

Despite a congenital arm deformity that prevented him from fully straightening his arm – a challenge that led him to adopt a distinctive putting style with a tall putter – Clark's skill and determination remained unwavering. His unique putting style became a defining characteristic of his game until rule changes eventually led to his retirement.

In major championships, Clark demonstrated his prowess with notable finishes: he placed 2nd at the 2006 Masters Tournament, 3rd at the 2003 PGA Championship, and tied for 3rd at the 2005 U.S. Open. His contributions to the sport were further recognized through his representation of the International Team in the Presidents Cup in 2003, 2005, and 2009.

Clark's career, marked by his resilience and success, is a testament to his exceptional talent and dedication to golf. His ability to overcome physical challenges while achieving at the highest levels of the sport makes his legacy truly inspiring.

CLARKE, NEVILLE SOUTH AFRICA

Neville Clarke is the chief operations manager of the Sunshine Senior Tour. His record includes wins in the Transvaal Amateur 1983; SA Amateur 1985, 1988; SA Open Freddie Tait trophy 1986, 1988, 1990; and the SA Stroke Play 1988, 2nd 1995. He was a Springbok in 1988

CLEMENCE, MARY UNION SOUTH AFRICA

Mary Clemence stands as a significant figure in South African women's golf, celebrated for her exceptional achievements in the late 1950s and early 1960s. Her career is marked by notable victories and an impressive presence in amateur golf.

Clemence earned Springbok colors in 1959, a prestigious recognition that highlighted her prominence in the sport. That same year, she claimed victory at the South African Ladies Amateur, setting the stage for a remarkable career. She would go on to win this title again in 1962, underscoring her consistent excellence on the golf course.

In addition to her successes at the South African Ladies Amateur, Clemence also excelled in regional competitions. She triumphed at the Natal Ladies Amateur in 1961 and secured the Transvaal Ladies Amateur title in 1962. Her performances in these tournaments further solidified her reputation as one of the leading female golfers of her time.

Clemence's career achievements are a testament to her skill and dedication to the sport, leaving a lasting impact on South African golf. Her success on the course during a pivotal era for women's golf is a testament to her talent and determination.

COETZEE, GEORGE (1986) SOUTH AFRICA

George Coetzee's golfing career is a testament to his skill and consistency, with notable successes across both the European and Sunshine Tours. With a total of 20 tournament victories, including five on the European Tour and fourteen on the Sunshine Tour, Coetzee has established himself as a prominent figure in the sport.

His journey in professional golf began with a strong showing in 2011 when he was the runner-up at the Johnnie Walker Championship at Gleneagles, setting the stage for his future successes. By 2013, Coetzee reached a career-high ranking of 41 in the Official World Golf Ranking, a significant milestone in his career.

In 2014, Coetzee secured his maiden European Tour title at the Joburg Open, overcoming strong competition from players like Justin Walters, Tyrell Hatton, and Jin Jeong. This victory marked the beginning of his successful run on the European Tour. The following year, he demonstrated his prowess by winning the Tshwane Open by a single stroke and also clinched the Sunshine Tour Order of Merit, highlighting his dominance on the local circuit.

Coetzee's success continued in 2017 when he won the Tshwane Open for the second time and claimed his second Sunshine Tour Order of Merit title. His performance in the PGA Championship, where he finished 7th, further underscored his ability to compete at the highest levels of the sport.

In 2020, Coetzee added to his European Tour achievements with a victory at the Portugal Masters. His final-round birdies on two of the last three holes secured the win, overcoming strong competitors like Laurie Canter and Tommy Fleetwood.

Coetzee's career is marked by consistent performances and significant victories, demonstrating his enduring impact on professional golf and his standing as a leading golfer on both the European and Sunshine Tours.

COHEN, BARRY (1952) SOUTH AFRICA

Barry John Cohen is a prominent figure in South African golf, renowned for his significant contributions both on and off the course. His dedication to the sport has left an indelible mark, fostering growth and preserving the rich heritage of golf in Southern Africa.

In 2006, Cohen co-founded the South African Golf Hall of Fame alongside Harry Brews, establishing a prestigious institution dedicated to honoring the achievements and legacy of South Africa's golfing legends. Building on this foundation, in 2009, he played a pivotal role in co-founding, designing, and creating the layout of the Hall of Fame Museum. Esteemed golfer Dale Hayes praised the museum's layout as one of the three best of its kind in the world, highlighting Cohen's commitment to excellence and innovation.

Cohen has been instrumental in funding various aspects of the Hall of Fame, including the Southern Africa Golf Hall of Fame induction banquets that celebrate new members. His vision and financial support were further demonstrated when he funded the relocation of the museum to the Cape Town Waterfront, enhancing its accessibility and prominence.

In recognition of his outstanding contributions to South African golf, Barry Cohen was honored with the Compleat Golfers' "Greatest Contribution to South African Golf" award in 2012. This accolade underscores his unwavering commitment to advancing the sport and supporting the golfing community.

Cohen is also a respected author in the golfing world, having written several influential books including *When We Were Champions*, *PAPWA*, and *Africa Who's Who of Golf*. His extensive knowledge and expertise make him an authority on Southern Africa's Black golf history, providing valuable insights and preserving the narratives of pioneering golfers.

Beyond his contributions as an author and philanthropist, he serves as a director for various golf trusts. His leadership roles include positions with the SA Golf Heritage Trust, The Little Golf Trust, and the Finding the Fair Way Foundation. Through these roles, he continues to advocate for the development and accessibility of golf, ensuring that the sport remains inclusive and vibrant.

His passion for golf is rooted in his early days as a player. Originally a scratch (0) handicap golfer, and where he coached the juniors for free every Saturday at Mount Coolum GC, Queensland during the 1980s. His firsthand experience and understanding of the game have fueled his efforts to enhance the golfing landscape in South Africa.

Cohen's multifaceted contributions – from founding and designing the South African Golf Hall of Fame to authoring key literature and leading important golf trusts – have significantly shaped the golfing environment in Southern Africa. His legacy is one of dedication, innovation, and a deep-seated love for the game, inspiring future generations of golfers and enthusiasts alike.

COLE, BOBBY "KING" (1948) SOUTH AFRICA

Bobby 'King' Cole was potentially one of the hot young golfers in the world, who won both the 1964 South Africa Junior Golf Championship and the Vaal Amateur. In 1966, Cole won the British Amateur at

Carnoustie, Scotland, and the Gold Illustrated Gold Vase (tied with Peter Townsend, and played for South Africa in the Eisenhower Trophy. In 1967 at the PGA Tour Qualifying School he earned medalist honors, and in 1974 he claimed both the team playing with Dale Hayes beating Japan (Isao Aoki and Masashi Ozaki) by 5 strokes, and the World Cup Individual Trophy. At the same time, he was the 1973-74 Sunshine Tour Order of Merit winner, and he is a two-time winner of the South African Open in 1974 beating Allan Henning, and 1980 from Nick Price.

In 1986, he won the South African PGA Championship from Teddy Webber. On the US PGA Tour, Cole won the 1977 Buick Open. He also won the 1985 Seattle-Everett Open from Dave Stockton. He had nine top-25 finishes in the major championships including 3rd in the PGA Championship, and 3rd in The Open 1975, one stroke out of playoff, 7th 1974. During the event, Cole shot back-to-back rounds of 66, setting and then matching the course record at Carnoustie. He also had 28 top-10 finishes on the PGA Tour. In all he had 14 professional wins. Cole was inducted into the Southern Africa Golf Hall of Fame in 2012. He presently has a teaching academy and plays Pro-Ams and other golf events. Professional golfer Eric Cole is his son.

COLEMAN, GEORGE NORTHERN RHODESIA, FEDERATION

Coleman's distinguished golfing career is a significant chapter in the history of the sport, especially within Northern Rhodesia (now Zambia). His contributions and achievements not only highlight his personal prowess but also reflect his dedication to the growth and development of golf in the region.

Coleman's amateur career was marked by several remarkable accomplishments. He clinched the Federation Amateur Championship in 1955 and was a dominant force in the Northern Rhodesia Amateur Championship, securing titles in 1943, 1945, 1951, 1955, and 1956. His consistent performance extended to the Copperbelt Amateur Championship, where he claimed victories in 1952 and 1953 and finished as a runner-up on several occasions.

In 1960, Coleman added another prestigious title to his collection by winning the Cock 'o North. His dominance at the Roan Antelope Golf Club is notable, with seven championships reflecting his long-standing excellence on the local stage.

Coleman's impact was not confined to individual competitions. As a key member of the 1957 Federation team, he played a pivotal role in the historic victory over the Springboks. His match against Rees and Bousfield (Great Britain), alongside teammate Treloar, was crucial in Northern Rhodesia's narrow win with a score of 6.5 to 5.5. This victory was a highlight of his career, showcasing his ability to perform under pressure.

His influence extended beyond the golf course as he served as the President of the Roan Antelope Golf Club from 1962 to 1964, demonstrating his leadership and commitment to the sport. Additionally, Coleman's numerous Northern Rhodesia caps and his role in managing the team further underscore his deep involvement and contribution to the golfing community.

Coleman's career is a testament to his skill, consistency, and dedication to the game. His legacy continues to inspire and set a high standard in the history of Northern Rhodesian golf.

COLLIS, HELEN RHODESIA, SOUTHERN RHODESIA

Helen Collis's career in golf is marked by significant achievements both as an amateur player and in administrative roles, showcasing her deep commitment to the sport and her impressive skills on the course.

In administration, Collis made a lasting impact through her service on the Rhodesia Ladies Golf Union (LGU) Executive for 15 years. Her leadership roles included serving as Vice-President of the Rhodesia LGU from 1959, and later as Vice-President and President of the Matabeleland Golf Club from 1960. Her tenure in these positions reflected her dedication to the development and management of golf in the region.

Collis's playing career was equally distinguished. She represented Southern Rhodesia and was part of the team that achieved a notable victory over the Springboks, a significant accomplishment in the sport's history.

Her list of amateur golf victories underscores her competitive spirit and skill. Collis won the Rhodesian Ladies Championship in 1957 and secured second place in 1953. At the Matabeleland Ladies Championship, she triumphed in 1955, 1956, 1957, and 1960, and earned a second-place finish in 1959. Her success extended to the Midland Ladies Championship where she claimed victory in 1952 and 1953, and was a runner-up in 1949 and 1956.

Collis also excelled in the Mashonaland Ladies Championship, winning in 1960 and finishing second in 1956 and 1961. Additionally, she won the Churchill Cup Ladies title in 1960 and the Bulawayo Diamond Jubilee Ladies Championship in 1958. Her performances in the Bulawayo Ladies Championship were particularly impressive, with victories in 1939, 1954, 1955, and 1961, and a second-place finish in 1960.

Helen Collis's extensive involvement in golf, through both her administrative roles and her competitive successes, highlights her significant contributions and achievements in the sport. Her legacy in golf is defined by her leadership and her remarkable achievements on the course.

CONYERS-KIRBY, H (WALTER) 'MUSSOLINI'
UNION SOUTH AFRICA

Conyers-Kirby stands out as a pivotal figure in the history of golf, celebrated for his extensive contributions to the administration and legislative aspects of the sport. His impact was deeply felt both in South Africa and internationally, shaping the governance and evolution of golf during his tenure.

Serving as the Secretary of the South African Golf Union (SAGU) for an impressive 26 years, from 1922 to 1947, Conyers-Kirby played a crucial role in the administration and development of golf in South Africa. His leadership during this period was instrumental in establishing the foundational structures and policies that guided the sport.

In 1936, Conyers-Kirby gained international recognition when he was appointed to the Rules and Interpretation Committee of the Royal and Ancient Golf Club of St Andrews (R&A). His role in this esteemed committee was pivotal in the evolution of golfing laws and etiquette, contributing significantly to the global standards and practices of the game.

His commitment extended to managing scoreboards at national tournaments, where he was actively involved in filling in details and making critical decisions on the finer points of golfing law. This meticulous attention to detail underscored his deep understanding and dedication to the sport.

Within the Western Province Golf Union (WPGU), Conyers-Kirby served as Vice-President and later as President in 1949, further demonstrating his leadership and influence in the regional golfing community.

At the Royal Cape Golf Club, his contributions were equally notable. He was a member of the Royal Cape Committee from 1911 and served as Captain from 1931 to 1932. His involvement continued as Vice-President in 1948, and he was honored as a Life Member in 1946, reflecting his enduring impact on the club.

Conyers-Kirby also held a prominent position as President of the South African Seniors Golfers' Association, showcasing his dedication to promoting and supporting senior golfers.

In recognition of his significant contributions to the sport, he was inducted into the inaugural class of the Southern Africa Golf Hall of Fame in 2009. This honor cemented his legacy as a key figure in the history of golf.

Known for his strict adherence to golf's etiquette and conventions, Conyers-Kirby earned the nickname 'Mussolini' due to his high standards. His extensive service and commitment to golf governance and administration have left a lasting and revered legacy in the sport.

D

DA SILVA, ADILSON JOSE (1972) SOUTH AFRICA, BRAZIL

Adilson José da Silva has carved out a notable and varied career in golf, showcasing his talents across multiple levels and regions of the sport.

Da Silva's journey began with impressive accomplishments as an amateur. He won the Brazil Amateur Open Championship in 1990 and 1991, followed by claiming the Zimbabwe Amateur Championship in 1992. These early victories set the stage for a successful professional career.

Turning professional in 1994, da Silva quickly made his mark. He secured his first tour title in 1997 and went on to accumulate a total of 19 professional tournament victories, including twelve on the Sunshine Tour. His consistency and skill were evident as he also secured four runner-up positions and topped the Vodacom Swing Challenge standings in 2006.

His career further expanded as he competed extensively on the Zimbabwean PGA Tour from 1996 to 2003, where he amassed over 30 titles and topped the Zimbabwean Order of Merit five times. This period solidified his reputation as a dominant force in the region.

Da Silva's versatility is highlighted by his current involvement in both the European Senior Tour, where he has won six titles, and the Sunshine Tour. His impact on the sport was underscored when he had the honour of hitting the opening tee shot in golf's return to the Olympics in Rio de Janeiro in 2016. Additionally, he represented Brazil at the World Cup in 2011 and 2013, further showcasing his international presence.

Adilson José da Silva's career reflects a remarkable blend of skill, adaptability, and success across different tours and formats, underscoring his significant contributions to the sport of golf.

DE JAGER, LOUIS (1987) SOUTH AFRICA

Louis de Jager's golf career is marked by a blend of impressive achievements both as an amateur and a professional.

De Jager's prowess first emerged during his amateur years, highlighted by his victory at the South African Amateur Championship in 2007. His success in this prestigious tournament, where he excelled in both stroke play and match play formats, showcased his versatility and skill on the golf course.

Transitioning to professional golf, De Jager quickly made his mark. He claimed his first professional victory at the Suncoast Classic in August 2009, a significant milestone that set the stage for a successful career. Over the years, he accumulated a total of eight professional tournament wins, underscoring his consistency and competitive edge.

One of the standout moments in his professional career came with his win at the 2019 Eye of Africa PGA Championship. This victory not only added to his impressive tally of wins but also solidified his reputation as a top player in the golf world.

Louis de Jager's career reflects a strong performance and dedication to the sport, showcasing his skill and consistency both in amateur and professional golf. His achievements continue to highlight his significant contributions to the game.

DE JONGE, BRENDON (1980) ZIMBABWE

Brendon Russell de Jonge has crafted a remarkable career in golf, distinguished by his achievements across amateur, collegiate, and professional levels.

De Jonge's journey in golf began with a strong foundation in amateur competition. He claimed the Zimbabwe Amateur Championship title in 1999 and represented his country at the 2000 Eisenhower Trophy. His

early successes hinted at the potential that would define his career.

During his collegiate years, de Jonge's talent shone brightly. He was honored as a two-time All-America selection by the Golf Coaches of America Association in 2002 and 2003. Additionally, he was named the Virginia Collegiate 'Player of the Year' for both of those years, reflecting his dominance in college golf. His achievements earned him a well-deserved spot in the Virginia Tech Sports Hall of Fame in 2014, cementing his legacy at the university.

Transitioning to professional golf, de Jonge quickly made a name for himself. In 2008, he was awarded the Nationwide Tour 'Player of the Year' after securing a victory at the Xerox Classic. His most successful year came in 2010, when he achieved seven top-10 finishes, ending the season 34th on the money list. Notably, in 2014, he finished as the runner-up in the McGladrey Classic, showcasing his competitive prowess.

On the international stage, de Jonge represented Zimbabwe at the World Cup in 2011 and 2013, and competed for the International team at the Presidents Cup in 2013. These experiences highlighted his ability to perform on a global stage and contribute to his country's golfing achievements.

Brendon Russell de Jonge's career is a testament to his skill and dedication, marked by a series of significant accomplishments that reflect his impact on the sport of golf.

DIAS, MRS MC PRATA MOZAMBIQUE

Mrs. Dias had a distinguished career in amateur golf, marked by several notable victories and international representation. Her achievements spanned across various championships and showcased her prowess on the golf course.

In 1966, Mrs. Dias represented Portugal, a significant milestone in her career. Her success in amateur golf was underscored by her impressive list of victories. She won the Portuguese Ladies Championship in 1966, establishing herself as a leading player in her home country.

Her triumphs extended beyond Portugal, with multiple wins in the Mozambique Ladies Championship, where she claimed victory in 1959, 1964, 1965, 1966, and 1969. Her consistent performance in this tournament highlighted her skill and adaptability across different courses and conditions.

Mrs. Dias also excelled at the Club da Polona Ladies Championship, securing wins in 1961, 1962, 1963, 1964, 1965, and 1966, and finishing in 2nd place in 1969. Additionally, she won the Beira Ladies Championship in 1955 and 1956, further demonstrating her competitive edge and success in amateur golf.

Her career reflects a blend of consistency, skill, and achievement, making her a notable figure in the history of amateur golf.

DICKSON, VERNON SOUTH AFRICA

Vernon Dickson made enduring contributions to the sport of golf, particularly through his work with junior golf development and administration. As the "father of the WP Junior Golf Foundation," Dickson played a pivotal role in expanding junior golf participation and providing valuable opportunities for young players. His efforts included initiating two family day competitions and a new Gala Day, both designed to raise funds for junior teams traveling to the annual Inter-Provincial.

Dickson's leadership was instrumental during his tenure on the WP Junior Golf Foundation executive from 1965 to 1976, and as Chairman from 1968 to 1976. His commitment to the growth of junior golf was recognized with the Vernon Dickson Memorial Trophy, awarded for achievements in junior golf within Western Province.

In addition to his administrative work, Dickson was an accomplished golfer, playing to a 1 handicap and representing Western Province in 1948. His contributions extended to serving as the Springbok manager in 1975, further demonstrating his dedication to the sport both on and off the course. Dickson's legacy is marked by his significant impact on junior golf and his contributions to the broader golfing community.

DITSEBE, RONALD UNION SOUTH AFRICA – APARTHEID

Ronald Ditsebe made notable contributions to golf, particularly within the non-European community during the mid-20th century. As a dedicated member of the 1953 Transvaal Non-European Golf Union committee, Ditsebe played a key role in advancing the sport during a period of significant challenge.

His achievements on the golf course were substantial. Ditsebe won the inaugural South Africa Non-European Championship in 1949 and continued to excel in subsequent years, securing 2nd place in 1957, 3rd place in 1953 and 1959, and 4th place in 1963. His success extended to other tournaments as well; he claimed victory at the Griqualand Non-European Championship in 1959 and won the Northern Transvaal Non-European Championship in 1953. In the Transvaal Non-European Matchplay, he finished 2nd in 1947.

Ditsebe also shone in regional competitions, winning the Viking Round Robin Tournament at Wynberg Golf Club in 1952 and at Pimville Golf Club in 1953. His achievements and contributions underscore his excellence in non-European golf and his influential role in promoting the sport during a challenging era.

DLAMINI, JOE 'MKHULU' (DIED 2015) SWAZILAND

Johannes 'Joe' Dlamini is a pioneering figure in Swazi and Southern African golf, leaving a lasting impact on the sport. As Swaziland's first professional golfer, Dlamini paved the way for future generations from his homeland. His long tenure as the Head Professional and Coach at the

Royal Swazi Country Club, where he served from 1981 to 2006, highlights his dedication to the development of golf in the region.

In recognition of his achievements, Dlamini was named Golfer of the Year in 1978 and was inducted into the Southern Africa Golf Hall of Fame in 2013. His prowess on the course is evident from his impressive record, including nine victories in the Swaziland Amateur Championship and over twelve professional wins. His professional victories encompass notable titles such as the 1983 Natal Non-European Championship and the 1988 Marley Classic on the TPA Non-European Tour, as well as the 1986 Royal Swazi Sun and the Pro-Shop Swazi Pro-Am on the Sunshine Tour. He also had a notable second-place finish in the 1989 Hollard Royal Swazi Spa.

Joe Dlamini's career is marked by his groundbreaking role as a professional golfer from Swaziland, his contributions to the Royal Swazi Country Club, and his significant impact on golf in Southern Africa.

DLAMINI, NOBUHLE SWAZILAND

Nobuhle Dlamini's story is one of exceptional talent and groundbreaking achievement in the world of golf. Born in Swaziland, now Eswatini, she emerged as a trailblazer in the sport, becoming the first black female professional golfer from her country. Her journey from a young golfer in Swaziland to a prominent figure in South African and international golf is a testament to her skill, perseverance, and the strong foundation laid by her coach and father, Joe Dlamini, who is revered as the "father of Swaziland golf."

Dlamini's amateur career was marked by remarkable success. She won the South African Women's Championship in 2009, and dominated the South African Women Strokeplay with titles in 2012 and 2013, and a runner-up finish in 2011. Her exceptional performances earned her a place in the world's top ten in 2012, where she achieved a career-high ranking of world number two, just behind Lydia Ko. She solidified her reputation as South Africa's leading female golfer by successfully defending her title at the Sanlam South African Women's Amateur Stroke-Play in 2013.

Transitioning to professional golf, Dlamini made her mark on the Sunshine Ladies Tour with a series of notable achievements. Her first professional victory came at the 2018 SuperSport Ladies Challenge, setting the stage for a series of successes. Over her career, she amassed eight titles on the Sunshine Ladies Tour. In 2019, she was crowned the Order of Merit winner, underscoring her dominance on the tour. Her notable victories include the SuperSport Ladies Challenge and the Investec Royal Swazi (Ladies) in 2018, and a string of victories in 2019, including the Dimension Data Ladies Pro-Am, Joburg Ladies Open, and multiple events at the Investec Royal Swazi (Ladies).

Known for her accuracy on the fairway, finesse around the greens, and near-flawless putting, Dlamini's prowess on the golf course is matched by her natural strength, as noted by her coach Llewellyn van Leeuwen. Her career is a shining example of talent and dedication, driven by her father's guidance and her own relentless pursuit of excellence. Today, as a member of the Ladies European Tour, Nobuhle Dlamini stands as one of the leading figures in African women's golf, continuing to inspire and pave the way for future generations of golfers.

DODDS, TREVOR (1959) NAMIBIA

Trevor George Dodds is a notable professional golfer with a distinguished career across multiple tours.

He is known for winning the 1998 Greater Greensboro Chrysler Classic shooting 68 in the last round. He won the Canadian Tour Order of Merit in 1995 and 1996. Dodds has compiled 13 wins on four different tours: the PGA Tour, Nationwide

Tour, Sunshine Tour and the Canadian Tour, and 8 runner-up positions. In 1990 he won the Protea Assurance South African Open, and the 1996 Canadian Masters. He participated in the 1996 World Cup representing Namibia.

Dodds' career is highlighted by his success on multiple tours, his victories in significant tournaments, and his representation of Namibia on the international stage.

DOWNS, MADGE SOUTH AFRICA

Madge Downs made substantial contributions to golf through her leadership and administrative roles across various golf unions. Her influence was particularly felt in the Free State Golf Union and the Natal Ladies Golf Union (LGU).

Downs' journey in golf administration began with the Free State Golf Union, where she served as President from 1969 to 1972, after being a member of the Executive Committee from 1967 to 1969. Her leadership during this period was crucial in shaping the direction and growth of golf in the Free State region.

Following her impactful tenure with the Free State Golf Union, Downs moved to the Natal Ladies Golf Union. Here, she took on multiple significant roles, starting as Secretary/Treasurer from 1972 to 1975, before advancing to Vice-President from 1975 to 1978. Her leadership culminated with her presidency of the Natal LGU from 1978 to 1980. In these roles, Downs played a pivotal part in the administration and promotion of golf within Natal, helping to enhance the sport's visibility and management.

Madge Downs' dedication to golf administration in both the Free State and Natal regions left a lasting legacy, reflecting her commitment to the development and growth of the sport.

DRYSDALE, JOHN RHODESIA, FEDERATION, NORTHERN RHODESIA

John Drysdale's name is etched in the annals of amateur golf history as one of the sport's greats in Rhodesia and Northern Rhodesia, now Zimbabwe and Zambia. His golfing career was marked by exceptional achievements and significant contributions to the sport, demonstrating his prowess and dedication on and off the course.

Drysdale first garnered attention in the mid-1950s and quickly established himself as a formidable competitor. In 1958 and 1960, he represented the Federation in international competitions, showcasing his skills on a broader stage. His selection for the Rhodesia national team in 1960 further cemented his status as a leading amateur golfer. Similarly, his participation in the Northern Rhodesia national team in 1959 and 1960 demonstrated his versatility and strength across regional teams.

Drysdale's individual achievements were nothing short of remarkable. He clinched victories at the Central African Amateur in 1956, 1959, and 1963, and secured the Northern Rhodesia Amateur title in 1959 and 1964. His wins at the Cock o' North in 1958 and 1963, the Broken Hill Open in both 1957 and 1958, and the Katanga Amateur in 1958 highlight his dominance in regional tournaments. His success extended into 1966 with a victory at the Nachanga Open, and he was also a runner-up at the Roan Antelope in 1959 and 1962.

Drysdale's competitive edge was particularly evident in team match performances. He played a pivotal role in Northern Rhodesia's historic victory over the Springboks, contributing significantly to their triumph in the first test match with a narrow score of 6.5 to 5.5. Drysdale's individual match wins included notable victories against high-profile players such as Jannie Le Roux, Gary Player, and Bobby Locke, underscoring his ability to compete at the highest level.

John Drysdale's impressive record in both individual and team golf, combined with his ability to challenge and overcome some of the sport's biggest names, solidifies his legacy as one of the era's premier amateur golfers. His career not only highlights his exceptional talent but also his dedication to advancing the sport in his region.

DUNNE, PHIL NORTHERN RHODESIA, SOUTH AFRICA

Phil Dunne, an accomplished amateur golfer, made significant contributions to the sport across multiple countries, including Northern Rhodesia, Zambia, and South Africa. His career is highlighted by his performances in both individual tournaments and team competitions. Dunne's international representation began in 1963 when he played for Combined Rhodesia in a match against the Springboks and Kenya. In 1964, he represented Northern Rhodesia at the World Cup, finishing in an impressive 13th place. After moving to South Africa, Dunne continued to excel, earning selections to represent the Springboks in 1972 and 1973.

Dunne's amateur career was distinguished by several notable victories. He won the Northern Rhodesia Amateur twice, in 1963 and 1965, and claimed victories in the Copperbelt Amateur and Lusaka Open in both 1963 and 1964. His success also included multiple wins at the Chinama Hill Open and Broken Hill Open during the early 1960s. In addition to these victories, Dunne reached the semi-finals of the 1967 Transvaal Amateur and won the South African Amateur Stroke Play in 1972. His achievements extended to the Swaziland Amateur, where he dominated with wins in 1972, 1973, and 1974, and he continued to demonstrate his competitive spirit by making it to the semi-finals of the 1978 South African Amateur.

Phil Dunne left a lasting impact on the sport through his impressive performances and dedication to amateur golf. Their careers reflect a high level of skill and commitment, contributing significantly to the golfing community in Africa.

DU PLESSIS, HENNIE (1996) SOUTH AFRICA

Hennie du Plessis has carved out a notable career in professional golf, marked by a blend of individual and team successes that have earned him recognition on both national and international stages.

In the world of professional golf, du Plessis has demonstrated a remarkable level of skill and consistency. His tenure on the Sunshine Tour highlights his competitive edge, with standout performances in 2016 and the 2017–18 season. He achieved five top-5 finishes in 2016, including a tie

for second place at the Vodacom Origins of Golf. His prowess continued into the following year, where he secured victories at both the Vodacom Origins of Golf and the Steyn City Team Championship, partnering with Jean Hugo to claim the latter title.

Du Plessis's career took a significant leap onto the global stage in 2022 when he competed in the LIV Golf Invitational London. His impressive performance at this tournament saw him finish as the runner-up, narrowly missing out on first place to compatriot Charl Schwartzel by just one stroke. This near-victory was particularly lucrative, earning du Plessis a substantial prize of $2,125,000. Additionally, his team success at the same event, where he joined forces with Schwartzel, Branden Grace, and Louis Oosthuizen, resulted in a team victory and an extra $750,000 in earnings.

With four professional victories and nine runner-up finishes, du Plessis's career reflects his ability to compete fiercely at the highest levels of the sport. His achievements on both the Sunshine Tour and the LIV Golf Series underscore his talent and competitiveness, marking him as a significant figure in professional golf.

DU TOIT, COMRIE SOUTH AFRICA

Comrie du Toit was a prominent figure in South African amateur golf during the 1960s, renowned for his exceptional skill and numerous accomplishments. His career was marked by consistent success across various prestigious tournaments and his contributions to South African golf.

Du Toit's impressive resume includes notable achievements such as representing the Springboks in 1966, 1967, and 1968. His most significant accomplishment came in 1966 when he won the esteemed South African Amateur Championship. That year was particularly notable for du Toit, as he also claimed victories in the Transvaal Amateur, Brazilian Amateur, Maccauvlei Match Play, and the Royal Johannesburg Silver Vase. His dominance extended into the following years, with victories in the Eastern Transvaal Amateur, Western Transvaal Amateur, Northern Transvaal Silver Salver, and a second win in the Transvaal Amateur in 1968. In 1969, he added the Oppenheimer Trophy to his list of achievements, further solidifying his status as one of the top amateurs of his era.

E

EASTON, BRYCE (1987) SOUTH AFRICA

Bryce Easton is a distinguished South African professional golfer known for his remarkable ability to perform under pressure and his knack for dramatic finishes. His career highlights include several notable victories that have cemented his reputation as a formidable competitor on the golf course.

Easton's professional career took off with a thrilling debut win at the 2012 Sun City Challenge. In an unforgettable conclusion to the tournament, Easton eagled the final hole to force a playoff. His dramatic flair continued as he eagled once more during the playoff, securing his first professional victory in a style that captured the attention of the golfing world.

Just two weeks after this initial triumph, Easton added to his growing list of achievements by winning the 2012 Vodacom Origins of Golf. This back-to-back success marked him as a rising star in the golfing community, showcasing his ability to maintain high performance and capitalize on momentum.

Easton's career continued to flourish, with a significant highlight being his victory at the 2018 Zimbabwe Open. In a closely contested event, Easton edged out Daniel van Tonder by a single stroke, demonstrating his composure and skill in high-stakes situations.

Bryce Easton's career is characterised by his dramatic performances and clutch victories. His ability to deliver spectacular moments when it counts has solidified his status as a leading figure on the Sunshine Tour and a prominent golfer in South Africa.

EASTON, RITA (LEVETAN) (DIED 2014) UNION SOUTH AFRICA

Rita Easton was a remarkable figure whose legacy spans both her exceptional achievements in golf and her unwavering commitment to social justice. Her career as a golfer was distinguished by a series of notable accomplishments, while her activism underscored her dedication to fighting against apartheid in South Africa.

Easton's golfing career was marked by a series of triumphs that established her as one of the foremost female golfers of her time. She claimed the South African Ladies Championship title an impressive seven times, in 1950, 1951, 1955, 1958, 1959, 1960, and 1968. Her dominance in the sport was evident over nearly two decades, with a notable second-place finish in 1967 highlighting her consistency. Internationally, Easton showcased her talent on a global stage, competing in Australia and reaching the finals at the British Open, demonstrating her prowess beyond South African borders.

Easton's journey in golf was also marked by significant milestones, including her brief stint as a professional golfer. She was one of the first women professionals in South Africa, a role she eventually left to return to amateur status, only to immediately reclaim the South African Ladies Championship. This feat underscored her extraordinary skill and adaptability. Renowned for her putting prowess, Easton was known for her meticulous practice routines, including putting through a jam tin at home, which became a hallmark of her game.

In 2009, Easton's contributions to golf were formally recognized when she was inducted into the inaugural Southern Africa Golf Hall of Fame alongside other golfing greats like Sally Little. This honor cemented her status as one of South Africa's greatest female golfers.

Beyond her accomplishments on the golf course, Easton's legacy is profoundly marked by her activism. She was deeply involved in the struggle against apartheid, serving as a dedicated member of the Black Sash, an organisation committed to peaceful protests and human rights advocacy. Her activism was hands-on; she ran the Black Sash office in Durban for five years and engaged directly with political figures such as Helen Suzman, a leader of the Progressive Federal Party. Easton was also a prolific writer, using her voice in the press to address political matters and advocate for justice.

Rita Easton's legacy is a testament to her dual commitment to excellence in sport and her courageous efforts to advance social justice. Her induction into the Southern Africa Golf Hall of Fame stands as a fitting tribute to her significant contributions both on and off the golf course.

ELKIN, BERT H. UNION SOUTH AFRICA

Bert Elkin was a standout figure in South African golf during the early 1920s, leaving a lasting mark on the sport with his exceptional skill and competitiveness. His career was highlighted by a series of impressive victories and consistent top finishes in major tournaments, solidifying his reputation as one of the leading golfers of his time.

Elkin's achievements in the South African Open are particularly noteworthy. He secured the title in 1924 and was a formidable competitor in subsequent years, finishing as runner-up in 1920, 1926, and 1927, and placing third in 1932. His dominance extended to other prestigious events, including the Western Province Open, where he emerged victorious in 1933 and was a runner-up in 1930 and 1931. His success continued with wins at the Transvaal Open in 1926 and the Free State & Basutoland Open in 1923, 1924, and 1927, further showcasing his versatility and skill across different courses.

In addition to these victories, Elkin triumphed in the South African PGA Championship in 1923, establishing himself as a leading player in the professional ranks. His competitive spirit was evident in his performances at the Lexington PGA Championship, where he finished as runner-up in 1934 and 1940. Elkin also achieved notable success in the South African

Professional Knock-out Championship, winning the title in 1908, 1923, 1924, and 1926, and finishing as runner-up in 1934, 1938, and 1940.

Elkin's career spanned a transformative period in South African golf, and his impressive list of achievements reflects his status as a prominent professional golfer before the rise of Jock Brews. His success across multiple tournaments and his consistent top finishes cemented his legacy as a key figure in the early history of South African golf.

ELKIN, MAJOR KEN UNION SOUTH AFRICA

Major Ken Elkin was a prominent figure in South African golf, having emigrated to the country in September 1911. He served as the professional golfer at Mowbray Golf Club for 34 years and at Hermanus Golf Club for 12 years. Beyond his playing career, Elkin was an accomplished course designer, creating 40 golf courses across South Africa. His contributions to the sport were recognized with the prestigious honor of being named a South African PGA Life Member.

Elkin's influence extended across numerous clubs, and his designs included notable courses such as Devonvale Golf, Parow, Durbanville, Shelley Point, Windhoek, Ceres, Paarl, Robertson, Stellenbosch, Swellendam, and Erinvale. His work left a lasting legacy on the golf landscape in South Africa.

As a player, Elkin's career was marked by significant victories. He won the South African PGA Championship in 1923 and the South African Open in 1924. His success continued in 1926, when he secured the Transvaal Open title, further cementing his place in South African golf history. Even in the later stages of his career, Elkin remained competitive, finishing as runner-up in the South African PGA Championship in both 1934 and 1940—remarkably, the latter at the age of 54. His dedication and achievements made him an enduring and respected figure in South African golf history.

ELS, THEODORE ERNEST 'ERNIE' (1969) SOUTH AFRICA

Theodore Ernest Els is nicknamed "The Big Easy" due to his physical stature along with his fluid golf swing. He held the number one spot in the Official World Golf Ranking June 1997 for nine weeks, and until 2013 held the record for weeks ranked in the top ten with 788, with 78 professional wins including 21 PGA Tour victories, 28 European Tour victories, and 16 Sunshine Tour wins.

Els is one of the greats of world golf, with best results in majors being the US Open 1994, 97; The Open Championship 2002, 2012 "It was my time for some reason," Els said. "A lot of people never thought I would win another one. I started believing this year." He lost 2004 playoff, and won the 2024 Senior Players Championship. He also came 2nd in the Masters 2000, 2004; and 3rd in the PGA Championship 1995, 1997. Other victories include South Africa Open (5), Players Championship (2), World Match Play (7), World Cup in 1996, 2001, World Cup Individual 1996, SA PGA (3), and the Nedbank Challenge (3).

His achievements include being inducted into the 2009 Southern Africa Golf Hall of Fame, and the 2011 World Golf Hall of Fame. He was the Southern Africa Tour Order of Merit winner 1991-92, 1994-95; European Tour Golfer of the Year 1994, 2002, 03; PGA Tour Rookie of the Year 1994; European Tour Order of Merit winner 2003, 04; Payne Stewart Award 2015; and the Old Tom Morris Award 2018.

As an amateur he won the Junior World Golf Championship in the Boys 13-14 category. Phil Mickelson was second that year. He won the South African Amateur a few months after his 17th birthday, becoming the youngest-ever winner of that event, breaking the record which had been held since 1935 by Bobby Locke. In 1989, he won the South African Amateur Stroke Play Championship.

As a professional, in 1994 Els won his first major championship at the U.S. Open. Els was tied with Colin Montgomerie and Loren Roberts after 72 holes and they went to an 18-hole playoff the next day. In spite of starting the playoff bogey-triple bogey, Els was able to match Roberts› score of 74, then he birdied the second hole of sudden death to win his first U.S. Open title. PGA Championship: Third place in 1995 and 1997.

2000 was the year of runners-up with three runner-up finishes in the Majors (Masters – also 2004, U.S. Open and The Open Championship). while 2002 was arguably Els's best year The premier moment of the season was surely his Open Championship. Els overcame a four-man playoff to take home the famous Claret Jug.

2004 was the start of the "Big Five era", the era in golf in which Tiger Woods, Vijay Singh, Ernie Els, Retief Goosen and Phil Mickelson dominated the game. The five switched up and down the top five positions in the World Golf Ranking, and for the most part, stayed in the top five spots from 2004 until the start of 2007. Els surprised the golfing world by winning the 2012 Open Championship in July by birding the 72nd hole.

Other Victories: South African Open: 5 wins; Players Championship: 2 wins; World Match Play Championship: 7 wins; World Cup: Winner in 1996 and 2001; World Cup Individual in 1996; South African PGA: 3 wins; Nedbank Challenge: 3 wins.

In preparation for the anchored putter ban in 2016, he switched back to the short putter in late 2015. Els's struggles with short putts, or the "yips," became the draw of much media attention in early 2016. At the 2016 Masters Tournament, his putting was again the source of negative publicity when he six-putted from 3 feet on his opening hole. In 2020, Els joined the PGA Tour Champions, and after coming close, in 2024 he won the Senior Players Major.

Els has designed 8 golf courses in Mauritius, China, USA, South Africa, UAE, Malaysia, with another 4 under construction in Hawaii, Bahamas, Vietnam, and Bahrain.

Since his son's autism diagnosis, Els and his wife have been active in charities devoted to that condition. In 2009, Els launched an annual charity golf event, the 'Els for Autism' Pro-Am for The Renaissance Learning Center. The couple also established the Els Center of Excellence, which began as a drive to build a new campus for the aforementioned school in Jupiter, Florida, but has since expanded into a $30 million plan to combine the school with a research facility.

Awards and Honors: Southern Africa Golf Hall of Fame: Inducted in 2009; World Golf Hall of Fame: Inducted in 2011; Southern Africa Tour Order of Merit: Winner in 1991-92 and 1994-95; European Tour Golfer of the Year: 1994, 2002, 2003; European Tour Order of Merit: Winner in 2003 and 2004; Payne Stewart Award: 2015; Old Tom Morris Award: 2018.

Ernie Els's legacy extends well beyond his impressive career on the course to include significant contributions to the game of golf and important charitable initiatives.

F

FALL, R.G. UNION SOUTH AFRICA

SA Golf Magazine: Began publication in June 1926 under the editorship of R.G. Fall; Official Mouthpiece of SAGU: By the 1929 AGM, SA Golf Magazine was unanimously adopted as the official journal of the South African Golf Union (SAGU). Delegates were encouraged to promote subscriptions to ensure the magazine's success and continuity.

Premier golf historian for Southern Africa, documenting the region's golf history from 1926 to 1986; Contributions: Fall's work with SA Golf Magazine made significant contributions to recording and preserving Southern Africa's golf heritage; Recognition: In 2009, he was inducted into the inaugural Southern Africa Golf Hall of Fame in acknowledgment of his valuable contributions to the sport.

R.G. Fall's dedication to documenting and preserving the history of golf in Southern Africa has left an enduring legacy, making him a key figure in the sport's historical record.

FERRIS, MRS E GRINDLEY UNION SOUTH AFRICA

Mrs. Grindley Ferris was a pioneering figure in Southern African golf, recognized for her significant contributions to the development of women's golf in the region. Her involvement began with her participation in the foundational committee of the Southern African Ladies Golf Union (SALGU) in 1910, where she helped draft the initial rules. Alongside prominent figures like Jooste and Gibb, she played a crucial role in the establishment of SALGU.

Her dedication extended to serving as the handicap manager for SALGU from 1918 to 1919, and she was actively involved in tournament management. She organized and managed the first SALGU tournament in 1920 and continued to oversee subsequent events through the mid-1920s. Her administrative roles included serving as Honorary Secretary of SALGU from 1919 to 1924 and later as President from 1924 to 1927 and again from 1932 to 1934. In recognition of her long-term commitment, she was named a Life Member of the SALGU Executive Council in 1927.

Beyond her work with SALGU, Mrs. Ferris was Vice-President of the Transvaal Ladies Golf Union (LGU) from 1915 to 1927 and served as President of the Rapenburg Golf Club (Mowbray Club) in 1925. Her extensive contributions to golf administration and tournament management played a pivotal role in laying the foundation for organized women's golf in Southern Africa, and her impact on the sport is widely celebrated.

FICHARDT, DARREN (1975) SOUTH AFRICA

Darren Richard is a distinguished South African professional golfer known for his successful career on both the European and Sunshine Tours. With a highest World Ranking of 75, Fichardt's achievements on the tour include notable victories and consistent performance.

Fichardt has twice won the Southern Africa Tour Order of Merit, first in the 1999/2000 season and again in the 2003/2004 season. He also represented South Africa in the WGC-World Cup in 2000, partnering with Retief Goosen.

In terms of professional victories, Fichardt has accumulated a total of 27 wins. His European Tour successes include five victories: the 2001 Brazil Open and Qatar Masters, the 2012 Saint-Omer Open, the 2013 Africa Open, and the 2017 Joburg Open. The Saint-Omer Open win in 2012 ended a nine-year title drought, while his victory at the Joburg Open added to his impressive tally.

On the Sunshine Tour, Fichardt has achieved 17 victories, with a notable win at the 2020 Betway Championship, where he secured the title with a final round of 64, narrowly defeating Ulrich van den Berg by one shot.

Fichardt's career is characterized by his consistent performance and significant achievements, both on the national and international stages.

FINLAYSON, KEN KENYA

Ken Finlayson stands out as a Kenyan golf legend renowned for his remarkable achievements in amateur golf during the mid-to-late 1950s. His success includes multiple wins at the Kenya Amateur Championship, where he claimed victory in 1958 and 1960, and was a runner-up in 1959 and 1961. Finlayson's prowess extended to other prestigious events; he won the Coronation Cup in 1956 and finished as a runner-up in 1958. Additionally, he was a runner-up in the Trans-Nzoia Amateur in 1958 and secured victory in the Singona Bowl (Kenya) in 1960. At the Karen Country Club (Karen Blixen's former home - film Out of Africa), Finlayson triumphed in 1958, 1959, and 1960, and also won the Kanya in 1958. His consistent performance and dominance in these tournaments highlight his exceptional skill and significant contributions to Kenyan golf.

FISHER JNR, TREVOR (1979) SOUTH AFRICA

Trevor Henry Fisher Jnr is a notable professional golfer with a total of ten career victories. His most significant win came at the Africa Open in 2015, a tournament co-sanctioned by both the Sunshine Tour and the European Tour. Fisher Jnr has also had several notable runner-up finishes, including at the Zimbabwe Open in 2012 and 2017, and the Eye of Africa PGA Championship in 2019. His career achievements reflect his competitiveness and skill on both the Sunshine Tour and the European Tour.

FOLLET-SMITH, BENJAMIN (1994) ZIMBABWE

Benjamin Follett-Smith has made a significant impact in professional golf, securing five career wins. Among his most notable victories are the Cape Town Open in both 2019 and 2023, both of which were co-sanctioned by the Challenge Tour. His professional achievements build on a strong amateur background, which includes winning the All-Africa Junior Championship in 2012 and representing Zimbabwe in the All-Africa Team Championships. Follett-Smith's international success also includes competing in the 2018 World Cup of Golf alongside fellow Zimbabwean Scott Vincent. In 2024, he added another prestigious title to his résumé by winning the D+D Real Czech Challenge, marking his second victory on the Challenge Tour.

FOTHERINGHAM, GEORGE LYALL (1883–1971) CAPE COLONY, UNION SOUTH AFRICA, SCOTLAND, USA

George Fotheringham was a towering figure in the early days of South African and American golf, leaving an indelible mark on both continents. Born in Carnoustie, Scotland, in 1883, Fotheringham's passion for the game began at a young age when he started caddying and apprenticing as a club maker, skills that would shape his future. He quickly grew in prominence, becoming a club champion in his hometown before making the life-altering decision to move to the Colony of Natal, South Africa, in 1903. Upon his arrival, he became the first professional at Durban Golf Club, now known as Royal Durban Golf Club.

Between 1905 and 1914, Fotheringham was nearly unbeatable on the South African golf scene. His greatest claim to fame came with his victories at the South African Open, which he won five times – in 1908, 1910, 1911, 1912, and 1914 – solidifying his legacy as one of the game's greats. He was a fierce competitor, reaching the runner-up position twice, in 1905 and 1909. Despite the passage of time, his love for golf never waned, as he continued competing in the South African Open well into his later years, even participating at the remarkable age of 75 in 1958.

Fotheringham's career, however, was far from confined to the African continent. In 1914, he crossed the Atlantic to the United States, accepting a professional position at the Williamsport Country Club in Pennsylvania. It was here that he played a pivotal role in the growth of professional golf in America. As one of the founding members of the PGA of America in 1916, he was instrumental in shaping the organization, serving on its first executive committee and chairing its inaugural meetings. Fotheringham competed in the first two PGA Championship tournaments, in 1916 and 1919, and though his career was beginning to wind down, he managed to defeat Eddie Loos in 1919, finishing tied for ninth overall.

Even as his playing career began to fade, Fotheringham's contributions to the game never stopped. He remained an active participant in the development of golf, both as a player and administrator. He finished second in significant tournaments like the Philadelphia Open in 1920 and the New Jersey Open in 1924, further cementing his place in golf history.

In recognition of his extraordinary achievements, George Fotheringham was inducted into the Southern Africa Golf Hall of Fame in its inaugural class in 2009. His story, from his humble beginnings as a caddy in Carnoustie to becoming a dominant force in South African golf and a founding member of the PGA of America, is a testament to his enduring influence on the game of golf.

FOURIE, JOHN (1939) SOUTH AFRICA

Jonathan Adriaan Fourie, a distinguished figure in South African golf, has been inducted into the Southern Africa Golf Hall of Fame for his exceptional contributions to the sport. Throughout his career, he achieved notable success both domestically and internationally.

As an amateur, Fourie represented South Africa in the Eisenhower Trophy in 1966, 1968, and 1970, securing a third-place finish in 1970. He also competed in the Canada Cup in 1966 and the Commonwealth Tournament in 1967. His South African Amateur titles include victories at the SA Open in 1963, the Freddie Tate Trophy in 1970, and multiple regional championships such as the Northern Transvaal Amateur and Silver Salver in 1966 and 1970. Fourie also set a record in the Transvaal Amateur Stroke Play with a score of 278 in 1967. His performance in international amateur tournaments was impressive, with notable results such as winning the British Amateur and Gold Vase in 1966, and reaching the semi-finals in the French Amateur and Canadian Amateur in the same year.

In his professional career, Fourie accumulated 18 wins, with significant victories including the Dunlop Masters in 1970, the Transvaal Open in 1973, and multiple wins at the WP Open and SA Masters. He also achieved a notable European Tour victory at the Callers of Newcastle Open in 1977.

As a senior golfer, Fourie continued to excel, winning the European Seniors Order of Merit in 1991 and claiming titles at the British Senior Open and the Belfast Telegraph Irish Senior Masters in the same year. He also won the SA Senior Open five times, cementing his legacy in senior golf.

FRANKLIN, BARRY SOUTH AFRICA

Barry Franklin, known for his early brilliance in golf, made a significant mark both as an amateur and a professional.

As an amateur, Franklin represented South Africa in the Springbok team in 1962 and 1963. He excelled in several notable amateur tournaments, securing titles at Schoeman Park in 1959, 1961, and 1962. He was a strong contender in the South African Open, finishing as the runner-up in 1961 and 1963. Franklin also won the Freddie Tait Trophy in 1961, 1962, and 1963, and clinched victories at the Northern Transvaal Amateur and Transvaal Amateur during the same period. He was a consistent performer in major tournaments, with twenty-six second-place finishes highlighting his competitive edge.

Transitioning to the professional circuit, Franklin achieved eight career wins. His victories include the Woodlawn Ramstein US Air Base in 1965, the Rhodesian Dunlop in 1966, the French Open in 1967, the German Open and Rhodesian Open in 1968, and the Swiss Open in 1971. Franklin also had notable runner-up finishes at the German Open in 1964 and the West German Open in 1968.

After retiring from competitive play, Franklin continued his involvement in golf as a club professional at Kempton Park, contributing his expertise to the sport even beyond his competitive years.

FRIEDLANDER, PAUL (1971) SWAZILAND

Friedlander had a successful college career winning the 1992 Elkins Lake Fall Classic, medalist at the 1993 Oklahoma State Amateur tournament, and won the 1994 UALR Intercollegiate.

As a Professional he won the 1995 IDC Development Classic in South Africa by 8 strokes, and that year he played for the Royal Swazi Sun Golf Club. The following year, he finished runner-up to James Kingston at the Bushveld Classic. In 1996, he also won the Asian Tour's 1998 Gadgil Western Dubai Creek Open, as well as winning the Stenham Royal Swazi Sun Open, an official event on the Sunshine Tour in his home country of Swaziland.

Despite these victories Friedlander did not have much else success, rarely recording other top ten finishes. In February 1999, frustrated after years of "wallowing in mediocrity," he announced his retirement from tournament golf at the age of 28. In all he has three professional wins.

FRITTELLI, DYLAN (1990) SOUTH AFRICA

Dylan Frittelli's golfing career has been marked by a series of impressive achievements both as an amateur and a professional.

As an amateur, Frittelli made his mark by winning the Callaway Junior World Golf Championships in 2007 for the 15-17 age group and the South African Boys' Championship in 2008. He represented South Africa in the Eisenhower Trophy in 2008 and 2010, showcasing his talent on an international stage. His college golf career at the University of Texas was notable for his decisive performance in the NCAA Championship in 2012.

Turning professional, Frittelli accumulated seven career wins. His professional journey began with a strong showing, finishing second in the Telkom PGA Championship in 2013. He secured his first Challenge Tour victory at the Kärnten Golf Open in 2014 and narrowly missed out on the Australian PGA Championship title in 2015, losing in a playoff.

In 2016, he earned a tie for second place in the Tayto Northern Ireland Open and won the Rolex Trophy, his second Challenge Tour victory. The following year, Frittelli achieved significant success on the European Tour, including a win at the Lyoness Open, a runner-up finish in the Turkish Airlines Open, and a tie for fourth in the DP World Tour Championship, Dubai. He also triumphed in the AfrAsia Bank Mauritius Open, securing the victory in a playoff and was named the 2017 European Tour Graduate of the Year.

Frittelli's achievements continued with his first PGA Tour victory at the John Deere Classic in 2019, where he shot 21-under par. In 2024, he marked a return to form with a win at the Bahrain Championship, his first European Tour victory in six years. Despite contemplating giving up the game before the final round, he clinched the title with a strong performance on the back nine, winning by two shots at Royal Golf Club.

FROST, DAVID LAURENCE (1959) SOUTH AFRICA

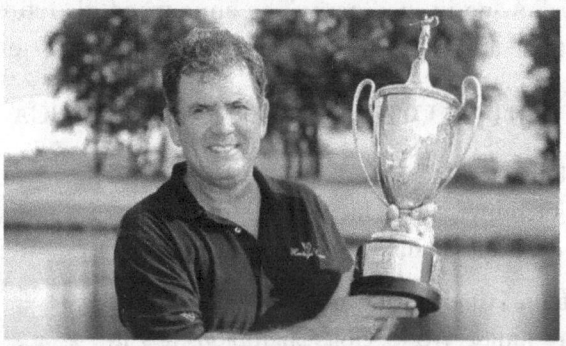

David "Frosty" Frost, despite a modest amateur career, developed an exceptional putting stroke that propelled him to a distinguished professional career. Frost amassed a total of 31 professional wins and reached a highest world ranking of 6.

On the PGA Tour, Frost secured ten victories, including notable wins at the World Series of Golf, the South African Open twice, the Nedbank Million Dollar Challenge three times, and the Canadian Open. His success extended to the European Tour, where he was part of the winning team at the Alfred Dunhill Cup in 1997 and 1998 alongside Ernie Els and Retief Goosen. He also claimed the Sunshine Tour Order of Merit for the 1998/99 season.

In major championships, Frost's highest finishes were 6th place at The Open Championship in 1987 and 5th place at The Masters in 1995. His achievements on the senior circuit include winning the Regions Tradition in June 2013, which was his first senior major, and he narrowly missed out on another major, losing in a playoff at the 2010 Senior PGA Championship.

Frost's career on the Champions Tour was marked by six titles, including a victory at the Mississippi Gulf Resort Classic in March 2015. His awards and recognition include the Byron Nelson Award in 1987, the Southern Africa Tour Order of Merit in 1998-99, and induction into the inaugural Southern Africa Golf Hall of Fame in 2009.

Additional notable achievements include winning the NEC World Series of Golf in 1989, where he defeated Ben Crenshaw in a playoff. He was ranked in the top 10 for 86 weeks between 1988 and 1994 and set a PGA Tour record for the fewest putts in 72 holes with 92 putts at the MCI Heritage in 2005.

Frost also made significant contributions to team golf, representing South Africa at the Alfred Dunhill Cup, where he captained the team to victory in 1997 and 1998. He played for the Rest of the World in the Hennessy Cognac Cup in 1984 and represented South Africa in the World Cup in 1994 and 1996, as well as being a member of the International Team in the Presidents Cup in 1994 and 1996.

G

GAILLE, ESTHER UNION SOUTH AFRICA

Esther Gaille made a significant impact both on and off the golf course. In her administrative roles, she was a dedicated member of the Transvaal Ladies Golf Union (TLGU) from 1946 to 1972, serving as an executive member and as President from 1963 to 1969. She also played a crucial role in the South African Ladies Golf Union (SALGU), where she served as an executive member, Vice-President, and President, totaling 24 years of service. Gaille was a prominent figure at the Royal Johannesburg Golf Club, where she was Captain in 1942, 1943, and 1946, and was later honored as a Lady Life-Member. Additionally, she represented South Africa on the World Council Ladies Golf from 1966 to 1976.

Her contributions earned her several honors, including being named Honourary Life President of both the TLGU and Royal Johannesburg LGC, receiving the Sport Merit Award in 1978, and being inducted into the Southern Africa Golf Hall of Fame.

Gaille's representation on the national stage was notable. She played for the Springbok Team in 1951 and 1953, and captained the team in 1957, 1966, 1970, and 1972, also serving as a manager during these years. Locally, she captained Transvaal in matches against the British team in 1951.

In her amateur career, Gaille achieved notable victories, including wins at the Transvaal Ladies Amateur in 1947, 1948, 1953, 1954, and 1956. She also excelled in Australian tournaments in 1953, with successes including leading qualifier at the Australian Championship and advancing to the semi-finals in several events. Her performance in the South African Ladies Amateur included a second-place finish in 1954 and semi-final appearances in 1947 and 1958.

GAMMON, MUSS RHODESIA, SOUTH AFRICA

Don Gammon's achievements in golf encompass both competitive successes and significant contributions to golf instruction.

Gammon represented internationally in the World Cups of 1971 and 1982. His amateur career included notable wins such as the Rhodesian

Amateur in 1965 and participation in the Flame Lily Bata Bush Babes in 1968. On the Sunshine Tour, he secured 25 top-ten finishes from 1968 to 1981.

In professional tournaments, Gammon accumulated nine wins in Rhodesian Pro Tournaments. He had several notable finishes, including second place in the Transvaal Open in 1969, the SA PGA and Welsh Open in 1971, and the Ellerines Pro 4 Ball in 1972, where he finished second with Allan Henning. Other significant finishes include fourth place in the Scottish Open in 1973, second place in the SA Open Seniors in 2003, and participation in the Ladies & Legends Royal Johannesburg in 2006.

Beyond his competitive career, Gammon made considerable contributions to golf as a teacher. He was the Lead Instructor at The Gammon Golf Academy and worked as a Club and Teaching Professional until 2019. He co-created the "Ultra Simple Golf" DVD series with his son Don, which gained television exposure.

GARCIA, NICOLE (1990) SOUTH AFRICA

Nicole's Garcia career highlights a blend of strong amateur and professional achievements. In 2013, she excelled in amateur tournaments by winning the Free State and Northern Cape Championship, the Gauteng Central Championship, and the Gauteng North Championship.

Her professional journey on the Ladies European Tour (LET) includes notable performances such as a runner-up finish at the 2015 Lalla Meryem Cup and a sixth-place finish at the 2016 Qatar Ladies Open. In 2017, she tied for seventh at the Andalucía Costa del Sol Open de España, where she famously saved par despite an unusual situation involving a referee's buggy. After facing a serious hip and back injury in 2018, which required surgery and extensive rehabilitation, she made a strong comeback in 2021. That year, she tied for third in the South African Women's Open and earned a spot at the U.S. Women's Open. In 2022, she led her team to victory at the Aramco Team Series – London, showcasing her leadership and competitive spirit. On the Sunshine Ladies Tour, she has secured three wins, adding to her impressive record.

GEDDES, DOUG UNION SOUTH AFRICA

Doug Geddes is renowned for his long-standing contributions to golf administration, particularly through his role as Secretary of the Natal Golf Union from 1937 to 1972, a remarkable 35-year tenure. His extensive service to the sport was recognized with honorary membership of the Royal and Ancient Golf Club of St Andrews (R&A), a prestigious accolade that underscores his significant impact and dedication to golf. Geddes' work in golf administration has left a lasting legacy in the sport.

GIBB, MAUD (TITTERTON) (1867–1932)
UNION SOUTH AFRICA, ENGLAND, SCOTLAND

Maud Titterton Gibb, originally known as Emily Maud Titterton, was a prominent amateur golfer who left an indelible mark on the sport, both in the UK and South Africa. Born in 1867, she is best remembered for her victory at the 1908 Women's Amateur Championship at the Old Course at St Andrews, where she triumphed over Dorothy Campbell in a dramatic extra-hole final. Throughout her career, she participated in numerous major championships and represented both Scotland and England in the Women's Home Internationals, achieving multiple victories.

Titterton's early years in competitive golf saw her reach the semi-finals of the 1897 Women's Amateur Championship at Gullane and the last-16 stages in several subsequent tournaments. She played consistently well but often lost to formidable opponents like Edith Orr, Bertha Thompson, and Lottie Dod. In 1902, she represented Scotland in the Women's Internationals, later switching to represent England in several events, including the Home Internationals in 1906, 1907, and 1908.

Titterton's 1908 victory at St Andrews was her most notable achievement, where she overcame a fierce challenge from Campbell in the final. That same year, she continued to perform strongly in the Scottish Women's Amateur Championship, though Campbell bested her in the quarter-finals.

In 1909 and 1911, personal tragedies, including the deaths of her fiancé and father, caused her to withdraw from major tournaments. However, she returned to golf with notable successes, including her participation in the 1910 Women's Home Internationals.

After marrying and becoming Maud Gibb, she moved to South Africa, where her influence on golf was profound. Gibb won the South African Championship in 1913 and 1914 and became the first president of the South African Ladies Golf Union. She also helped establish regional golf unions and the first ladies' interclub league, profoundly shaping women's golf in South Africa. Her leadership roles extended beyond the course, as she held the presidency of the South African Ladies Golf Union from 1914 to 1916 and again from 1919 to 1923.

Maud Gibb's impact on golf, especially in South Africa, is remembered through her organisational efforts, championships, and as the driving force behind the establishment of ladies' golf unions in the country. Her contributions earned her induction into the Southern Africa Golf Hall of Fame, cementing her legacy as one of the most influential figures in women's golf of her era.

GLENNIE, RONNIE UNION SOUTH AFRICA

Ronnie Glennie is renowned for his exceptional contributions to golf as an amateur. His professional highlight came with a victory in the South African Open in 1947. As an amateur, Glennie's achievements are numerous and distinguished. He won the South African Amateur in 1949 and was a runner-up in 1952, reaching the semi-finals in 1946. His victory in the People of Britain tournament in 1946 further underscored his prowess. Additionally, he excelled in regional competitions, winning the Western Province Amateur on multiple occasions and the Western Province Stroke Play four times. He also triumphed in the Cape Province Amateur and secured victories in the South African Seniors in 1974 and was a runner-up in 1973. Glennie's remarkable career and consistent performance across various tournaments earned him a well-deserved place in the Southern Africa Golf Hall of Fame.

GODBOLD, A.B. CAPE COLONY, UNION SOUTH AFRICA

A.B. Godbold is celebrated for his pivotal role in the development of golf in Southern Africa, particularly through his foundational work with the South African Golf Union. Inducted into the Southern Africa Golf Hall of Fame in 2009 as part of its inaugural class, Godbold's legacy is deeply rooted in his leadership and organizational contributions.

In 1909, Godbold played a crucial role in the formation of the South African Golf Union during a meeting in Potchefstroom. He was a key member of a special committee tasked with drafting the union's constitution, alongside H. Gunn and F. Black. The inaugural meeting was held at Cape Golf Club, where Lord Gladstone, the Governor-General, was elected as the Union's President. Godbold was elected Vice-President, bringing with him extensive experience from his presidency of the Football Association.

Godbold's influence extended well beyond the formation phase. From 1910 to 1930, he was widely recognized as the de facto President of the

South African Golf Union. In 1919, his role as President was officially formalized, a position further endorsed by the Governor-General's appointment as the Union's Patron. In 1933, Godbold also served as Captain of the Royal Cape Golf Club.

His enduring contributions and leadership were instrumental in shaping the structure and growth of golf in Southern Africa, leaving a lasting impact on the sport's development in the region.

GOOSEN, RETIEF (1969) SOUTH AFRICA

Retief Goosen's career is a tale of resilience, skill, and a quiet determination that earned him a place among golf's elite. Born in Pietersburg, South Africa, in 1969, Goosen's journey to the pinnacle of the golfing world is a story shaped by both triumph and adversity.

In 1987, Goosen's life took a dramatic turn when he was struck by lightning while playing at Pietersburg Golf Club. The incident, which left him with burned clothing and severe injuries, could have ended his career before it even began. But for Goosen, it was a defining moment that contributed to his famously calm demeanor on the course, earning him the nickname "The Iceman."

Goosen turned professional in 1990, having already made his mark by winning the South African Amateur Championship. However, his rise to global prominence took time. Early in his professional career, he played primarily on the Sunshine Tour and the European Tour, gradually building a reputation for consistency and composure under pressure. In 1997, Goosen secured his first European Tour victory at the Peugeot Open de France, a win that foreshadowed the success to come.

The turning point in Goosen's career came in 2001 when he captured his first major championship at the U.S. Open. On the challenging Southern Hills course, Goosen demonstrated the steady, unflappable temperament that had become his trademark. After a dramatic final round in which he missed a two-foot putt to win outright, Goosen faced off against Mark Brooks in an 18-hole playoff. The next day, he dominated the playoff, securing his first major title and proving he had the nerve to compete at the highest level.

That same year, Goosen's confidence soared, and his performances followed suit. He won the Scottish Open with a wire-to-wire victory, solidifying his place among the world's best. By the end of the season, he had topped the European Tour Order of Merit and risen to a career-high ranking of 11th in the world. Teaming up with fellow South African star Ernie Els, Goosen also added the WGC-World Cup to his growing list of accolades, further cementing his status as one of the game's greats.

Goosen's success continued into 2004, a year in which he won his second U.S. Open title. This time, the victory came at Shinnecock Hills, where he produced one of the most memorable clutch putting displays in major championship history. With treacherous greens testing the world's best players, Goosen calmly navigated his way to victory, once again demonstrating the poise that had become his hallmark. That same year, he also claimed the European Open, highlighting his ability to compete on both sides of the Atlantic.

Beyond his two U.S. Open victories, Goosen's career includes an impressive array of achievements. He has seven PGA Tour victories, five Asian Tour wins, and six Sunshine Tour titles, including two South African Opens. He also spent more than 250 weeks in the top ten of the world rankings between 2001 and 2007, a testament to his consistency and excellence over an extended period.

In recognition of his illustrious career, Goosen was inducted into the Southern Africa Golf Hall of Fame in 2009 and the World Golf Hall of

Fame in 2019. His legacy extends beyond his playing career, with his golf course designs, including Lizard Point and Legends in South Africa, showcasing his contributions to the sport's future.

Goosen's remarkable journey from a lightning strike survivor to a two-time U.S. Open champion is a testament to his resilience and perseverance. Known as "The Iceman" for his calm demeanor under pressure, Retief Goosen remains one of golf's most enduring and respected figures, a player whose achievements will be celebrated for generations to come.

GORDON-STEWART, H. CAPE COLONY, UNION SOUTH AFRICA

Gordon-Stewart was a force to be reckoned with in amateur golf from 1909 to 1929, establishing himself as one of the most formidable players of his time. Known for his consistency and competitive spirit, Stewart's golfing journey was marked by numerous victories and memorable performances that left an indelible mark on South African golf history.

His breakthrough moment came in 1909 when he not only claimed his first Western Province Amateur title but also finished as the runner-up in the prestigious South African Amateur Championship. This early success set the stage for an illustrious career, as Stewart quickly became a dominant figure in amateur golf. Over the next two decades, he captured the South African Amateur title three times, in 1912, 1919, and 1921, while finishing as a runner-up twice and taking third place on two other occasions.

Stewart's performance in the Western Province Amateur Championship was equally impressive. He claimed the title an astonishing eight times, including back-to-back wins from 1927 to 1929. His dominance extended beyond the Western Province, as he also captured multiple victories in the Transvaal Amateur Championship and the Cape Golf Club Championship, where he won a remarkable nine times between 1907 and 1929.

In 1919, Stewart nearly added another major title to his resume when he finished as the runner-up in the South African Open, showcasing his ability to compete against the best of the best. His continued success at both the national and provincial levels demonstrated his unwavering dedication to the game and solidified his place as one of South Africa's greatest amateur golfers.

What set Stewart apart was not only his ability to win but his consistency across multiple decades. His third-place finishes in the South African Amateur in 1908 and 1923, and his runner-up finishes in the Western Province Amateur in 1925, illustrate the longevity of his career and his ability to remain competitive against younger players.

Stewart's contribution to South African golf went far beyond just his victories. He played a pivotal role in raising the profile of amateur golf in the country, inspiring future generations of golfers. His remarkable achievements over a 20-year span, coupled with his sportsmanship and passion for the game, made him a true legend in the early days of South African golf.

In an era where professionalism was still in its infancy, Gordon Stewart's name stood tall among the amateurs, and he was inducted into the Southern Africa Golf Hall of Fame. His legacy as one of the game's early champions continues to be remembered to this day.

GOUGH, JAMIE SOUTH AFRICA

Jamie Gough is a distinguished golf coach with over 34 years of experience, renowned for his significant contributions to the game. His exceptional career has been marked by numerous accolades and a reputation as one of the world's leading golf instructors.

In 2017, Gough received the prestigious John Jacobs Award for Teaching & Coaching at the PGAs of Europe's Annual Congress Gala Awards, highlighting his exceptional coaching prowess. Throughout his career, he has mentored numerous elite players on the European Tour, including 17 tournament winners. His deep understanding of the game and his ability to guide professionals have solidified his status as a sought-after coach.

Gough's influence extends beyond South Africa, having coached the South African Eisenhower Team in 2006 and worked with players in major golf events like the Ryder Cup and World Golf Championships. Currently, he coaches top golfers such as Brandon Stone, Richard Sterne, Andy Sullivan, and Hao Tong Li, helping them maintain their competitive edge.

His impressive list of former clients includes notable names such as Miguel Angel Jimenez, Thomas Bjorn, Alex Noren, Jose Maria Olazabal, Anders Hanson, David Howell, Charl Schwartzel, Brett Rumford, Haydn Porteous, and George Coetzee. These players have achieved significant success, benefiting from Gough's coaching philosophy and technical insights.

Gough's contributions have earned him recognition from Golf Digest, which named him the No. 1 teacher in South Africa. He also founded and operated the largest and most successful chain of golf schools in the country, reflecting his commitment to growing the sport and developing talent.

Gough's coaching philosophy emphasizes mastering the fundamentals, particularly grip, setup, and posture. He incorporates ball flight observation into his teaching, inspired by John Jacobs, to help players translate technical skills into improved performance on the course. Jamie Gough's remarkable career and dedication to coaching have left a lasting impact on the game of golf, showcasing his exceptional ability to nurture and develop talent at all levels.

GOVENDER, HENRY SOUTH AFRICA – APARTHEID

Henry Govender played a pivotal role in transforming South African golf during a critical period of socio-political change. His leadership and commitment were instrumental in advancing the sport's inclusivity and unification in the post-apartheid era.

As president of the South African Non-White Golf Association from 1980 to 1992, Govender championed the promotion and development of golf within non-white communities amidst the challenges of apartheid. His efforts were crucial in keeping the sport relevant and accessible during a time of significant segregation.

In 1992, Govender became the deputy president of the South African Golf Federation, playing a key role in the transition from the segregated golf organizations to a unified national body. His leadership continued as he assumed the presidency of the South African Golf Federation in 1993. During this time, he guided the federation through the complexities of integrating golf in the post-apartheid landscape, ensuring that the sport became more representative of South Africa's diverse population.

Govender also served as president of the Natal Golf Association in 1981, contributing to regional efforts to address local needs and foster unity within the golf community. His involvement with the Durban Indian Golf Club underscored his dedication to grassroots development, working to make the sport accessible at the local level.

Henry Govender's legacy lies in his crucial role in reshaping South African golf. His efforts to promote inclusivity, facilitate the transition from apartheid, and unify the sport were instrumental in creating a more inclusive and representative golfing community in South Africa.

GRACE, BRANDEN JOHN (1988) SOUTH AFRICA

Branden Grace has established himself as a prominent figure in the world of golf through a series of remarkable achievements across multiple tours. His career is highlighted by numerous victories on the European Tour, including prestigious events such as the Alfred Dunhill

Links Championship, Commercial Bank Qatar Masters, Nedbank Golf Challenge, South African Open, and the Alfred Dunhill Championship. Grace also secured a notable win on the PGA Tour with his triumph at the 2016 RBC Heritage, where he clinched the title with a final-round 66.

Grace's performance in Major Championships has been consistently strong. He has achieved impressive finishes, including a tie for 4th place at the 2015 U.S. Open, 4th place at the 2016 PGA Championship, 6th place at the 2016 Open Championship, 5th place at the 2017 U.S. Open, and 7th place at the 2021 U.S. Open. These results underscore his ability to compete at the highest levels of the sport.

In team competitions, Grace represented the International Team in the Presidents Cup in 2013, 2015, and 2017, and played in the 2013 World Cup of Golf. He achieved a career-high Official World Golf Ranking of 10 in 2016 and made history by becoming the first player to win his first four European Tour titles in a single year (2012). Grace also claimed the South African Amateur Stroke Play Championship in 2006 and was the Sunshine Tour Order of Merit winner in 2012.

Despite experiencing a dip in performance between 2018 and 2020, Grace has demonstrated resilience and a return to form with a recent victory on the LIV Golf Tour. His career remains distinguished by consistent high-level performances and significant victories, reflecting his enduring talent and competitive edge in the world of golf.

GRAY, ALAN TRANSVAAL REPUBLIC, ENGLAND

Allan Gray was a prominent club professional from England who made a significant impact on South African golf in the early 20th century. He won the South African Open in 1905 after a playoff against George Fotheringham and secured the title again in 1906. Gray's consistent performance continued as he finished in second place in 1910, this time trailing George Fotheringham by five strokes. His achievements during this period highlight his skill and competitiveness in the sport.

GREEN, REGGIE UNION SOUTH AFRICA

Reggie Green was a dominant figure in women's golf during the 1950s, known for her remarkable achievements and consistent performance. Throughout her career, she won numerous prestigious tournaments and provincial championships.

In major tournaments, Green claimed victory in the South African Ladies Amateur on multiple occasions – 1947, 1950, 1952, and 1954. She also earned second place in 1953. Her success extended to the Rhodesian Ladies Amateur, where she won in 1945, 1947, and 1949, and secured second place in 1946, 1961, and 1962. Additionally, she won the Rhodesian Ladies Match Play in 1946.

Green's provincial achievements were equally impressive. She dominated the OFS Ladies Amateur with victories in 1951, 1952, 1955, 1956, 1957, and 1958, and was the runner-up in 1959. She also won the North Transvaal championship in 1958 and 1959. Her success continued in the Transvaal Ladies Amateur with wins in 1939 and 1952, and she was the runner-up in 1947 and 1951. In the Natal Ladies championship, she secured second place in 1962. Moreover, she was a consistent performer in the West Transvaal and East Transvaal championships, winning multiple times and placing second on several occasions.

Green's dominance extended to her club performances, where she won her club championship 38 times, further solidifying her legacy as one of the leading women golfers of her era.

GRIMSDELL, ROBERT 'BOB' (1896–1986)
UNION SOUTH AFRICA

Bob Grimsdell was a highly regarded golf course architect who made significant contributions to the sport through his design work and competitive achievements. Studying under the esteemed Harry Colt and Charles Alison, Grimsdell's design portfolio boasts over 20 courses, including notable venues such as Blackcap Country Club, Bosch Hoek Golf Club, Hans Merensky Country Club, and St. Francis Bay Golf Club.

In addition to his design achievements, Grimsdell was an accomplished amateur golfer. He achieved notable finishes in prestigious tournaments, including second places in the South African Open in 1931 and 1932. He also secured second place in the South African Match-Play on four occasions between 1925 and 1932 and finished as runner-up in the Free State & Basutoland Open in 1927.

Grimsdell's dual impact on golf – through his innovative course designs and his competitive spirit – has left an enduring legacy in the sport.

GROENEWALD, VAUGHN (1974) SOUTH AFRICA

Vaughn Groenewald has had a distinguished career on the Sunshine Tour, marked by several notable victories and consistent performances. He has secured victories in the Vodacom Origins of Golf on two occasions, in 2006 and 2016, and also achieved second place finishes in 2012 and 2015. In addition to his success in the Vodacom Origins of Golf, Groenewald won the Zambia Sugar Open in 2015. His impressive track record includes four runner-up positions, demonstrating his ability to remain competitive at the highest levels of the Sunshine Tour. Groenewald's achievements highlight his significant impact on the tour and his status as a prominent figure in South African golf.

GUTHRIE, SANDY UNION SOUTH AFRICA

Sandy Guthrie was a prominent professional golfer who achieved significant success in South African golf during the mid-20th century. His notable accomplishments include multiple high finishes in major tournaments. Guthrie was a consistent contender at the South African Open, finishing as runner-up on four occasions: in 1948, 1950, 1952, and 1957, with his 1948 and 1957 finishes coming after play-offs.

In addition to his strong performances in the South African Open, Guthrie won the South African PGA Championship and the South

African Masters, both in 1947. He also claimed victories in regional tournaments, winning the Transvaal Open in 1952 and the Natal Open in 1951 and 1952. His contributions and successes in South African golf are well-remembered and reflect his prowess as a leading golfer of his time.

H

HAIG, ANTON (1986) SOUTH AFRICA

Anton Haig is a notable figure in golf with a distinguished career both as an amateur and a professional. His most significant achievement came in March 2007 when he won the Johnnie Walker Classic, a multi-tour event that secured him full membership on the European Tour and elevated him into the top 100 of the Official World Golf Rankings. In total, Haig has secured 11 professional victories throughout his career.

Despite his success, Haig faced challenges, including a period of retirement due to back injuries announced in November 2011. However, he made a comeback to professional golf in March 2012. As an amateur, Haig was also highly accomplished, having won the South African Amateur in 2003 and the South African Boys Championship. His career reflects both notable highs and significant comebacks, underscoring his resilience and skill in the sport.

HARDING, JUSTIN (1986) SOUTH AFRICA

Justin Harding, a South African golfer, began his professional career with notable success. Although his amateur career did not feature significant milestones, Harding quickly established himself on the professional circuit with consistent victories. He won a tournament in each of his first three seasons on tour, from 2010 to 2012. His success continued with additional wins in 2015 and 2016. In 2018, Harding demonstrated his prowess by securing two victories within two weeks, including the Bank BRI Indonesia Open on the Asian Tour and the Royal Cup, where he won by six strokes.

In 2019, Harding earned his first European Tour victory at the Commercial Bank Qatar Masters, triumphing by two strokes. He also finished as a joint runner-up at the Kenya Open, which helped him break into the world top 50 and qualify for the 2019 Masters Tournament, where he finished 12th. Harding continued his strong performance in 2021 with a win at the Magical Kenya Open and a runner-up finish at the Cazoo Open on the European Tour.

Harding's career is marked by his ability to win across various tours and make a notable impact on the international stage, including a strong showing at the Masters Tournament. His consistent performance and achievements underscore his rise within the world golf rankings and his influence in the sport.

HARVEY, GEORGE RHODESIA

1975 Denis Watson and George Harvey

George Harvey, a prominent figure in Rhodesian golf, is renowned for his exceptional achievements during the 1970s. As an amateur, he excelled in numerous competitions, including winning the Eisenhower Trophy in 1973 while representing Rhodesia. His success continued with multiple victories in the Rhodesia Amateur from 1973 to 1977, the Multi-National

Championship in 1973, and the South African Amateur Stroke Play in 1973 and 1976. Harvey also triumphed in the Proudfoot Trophy in 1973 and the Southern Rhodesian Amateur from 1971 to 1975. Notably, he partnered with Denis Watson to win the World Pairs Championship in 1975.

Turning professional in the late 1970s, Harvey achieved a notable second place in the 1979 SA PGA Order of Merit. His contributions to the sport were recognized through accolades such as Rhodesian Golfer of the Year in 1971 and Rhodesian Sportsman of the Year in 1975. Harvey also represented Rhodesia in several Eisenhower Trophies and was part of the No. 1 International 8-Man Team in 1973. Beyond his playing career, he is remembered as a respected coach in Mnt Edgecombe, continuing to impact the game through his expertise and mentorship.

HASSANEIN, HASSAN (1916–1957) EGYPT – DISCRIMINATED

Golfer Hassanein and lodged ball.

Hassan Hassanein is a seminal figure in golf history, renowned for his pioneering role as an African golfer on the international stage. Despite relative obscurity today, Hassanein was a major force in his time, often considered Africa's greatest golfer of colour. His achievements are especially remarkable given the racial barriers he faced, including the exclusion of Black golfers from PGA tournaments in the United States.

Hassanein's journey in golf began at the Heliopolis sand course in Cairo, where he started as a barefoot caddy. Turning professional in 1946, he quickly made a name for himself with significant victories. Notably, he won the Egyptian Open four times between 1949 and 1952, overcoming prominent players like Max Faulkner and Norman Von Nida. His exceptional 1951 season saw him win the Egyptian Open, the Egyptian Match-Play Championship, the French Open, and secure a second-place finish in the Belgian Open. His career tally includes 17 professional wins, with other major victories such as the Italian Open and the Desert Open.

Hassanein's impact extended beyond his tournament successes. He was celebrated for his exceptional balance and swing technique, honed from his unique beginnings playing on sand and in bare feet. This technique earned praise from British Open champion Max Faulkner, who described Hassanein's swing as one of the finest he had ever seen.

Despite his accomplishments, Hassanein's career was hindered by racial discrimination. Although he participated in a few U.S. tournaments in the early 1950s, his opportunities were restricted due to the exclusionary practices of the PGA of America. Nevertheless, he managed to compete in the All American Open, thanks to invitations from businessman George S. May, who welcomed international players.

Hassanein also represented Egypt in the World Cup (formerly the Canada Cup) in 1955 and 1956. His career was cut tragically short when he died in an oil stove explosion at his home in Cairo in 1957, at just 40 years old.

Hassan Hassanein's legacy as a trailblazing golfer is defined by his resilience and remarkable skill in overcoming racial barriers, making a lasting impact on the sport and inspiring future generations of African golfers.

HAST, RAE (1952) SOUTH AFRICA

Rae Hast's career is distinguished by her achievements as both an amateur and professional golfer, as well as her contributions to the sport through coaching and administration. As an amateur, Hast represented South Africa in the World Amateur Championships in 1980 and 1982 and achieved notable victories in the South African Strokeplay and Matchplay Championships in 1980 and 1982. She also excelled in the Castle Champions of Champions, winning titles in 1980, 1982, and 1983, and secured the Western Province Strokeplay Championship and Border Strokeplay and Matchplay Championships in 1983.

Turning professional, Hast made her mark on the Ladies European Tour with a win at the United Friendly Insurance Open in 1984, and she also triumphed in the WPGA Championship on the South African Tour. Her contributions to the sport extend beyond playing, as she has served as a teaching professional at Erinvale Golf Estate since 1997 and was recognized as the National Coach of the Year. Additionally, her leadership was evident during her tenure as President of the Western Province Golf Association from 2010 to 2012.

Rae Hast's career is characterized by her exceptional performance on the golf course, her influence as a coach and teacher, and her leadership within the golfing community.

HAWKES, JEFF (1953) SOUTH AFRICA

Jeff Hawkes had a distinguished career on the European Tour, spanning over two decades. He was consistently ranked in the top 100 of the Order of Merit from 1977 to 1991. His notable achievement came with a single European Tour victory at the 1991 Canon European Masters Swiss Open, where he narrowly edged out Seve Ballesteros by a stroke.

In addition to his success on the European Tour, Hawkes also made an impact on the Southern Africa Tour, securing three victories against notable players such as John Bland in 1988, Tony Johnstone in 1989, and both John Daly and Joe Dlamini in 1989. Over his career, he won a total of five professional tournaments and reached a world ranking of 89 in 1989.

Hawkes also represented South Africa as an amateur in the Eisenhower Trophy in 1974 and later competed in the Hennessy Cognac Cup for the Rest of the World in 1982. After retiring from competitive play, he transitioned to a career as a golf commentator and analyst for Sky Sports in the United Kingdom.

HAYES, DALE (1952) SOUTH AFRICA

Dale Hayes, renowned for his dynamic and powerful swing, was a significant figure in golf during the early 1970s. Known for his aggressive style and remarkable talent, Hayes was a major force on the golf course, achieving considerable success before retiring from major professional

tournaments at just 29 due to the restrictive policies of apartheid-era South Africa.

As an amateur, Hayes had a standout career, winning the Junior World Golf Championships in the 1960s and capturing titles in the South African Strokeplay, Scottish Amateur, and German Amateur. He was also a runner-up in the 1970 Eisenhower Trophy. His transition to professional golf was equally impressive. Hayes dominated the South African Tour, leading the Order of Merit in 1972/73 and securing multiple runner-up finishes in subsequent years.

In Europe, Hayes achieved notable victories, including winning the Spanish Open in 1971 at the age of 18, and again in 1979. He topped the European Tour Order of Merit in 1975 and won the Vardon Trophy the same year. His professional career also included victories in the South African Open, the World Cup of Golf with Bobby Cole, and the Italian and French Opens in 1978.

Despite his early retirement, Hayes has remained active in the golf world. He has worked as a broadcaster for South African television and the Golf Channel, edited a golf magazine, and contributed to golf course design through Matkovich & Hayes. Hayes is also a public speaker known for his humor, owns Zwartkop Golf Club, and continues to write about golf and host a podcast. His achievements are recognized by his inductions into the Southern Africa Golf Hall of Fame and the South African Sport Hall of Fame. Hayes' legacy reflects his exceptional skill on the course and his continued influence in the sport.

HAYES, JOHN SOUTH AFRICA

John Hayes was a prominent South African amateur golfer whose career in the early 1960s showcased his remarkable talent and competitive spirit. Representing South Africa as a Springbok team member in 1962 and 1963, Hayes achieved notable successes both locally and internationally.

In South Africa, he secured victories in prestigious tournaments such as the Pretoria Open in 1959 and the South African Amateur in 1962, where he also finished as a runner-up in 1961 and 1963. His excellence extended to other notable events, including wins at the Rhodesian Amateur and the Proudfoot Trophy in 1963, as well as the WP Amateur in 1961 and 1962.

Hayes also made an impact on the international stage, winning the Australian Amateur in 1963 and placing second in the Queensland Open and Rhodesian Dunlop in 1964 and 1968, respectively. His performance in the German Open in 1962, where he finished third, highlighted his competitive edge on a global level.

Despite his early passing, Hayes' achievements in amateur golf left a lasting impression. His contributions to the sport during his brief but impactful career continue to be remembered for their significance and excellence.

HAYES, OTWAY (DIED 2002) UNION SOUTH AFRICA

Otway Hayes was a prominent figure in South African golf, known for his extensive career both as a professional and an amateur. He made a significant impact as the first golf professional at Zwartkop Golf Club, serving from 1940 to 1996. Hayes was also part of the inaugural Springbok Golf Team in 1937. His professional achievements include a notable second-place finish in the SA Open in 1953, where he lost in a playoff, and a third-place finish in 1950. In 1960, he won the Mills Tournament, defeating Bobby Locke in the semi-final, and accumulated eight professional titles throughout his career.

In his amateur days, Hayes earned numerous accolades, including victories in the Western Province Amateur in 1936 and 1938, the Natal Amateur in 1938, and the South African Amateur in 1939. He also won

Otway Hayes and the boys

the Western Province Open three times 1947, 1948, 1949 and the Natal Open twice 1938, 1946.

Hayes' contributions to the sport were recognized with several honors. He was named an Honorary Life Member of the Professional Golfers Association of South Africa and received the Compleat Golfer Contribution to Golf Award in 1996. The Otway Hayes Trophy, awarded annually to the Club Professional of the Year, was established in his honor. His legacy is also reflected in his family's deep involvement in golf, with three professional sons and three grandsons collectively contributing over 200 years to the sport.

HENNING, ALLAN "DOC" (1944) SOUTH AFRICA

Allan Henning was a highly accomplished golfer in Southern Africa during the 1960s and 70s, known for his impressive career both on the main tour and the Senior Tour. His standout victory came at the South African Open in 1963, a notable achievement considering he was only 19 at the time. Henning also had a significant impact on the Sunshine Tour, winning the Order of Merit titles in the 1974/75 and 1975/76 seasons. His remarkable performance on the course included setting a record with a score of 61 at Glendower Golf Club during the Toro Classic in 1976.

Throughout his professional career, Henning accumulated 20 victories in Southern Africa and 13 wins on the Senior Tour. His victories included multiple wins at prestigious events such as the South African Open, Western Province Open, Rhodesian Dunlop Masters, and Transvaal Open. He also achieved notable second-place finishes and represented South Africa in international tournaments like the World Cup of Golf and the World Series of Golf.

Henning's influence extended beyond playing, as he served as a teaching professional at Royal Johannesburg & Kensington Golf Club for 42 years. His contributions to the sport were recognized with an Honorary Membership from the South African Professional Golfers' Association (SAPGA) and the Master Professional award. In 2008, he was named Club Professional of the Year. Known for his resilience and ability to come from behind with impressive final-round scores, Henning left a lasting legacy in the world of golf.

HENNING, BRIAN "BRUNO" (DIED 2023) SOUTH AFRICA, USA

Brian 'Bruno' Henning made significant contributions to golf, particularly through his role in shaping the Senior PGA Tour. After relocating to the USA in 1976, Henning initially worked in modest positions, such as a locker-room attendant and golf cart operator. However, his career took a pivotal turn when PGA Tour Commissioner Deane Berman offered him the opportunity to oversee the emerging Senior PGA Tour.

Allan, Harold, Brian, Graham Henning

Starting as Director of Tournament Administration, Henning's dedication and expertise led him to become Vice President of Competitions. His leadership was instrumental in the tour's expansion, growing from 11 tournaments in 1982 to 39 by 2000. Henning authored the 'Senior Tour Bible,' a comprehensive guide for tournament directors that became a standard reference in the industry.

In recognition of his impactful contributions, the PGA Tour Champions Tournament Association established the 'Bruno Award', named in his honor. This award is presented annually to individuals or organizations that have made exceptional contributions to the Senior PGA Tour. Henning's legacy is marked by his instrumental role in the tour's growth and organization, and the Bruno Award serves as a testament to his lasting influence on the sport.

HENNING, GRAHAM SOUTH AFRICA

Graham Henning emerged as one of South Africa's leading golfers in the late 1960s and early 1970s, marked by several impressive performances in international and local tournaments. His breakthrough came with a remarkable victory at the 1967 Engadine Open, where he shot a final round 62 to secure a commanding win, overcoming Australia's Randall Vines by ten strokes.

Henning's strong showing on the global stage was further highlighted by his qualification for South Africa's 1969 World Cup team, a testament to his consistent excellence. In the same year, he recorded notable victories

at the General Motors Open in Port Elizabeth and tied with Alex Caygill at the Martini International. Despite a narrow defeat at the Rhodesian Masters and the Agfa-Gevaert Tournament, where he finished second, Henning's performances established him as a significant player on the international circuit.

He continued to excel with a runner-up finish at the 1971 Transvaal Open and achieved a total of seven professional wins throughout his career. Beyond his tournament success, Henning contributed to the golfing community as the club professional at Wanderers, influencing the sport at a local level.

Henning's legacy is defined by his strong international performances, his role in the 1969 World Cup team, and his dedicated service to golf through his club professional role. His career achievements and contributions have left a lasting impact on South African golf.

HENNING, HAROLD "THE HORSE" (1934–2004)
UNION SOUTH AFRICA

Harold Henning, affectionately nick-named "The Horse," was celebrated for his understated yet fiercely competitive approach to golf. Turning professional in 1953, Henning quickly established himself as one of South Africa's top golfers and a formidable presence on the international stage. His notable achievements include winning the South African Open twice, in 1957 and 1962, and clinching the Canada Cup with Gary Player in 1965, a significant milestone as it marked the first time the USA had lost the World Cup.

Harold Henning was a truly global figure in the world of professional golf, known for his relentless competitiveness and remarkable ability to achieve success on various international circuits. His career highlights included three wins at the Swiss Open (1960, 1964, 1965) and a victory at the 1957 Italian Open. Henning also tied in several prestigious tournaments, such as the Daks and Yorkshire Evening News Tournaments in 1958, competing against legends like Peter Thomson and Eric Brown.

Henning's victories extended beyond Europe, as he claimed titles across Africa, the Far East, and New Zealand. Notable wins included the 1966 Malayan Open and the 1958 Wiseman's Tournament in New Zealand. While he did not secure a major championship title, Henning made a strong impression at The Open Championship, finishing third in both 1960 and 1970, and earning several other top-10 finishes.

Later in his career, Henning found success on the PGA Tour with wins at the 1966 Texas Open and 1970 Tallahassee Open. Though he stepped away from full-time competition in the early 1970s, Henning returned to form in the 1980s, winning the 1981 Dutch Open on the European Tour and adding victories on the Champions Tour, including the 1985 Tucson Senior Match Play Championship and the 1991 First of America Classic.

From his humble beginnings as a caddie to becoming a world-class player, Harold Henning's journey embodied perseverance and passion for the game. His legacy is one of resilience, longevity, and a profound impact on South African and international golf.

His legacy includes a total of 54 professional victories worldwide, with a career marked by significant contributions to the game and a style of play that combined simplicity with competitive brilliance. His career accomplishments and enduring influence make him one of the most celebrated golfers in South African history.

HENNING, NICK (1969) SOUTH AFRICA

Nick Henning, hailing from a distinguished golfing family with his father Graham and three uncles all being professional golfers, made a significant mark in the sport early in his career. He began gaining attention with a runner-up finish at the Zimbabwe Open early in the 1993–94 season, setting the stage for his future successes.

Henning's major career victories include winning the Vodacom Players Championship in 1999, where he triumphed over Darren Clarke in a playoff. He continued to build on his success with notable wins at the Royal Swazi Sun Classic in 2003 and the Capital Alliance Royal Swazi Sun Open in 2004. His final win came on the Vodacom Origins of Golf Tour in 2005.

Throughout his career, Henning also achieved commendable finishes, such as representing South Africa in the World Cup in 1998 and finishing second on the South African Tour's Order of Merit for the 1999–2000 season. His career featured several close calls, including losing in playoffs at the Seekers Travel Pro-Am in October 2005, the Nashua Golf Challenge in 2008, and the MTC Namibia PGA Championship in 2008.

Nick Henning's career, marked by his significant victories and near-misses in playoffs, underscores his competitive spirit and solidifies his place in the Henning family's golfing legacy. His contributions to the sport continue to be recognized and celebrated within the golfing community.

HESS, RODNEY SOUTH AFRICA

Rodney Hess has made significant contributions to golf development in South Africa through his pioneering work and unwavering dedication. In the late 1990s, he undertook the prestigious International European Golf Teaching Instructors (EGTI) course, becoming the only South African to do so despite the high costs and competition. His early career also involved training with Claude May, where he learned about golf club repair and technical aspects of the sport, although this period provided no financial return.

Hess's most notable impact has been in the realm of golf development. Around 2009, he took on the role of manager for the Western Province Chapter of the South African Golf Development Board (SAGDB). In this capacity, he played a crucial role in establishing and managing the WP Golf Development Programme. He also initiated golf programs in schools, including Square Hill PS and schools in Grassy Park, aimed at providing children from disadvantaged backgrounds with access to the sport. Additionally, he improved facilities access at notable locations such as the River Club and established connections with other key driving ranges.

Hess's commitment to making golf accessible to all is evident in his efforts to ensure that children from diverse backgrounds had equal opportunities in the sport. He organized junior foundation competitions that provided equal opportunities for participants from both affluent and less privileged areas. He secured club memberships for young golfers at Rondebosch and Mowbray Golf Clubs and the River Club, which facilitated their development and competition. Furthermore, his mentorship influenced programs like the WP Ladies development programme and the Mountain Academy, where he shared his knowledge and skills with the next generation of golfers.

Rodney Hess's work has profoundly impacted many young golfers by breaking down barriers and providing opportunities that were previously out of reach. His dedication to transforming golf and making it more inclusive underscores his passion and commitment to the sport.

HIGGINSON, JOHN TANGANYIKA

John Higginson enjoyed a distinguished career in amateur golf from the 1930s through the early 1960s, although his career was interrupted by World War II. He is celebrated for his remarkable achievements in the sport, particularly in East Africa. Higginson's success was highlighted by his impressive record in the Kenya Amateur, where he triumphed in 1938 and 1939, and again in 1946, with a second-place finish in 1951. His dominance extended to the Tanganyika Amateur, where he secured victories in 1958, 1959, 1960, and 1961. Higginson's accomplishments solidify his legacy as one of the greatest golfers from Tanganyika, showcasing his skill and dedication to the game.

HIGGO, GARRICK (1999) SOUTH AFRICA

Garrick Higgo has quickly made a name for himself on the international golf scene since turning professional in early 2019. His debut season on the Sunshine Tour was remarkable, with wins at the Sun City Challenge and the Tour Championship, alongside a runner-up finish at the Challenge Tour Cape Town Open. His performance earned him the Rookie of the Year title and a 6th-place finish on the Order of Merit.

Higgo's success continued on the European Tour in 2020, where he claimed three significant victories. He won the Open de Portugal with a bogey-free final round of 65, the Gran Canaria Lopesan Open with a record-breaking aggregate score of 255, and the Canary Islands Championship with a commanding final score of 257, 27 under par.

In June 2021, Higgo made his mark on the PGA Tour by winning the Palmetto Championship in South Carolina. This victory earned him over $1.3 million and further established his reputation. With a total of eight professional wins and a World Ranking of 39 as of 2021, Garrick Higgo is recognized as a rising star in the world of golf.

HLAPO, SIMON 'COX' (1926–1986) UNION SOUTH AFRICA – APARTHEID

Simon 'Cox' Hlapo is a celebrated pioneer in South African golf, renowned for his remarkable achievements and enduring legacy. Before the inclusion of black golfers in mainstream golf courses with the arrival of Papwa Sewgolum in 1960, Hlapo was a dominant figure in the sport. He was consistently at the top of the leaderboard, often found in the top three, and was a symbol of excellence and resilience in black golf.

Known as the "King of the Sand Greens," Hlapo's prowess on the golf course was legendary. His ability to master the sand greens and his consistent performance in tournaments earned him a reputation as one of the most reliable African golfers of his time. Despite his unassuming appearance – dressed in ordinary attire and known for his trademark beret – Hlapo's imposing presence and skill on the course set him apart. He was noted for his unique playing style and his focus, which made him a formidable opponent.

Hlapo's early life was marked by significant challenges. As a Putco bus driver working morning shifts, he would often hit the golf course at Alexandra in the afternoon. Financial constraints sometimes prevented him from participating in tournaments due to the entry fees, but his determination and skill led him to achieve notable successes.

His career highlights include multiple victories in prestigious tournaments such as the SA Non-European Open, where he won in 1955, 1957, and 1959, and the Orange Free State Open, with wins in 1953, 1960, 1961, 1962, and 1963. His last major win came in 1972 at the Luyt Lager Tournament, and he continued to perform impressively into his later years, including a victory in the 3M Classic in 1983 at the age of 56.

Hlapo's legacy extends beyond his tournament wins. He became an inspirational figure for many black golfers, demonstrating exceptional talent and perseverance during an era of significant racial discrimination. His contributions to the development and administration of black golf were invaluable.

In recognition of his impact on the sport, Hlapo was inducted into the Southern Africa Golf Hall of Fame in 2011 and received the Andrew Mlangeni Green Jacket Award from the Minister of Sport Tokozile Xasa in 2018. Simon 'Cox' Hlapo remains a celebrated and influential figure in the history of South African golf.

HOBDAY, JUSTIN (1963) SOUTH AFRICA

Justin Hobday is a prominent figure in South African golf, known for his achievements both as an amateur and professional. During his amateur career, Hobday earned Springbok colors four times from 1981 to 1984, a testament to his skill and dedication to the sport. He was also recognized as the Rookie of the Year in 1986, receiving the prestigious Bobby Locke Trophy, which marked the beginning of his promising career.

As a professional golfer, Hobday made a notable impact on the Sunshine Tour, where he accumulated 13 victories. His first professional win came in 1989, and he continued to secure additional titles throughout his career, with ten more tournament wins between 1989 and 2001. His performance on the European Tour was also impressive, highlighted by a third-place finish at the 1992 Peugeot Spanish Open.

Hobday is also connected to another golfing legend, Simon Hobday, as his nephew. This family connection underscores a notable golfing lineage, contributing to Justin Hobday's distinguished career. His consistent performance and early recognition set him apart as a significant figure in South African golf.

HOBDAY, SIMON (1940–2017) ZAMBIA, SOUTH AFRICA

Simon Forbes Newbold Hobday, widely known as Simon Hobday, is celebrated for his colorful and influential career in golf. His early career was notable for representing Zambia in the 1966 Eisenhower Trophy and making a significant impact in the 1969 Kenya Open, where he shot a course-record 66 to finish as the runner-up.

Hobday's professional career saw considerable success across various tours. He claimed six titles on the Southern Africa Professional Tour and achieved victories on the European Tour, including the German Open in

1976 and the Madrid Open in 1979. His performance was highlighted by reaching the semi-finals of the British Match-Play in 1976 and finishing tenth and eleventh on the European Order of Merit in 1978 and 1979, respectively.

Despite facing political and economic challenges, such as having his earnings frozen due to sanctions against Rhodesia, Hobday adapted by changing his sporting nationality to South Africa. His resilience continued as he moved to South Africa in 1981, where he transitioned to a new role at Wingate Park Club in Pretoria.

In the latter part of his career, Hobday excelled on the Senior PGA Tour (now Champions Tour), securing five titles between 1993 and 1995, including the 1994 U.S. Senior Open, which is considered one of his greatest victories.

Hobday's career is marked by his vibrant personality, which set him apart from many of his peers. His open-handedness and engaging demeanor earned him admiration and recognition, including being named Rhodesian Sportsman of the Year in 1979. His journey from a farmer in Zambia to a celebrated golfer reflects his adaptability and enduring talent.

HOCKEY, ANGELA (BURWELL) UNION SOUTH AFRICA

Angela Hockey's career in golf is distinguished by both significant achievements on the course and substantial contributions off it. She was deeply involved in the administration of golf, serving on her club committee for many years and as an executive member of the Western

Province Ladies' Golf Union from 1959 to 1966.

In terms of amateur accomplishments, she made a remarkable impact in Western Province ladies' golf. She won the S.A. Ladies Amateur Championships twice, in 1933 and 1938, and was a runner-up in 1927 and 1929. Her dominance extended to the Western Province Ladies Championships, where she secured victories in a span of years from 1923 to 1938 and was a runner-up on several occasions. At the Royal Cape Ladies Championships, she also had a prolific record, winning numerous titles between 1923 and 1959. Her success continued into her senior years with wins in the WP Senior Women's Championships in 1956, 1959, and 1960.

Her long-standing influence in Western Province ladies' golf, coupled with her significant administrative roles, underscores her dedication and impact on the sport.

HOLLAND, VAL SOUTH AFRICA

Val Holland has made notable contributions to golf through both her competitive and coaching careers. She represented South Africa as an amateur player for many years, showcasing her skills on the national stage. Among her achievements, she won the South African Ladies Strokeplay Championship in 1987 and became a member of the PGA of South Africa in 2003.

Holland's coaching career has been distinguished by her roles as the South African Women's National Coach since 2004 and as the head coach of the Louis 57 Junior Golf Academy since 2012. Her coaching philosophy emphasizes the importance of creating a simple understanding of good fundamentals to achieve long-lasting results for golfers at all levels.

Her impact extends beyond national borders, as she has provided coaching for players on both the European and Sunshine Tours. Notably, under her influence, South Africa was well-represented at the Presidents Cup Junior Team in 2019, with three of the five amateur players coming from her guidance: Lee-Anne Pace, Vaughn Groenewald, and Tjaart van der Walt. Holland's contributions have significantly shaped the development of junior golf and the sport in the southern Cape, demonstrating her profound influence on the game.

HORAK, VIVIAN SOUTH AFRICA

Vivian Horak took over as secretary from stalwart secretary Esther Cutler of the then "South African Ladies Golf Union (SALGU)" in 1997. She had not been involved in golf administration before, and came out of the corporate world. She set about methodically organising all aspects of amateur women's golf administration, computerised the central secretarial function and pioneered the establishment of internet communication between all unions and the SALGU. In 1999 Vivian took on this position as treasurer as well.

She was instrumental in organizing the new emerging provinces to serve on a main SALGU executive committee. Prior to the establishment of the Development Board, she sourced a major sponsorship which enabled WGSA to implement grassroots development in all the unions. With the formation of the SAGDB, she represented WGSA on the board, promoting cooperation with the stakeholders, while still driving WGSA's own development program in the unions, while she forged close ties with the National Nomads in promoting junior golf development, which still prevail today.

She was instrumental in establishing the SA Girls Championship and in reviving the Junior Rose Bowl Tournament which the Junior Golf Foundation had shelved. Vivian developed a close relationship with the WPGA to facilitate the move of young players from the amateur to the professional ranks.

She oversaw the transition from the "South African Ladies Golf Union" with all its old connotations of colonial elitism to the vibrant all inclusive "Womens Golf South Africa" which we have today. This transition relevant in particular in South Africa where sport had become an essential tool in nation building. Vivian insisted that the newly established WGSA build its brand and take advantage of the growing popularity of the sport in order to attract better sponsorships.

During Vivians tenure, South Africa very successfully hosted a number of international events. From the All Africa Challenge Trophy in 1998 to the Five Nations Tournament in 2007 when the global perception of Johannesburg was at an all-time low.

She achieved as much if not more on the administration front than any of the women golfers achieved on the fairways.

HORNE, KEITH (1971) SOUTH AFRICA

Keith Horne has had a distinguished career in professional golf, marked by significant achievements and consistency on the Sunshine Tour. His amateur success included a notable performance in 1993, where he won a Silver Medal at the World Games in Spain.

Turning professional, Horne's first major win came in 1998 at the Vodacom Series: Kwazulu Natal. Over the years, he built on this success with a series of victories and strong performances. In 2007, he clinched the MTC Namibia PGA Championship with a remarkable final round of 63. His win at the Nashua Golf Challenge in 2008 further established his reputation.

Horne's achievements continued with a runner-up finish in the 2010 Joburg Open and a victory at the Telkom PGA Championship in 2012, adding his fifth Sunshine Tour win. His career continued to flourish with additional victories in 2014, 2015, and a final win in 2024, bringing his total professional wins to 13. Horne's career is a testament to his skill and longevity in the sport.

HOOPER, R.W. KENYA

R.W. Hooper is a pivotal figure in the history of Kenyan golf, known for his impressive achievements and contributions to the sport. He secured multiple victories in the Kenya Amateur Championships, winning the title in 1932, 1934, 1936, 1952, and 1953, and was a runner-up on several occasions from 1931 to 1937. In addition to his success at the national level, Hooper also claimed the Uganda Amateur Championship in 1953.

His representation of Kenya in 1952, notably in a match against the British team, underscored his prominence in the sport. Hooper's legacy is marked by his comprehensive record and significant impact on the development of golf in Kenya and its neighboring countries, solidifying his role as a key figure in the region's golfing history.

HUGO, JEAN (1973) SOUTH AFRICA

Victor Jean Hugo has had a distinguished career in golf, transitioning seamlessly from a successful amateur to a notable professional. As an amateur, he represented South Africa in the 1998 Eisenhower Trophy and achieved significant victories, including winning the South African International Amateur Match-play Championship in 1998 and the South African Amateur Stroke Play Championship in 1999.

Turning professional, Hugo amassed a total of 22 wins, with several notable accomplishments. His first major professional win came at the 1999 Zimbabwe Open. He continued to excel with victories in the 2000 Volvo Finnish Open and multiple wins in the Vodacom Origins of Golf series, including in 2006, 2008, 2010, 2011, 2013, 2014, 2015, and 2016. Noteworthy among these was his win in the Vodacom Origins of Golf Final in 2011 and the Nashua Masters in 2007. Hugo's career reflects a blend of early promise and sustained success, particularly within the Vodacom Origins of Golf series.

HUTCHINGS, IAN (1968) ZIMBABWE

Ian Hutchings has built a noteworthy career in golf, marked by significant achievements both in South Africa and internationally. He is currently a member of the Sunshine Tour, having previously competed on the Canadian Tour. Hutchings enjoyed success on both tours, with two victories in South Africa in 1994 and 1996, and four wins in Canada. His Canadian Tour wins include the 1994 Klondike Klassic, the 1995 Alberta Open, the 1997 Calgary Open, and the 1998 BC TEL Pacific Open. In addition to his tour successes, Hutchings has earned over R1,500,000 in career earnings on the Sunshine Tour, with his best finish on the Order of Merit being 14th in 1994. He also boasts 12 amateur wins and represented South Africa as a Springbok in 1987/1988. His career reflects a blend of domestic and international success, highlighting his skill and versatility as a golfer.

HUTCHINSON, DENIS (1932) SOUTHERN RHODESIA, SOUTH AFRICA

Denis John Hutchinson is a highly regarded figure in the world of golf, recognized for his accomplishments both as a player and in his post-playing career. His amateur career was highlighted by notable successes, including representing South Africa in prestigious events such as the Commonwealth Tournament and the Eisenhower Trophy. He also had notable successes in professional tournaments while still an amateur, including a win at the 1959 South African Open, a significant achievement in his amateur career.

Turning professional in 1960, Hutchinson's career was marked by consistency and notable victories. He won 16 professional tournaments, including prestigious events such as the South African Masters, the French Open, and the South African PGA Championship. His professional career also included a successful stint on the PGA Tour, where he had a top-10 finish at the Oklahoma City Open Invitational. He was particularly successful in the Vodacom Origins of Golf series and won the Woodlawn International Invitational twice.

After retiring from competitive golf, Hutchinson made a significant impact as a golf commentator for Sky Sports, earning the nickname "Voice of Golf" in South Africa. His contributions to the sport were further recognized with several honors, including being named Honorary Life President of the South African PGA and being inducted into the Southern African Hall of Fame.

In addition to his work in commentary and administration, Hutchinson has been honored with the creation of the Denis Hutchinson Challenge Trophy, which will be held annually at his home course, Royal Johannesburg and Kensington Golf Club. This tournament will feature a mix of Sunshine Tour professionals, PGA of South Africa professionals, and GolfRSA amateurs in a prestigious challenge match.

Overall, Denis Hutchinson's career is celebrated for his impressive achievements on the golf course, his influential role in golf administration and commentary, and his lasting impact on the sport through both his playing and post-playing endeavors.

I

IMMELMAN, MARK (1970) SOUTH AFRICA

Mark Immelman has made significant contributions to the world of golf through various roles as a coach, commentator, and author. He currently hosts the "On the Mark" podcast on pgatour.com and provides live golf commentary for the PGA Tour on ESPN+ and CBS Sports. Additionally, he contributes analysis to the CBS Sports digital podcast "The First Cut" and CBS Sports HQ.

In golf coaching, Immelman is well-regarded for his achievements, including being named the NCAA Division II Coach of the Year in 2009. He founded the Mark Immelman Golf Academy in 2015, which is known for its exceptional coaching and college preparatory education. His coaching resume includes working with prominent players such as his brother Trevor Immelman (2008 Masters Champion), Larry Mize (1998 Masters Champion), and Louis Oosthuizen (2010 British Open Champion), among others. He also served as the non-playing captain of the Palmer Cup International Team in 2019.

Immelman's playing career includes a notable college stint at Columbus State University, where he earned three All-American honors (1992, 1994, 1995) and was a two-time Academic All-American. He helped lead the team to national championships in 1992 and 1994. His contributions to the sport were further recognized with his induction into the Columbus State Athletics Hall of Fame in 2017.

Mark Immelman is also an accomplished author, having contributed to golf literature, showcasing his deep knowledge and passion for the sport. His diverse career in coaching, broadcasting, and writing underscores his substantial impact on the golf industry.

IMMELMAN, TREVOR (1979) SOUTH AFRICA

Trevor Immelman has had a distinguished career both as a golfer and in broadcasting. He won his sole major championship at the 2008 Masters Tournament, and 6th in the 2007 PGA Championship with a highest World Ranking of 12. In 1997 he won the South African Amateur, and a year later in 1998 he won the U.S. Amateur Public Links.

In 2003 Immelman won the WGC-World Cup for South Africa in partnership with Rory Sabbatini. 2005 he was a member of the losing International Team at the Presidents Cup. 2006 he won his first PGA Tour event at the Cialis Western Open, a result that moved him into the top 15 in the Official World Golf Rankings. He won the Sunshine Tour Order of Merit in 2002/03.

He finished 2006 in the top 10 of the PGA Tour money list and was named Rookie of the Year. In September 2007, Trevor was picked by Gary Player to participate in the 7th Presidents Cup.

He came back to win the 2008 Masters Tournament. Despite scoring a double bogey on the 70th hole, the par 3 16th, Immelman finished with a score of 8 under par, beating favourite Tiger Woods by three strokes and a new world ranking 12. 2013 he won the Hotel Fitness Championship, the first of four Web.com Tour Finals tournaments, and finished the Finals in sixth place to regain his PGA Tour card for 2014. 2018 saw a resurgence in Immelman's career. Focusing on the European Tour, he made the cut in 8 out of 13 events, with a best finish of T3 at the Scottish Open. September 2022, Immelman captained the International team in the 2022 Presidents Cup at Quail Hollow Club. The U.S. team won 17.5-12.5.

In 2017, 2018 and 2019, Turner Sports utilised Immelman as an analyst for coverage of the PGA Championship on TNT. In December 2019, he joined the PGA Tour on CBS commentating team.[1] After Nick Faldo retired from CBS in 2022, Immelman was named the new lead golf analyst for 2023.

Immelman's career reflects a balance of notable on-course achievements and significant contributions to golf broadcasting.

INGGS, HUGH (1938) SOUTH AFRICA

Hugh William Inggs enjoyed a career characterised by perseverance and notable achievements in both South African and European golf. Turning professional at the age of 20, Inggs began his career with a strong performance, finishing 3rd in the 1965 South African Open behind Gary Player. He continued to make an impact, notably finishing 2nd in the 1969 General Motors Open.

Inggs secured his first professional win at the 1969 Rhodesian Masters, where he narrowly defeated Graham Henning. He successfully defended this title the following year. His PGA Tour career began after he qualified at the Spring 1969 PGA Tour Qualifying School. Although he did not secure a win on the PGA Tour, he achieved notable finishes, including a joint runner-up position at the 1969 Minnesota Golf Classic.

In the latter part of his career, Inggs competed on the European Senior Tour from 1992 to 2001. He played part-time in the early seasons with modest success. Notable performances include finishing as the runner-up at the 1995 London Seniors Masters and placing 3rd in the 1998 Lawrence Batley Seniors. Inggs's career is distinguished by his consistent ability to compete at a high level, particularly during his years on the European Senior Tour.

INGRAM, COLIN WRAY RHODESIA, FEDERATION

Colin Wray Ingram had a notable career as both a golf administrator and player. As the first President of the Central African Golf Union, a position he held from its establishment in 1955 until 1963, Ingram played a key role in shaping the development of golf in the region.

On the course, Ingram achieved significant success. He represented All Rhodesia in a 1947 match against the South African Touring Team, where he secured a victory over Ronny Glennie. His tournament successes include winning the Croydon Amateur in the UK in 1948 and the South Rhodesia Amateur in 1947, with additional strong finishes including 2nd place in 1938 and 1940. He also claimed victory at the Manicaland Amateur in 1951 and won the Royal Salisbury tournament multiple times, in 1936, 1938, 1939, 1940, and 1949. Ingram's dual impact on the sport—through administration and his competitive achievements—highlights his significant contributions to golf in Central Africa.

J

JAMES, DEREK (1960) SOUTH AFRICA

Derek James had a notable golf career, beginning with his amateur achievements. He played in the 1982 Eisenhower Trophy and secured his biggest amateur win as the 1984 South African Strokeplay champion. After turning professional later that year, he joined the Sunshine Tour, where he claimed his first title in 1991. Over the next few years, he added six more victories to his name 1992 Iscor Newcastle Classic, Kalahari Classic, Mercedes Benz Golf Challenge; 1993 Lombard Tryes Classic, Momentum Life Classic; 1994 Sanlam Cancer Challenge, with a particularly strong run between 1991 and 1994. James also finished as runner-up in the 1992 South African Open and achieved international success by winning the Canadian Tournament Players' Championship in 1994. Additionally, he picked up three minor tournament victories in the United States before retiring from competitive golf in 1997. Professional wins 11. Today, he serves as the head professional at Southbroom Golf Club.

JANGLE, FRED UNION SOUTH AFRICA

Fred Jangle made history in South African golf when he was appointed the golf professional at Metropolitan Golf Club in 1917, earning a modest salary of £3 per month. His career reached a significant milestone in 1922 when he entered the South African Open, held at the Royal Port Alfred. Jangle became the first South African-born golfer to win this prestigious tournament, the second oldest in the world after The Open Championship, with a score of 310. His victory was particularly noteworthy as it ended the dominance of Jock Brews, marking a new era in South African golf.

JANKS, MICKEY UNION SOUTH AFRICA

Mickey Janks, a cousin of the renowned Sid Brews, had an illustrious amateur golfing career in South Africa. In 1952, he represented South Africa in a match against Great Britain, showcasing his talent on an international stage. Janks' most notable victory came in 1948 when he won the South African Open as an amateur, also earning the Freddie Tait Trophy for being the leading amateur. He finished fourth in the 1947 South African Open and won the Proudfoot Trophy in 1951. In 1958, he came close to another major victory, finishing second in the Southern Rhodesia Open.

Janks also had a successful run in amateur championships. He won the South African Amateur title twice, in 1948 and 1952, and was runner-up in 1951 and 1953, reaching the semi-finals on four occasions. His success extended to regional tournaments as well, winning the Natal Amateur in 1951 and finishing second in 1952. He also won the Transvaal Amateur in 1937 and 1953 but was runner-up five times, earning him the unofficial title of the "best runner-up." Despite his many successes, Janks also had several near misses, including losing in the semi-finals to Bobby Locke in 1934.

JEPHCOTT, EDITH SOUTHERN RHODESIA

Edith Jephcott was a distinguished Rhodesian amateur golfer, renowned for her numerous victories and consistent performances across various tournaments. She dominated the Rhodesian Ladies Championship, winning the title multiple times in 1937, 1938, 1939, 1943, 1946, and 1950, with runner-up finishes in 1948 and 1949. In 1946, she added the Rhodesian Ladies Match Play title to her impressive list of achievements.

Jephcott also excelled in regional competitions, winning the Manicaland Ladies Championship in 1956 and finishing as runner-up in 1950, 1951, 1952, and 1954. She claimed the Mashonaland Championship in 1951, with additional second-place finishes in 1948, 1949, 1954, and 1957. Her success extended to the Royal Salisbury Ladies Championship, where she secured victories in 1944, 1946, 1947, 1948, 1949, and 1957. Jephcott's remarkable career made her one of the leading figures in Rhodesian women's golf during her era.

JOHNSON-SEDIBE, EDWARD (1932) SOUTH AFRICA – APARTHEID

Edward Johnson-Sedebi, often referred to as Eddie, made significant contributions to golf despite facing numerous challenges:

He met the game through barbed wire fences that separated the posh 'white' areas from his poor township. Eddie, as he was referred to, first stormed onto the local golf scene in the late 1940s. In 1947, 1951, and 1952 he won the Non-European Transvaal Championships, in 1951 and 1952 the Non-European South African Championships, 2nd 1964, 3rd 1962, 5th 1961; Northern Transvaal Non-European Championship 1953; Kroonstad Non-European 2nd 1959, 1964; Natal Non-European Open 3rd 1962; Griqualand Non-European Open 3rd 1965.

Given the lack of prospects for black golfers in South Africa, Eddie decided to decide to try his luck in Europe and somehow with the help of some well-meaning white friends managed to fund his first trip. In 1956, he showed up at the golf club of Frankfurt am Main, where the German Open was being held. Without the means for accommodation he shared a tent with the future German golf teacher Hans Heiser. Unfortunately Eddie had come without his golf clubs. *"They didn't arrive with the plane,"* he explained. What he did bring with him, though, was an incredible ability to make things appear positive. And although he never received proper training as a golf teacher, and charisma that would soon help him set up in Europe. After the tragic early death of his wife in 1959 this self-annointed professional from Alexandra Township GC – an open stretch Johannesburg-Pretoria, remained in Europe becoming a leading golf coach in Germany.

Although still banned from membership in the South African PGA, Eddie became the first native-black player to play in 1959 in The Open. Only the second person of colour from South Africa where he was not allowed to play on 'white' golf courses or PGA tournaments.

Notable Tournament Performance: At the 1960 Wentworth Ballentine Bigger Ball tournament, he led the first round with a score of 65. Despite falling back in later rounds, his performance was impressive given the limitations he faced.

Eddie also finished 26th in the 1960 Italian Open, and 30th in the Portuguese Open; and in 1961 he finished 26th in the Spanish Open. He also won some minor tournaments in Portugal and England.

Johnson-Sedebi's story is one of resilience and talent overcoming significant barriers, and he played a key role in challenging the perceptions and restrictions placed on black golfers during his time.

JOHNSTONE, TONY (1956) RHODESIA

Anthony Alastair Johnstone, a prominent figure in Rhodesian and Zimbabwean golf, enjoyed a highly successful professional career, securing 25 victories and achieving a peak world ranking of 22. He was part of the golden age of Rhodesian golf, alongside other notable golfers such as Denis Watson, Simon Hobday, George Harvey, Teddy Webber, Mark McNulty, and Nick Price. Johnstone first gained widespread attention in 1981 when he nearly won the Swiss Open, tying with Manuel Piñero and Antonio Garrido after rounds of 69, 69, 71, and 69, only to lose to Piñero in a playoff. His distinctive body movement during his address earned him the nickname "Elvis" on the tour.

Johnstone's career was marked by significant achievements, including six victories on the European Tour, with his most prestigious win coming at the 1992 British PGA Championship at Wentworth after a stunning final round 65. That year, he also achieved his career-best seventh place on the European Tour Order of Merit. On the Southern African Tour, he won 17 times, topping the Order of Merit in both the 1988–89 and 1993–94 seasons. Some of his notable victories on the Sunshine Tour include winning the South African Open in 1984 and 1993, the South African PGA Championship in 1989 and 1998, the South African Masters in 1984 and 1993, and the Zimbabwe Open in 1993.

Johnstone's excellent short game was a hallmark of his play, and he led the European Tour's short game statistics in 1998, 1999, and 2000. His team appearances include representing Rhodesia in the Eisenhower Trophy in 1976, the Rest of the World in the 1982 Hennessy Cognac Cup, and Zimbabwe in the Alfred Dunhill Cup from 1993 to 2000 and the World Cup from 1994 to 2001. He was also part of the winning Southern Africa team in the 1995 Alfred Dunhill Challenge.

At the age of 49, Tony's life took a turn that makes his new role with EDGA particularly significant. He was diagnosed with multiple sclerosis. With a revolutionary drug treatment, his MS went into remission and Tony would make his European Seniors Tour debut in 2006, winning the Jersey Seniors Classic in 2008 and the Travis Perkins plc Senior Masters in 2009.

Today, Tony is a respected and popular golf analyst with Sky Sports, providing expert insight at many professional tournaments. He is also an active Ambassador for the UK's MS Society, raising significant funds for this society through golf.

In 2020 Tony Johnstone was welcomed as an official ambassador for European Disabled Golf Association, the international body that encourages people with disability to thrive through golf.

In recognition of his contributions to the sport, Johnstone was inducted into the Southern Africa Golf Hall of Fame in 2015. After retiring from competitive golf, he transitioned into a career as a golf commentator for Sky Sports. He also presented a television series called "Bush Hacking," which featured short, two-minute episodes filmed in the Kruger Park and Shamwari in South Africa, aired as fillers during live golf coverage on Sky Sports and also broadcast on SuperGolf on SuperSport

JONAS, PHILIP SOUTH AFRICA, CANADA

Philip Jonas was once hailed as the hottest junior golf prospect to emerge from South Africa since Dale Hayes. Despite the high expectations and numerous victories as a junior, his success on the PGA Tour did not fully match his early potential. However, Jonas found his niche on the Canadian Tour, both as a player and a coach. Drawing from his own experience in South Africa's strong junior golf program, he has dedicated himself to helping young golfers realize their potential.

As an amateur, Jonas built an impressive resume. He won the South African Junior Championship in 1976, 1978, and 1979 and was recognized as the Leading International Player at the Junior World Championship five times. In 1977, he was named South Africa's Young Sportsman of the Year. He represented South Africa in the World Amateur Team Championship in 1980. His collegiate career at Lamar University in Texas from 1982 to 1986 was marked by seven tournament victories, and he was named a First Team All-American in the NCAA Division 1 in 1986.

Jonas has also received numerous honors throughout his career. He was inducted into the Golf Hall of Fame of British Columbia in 2019 and was a two-time medalist at the US Senior Open in 2017 and 2018. Other accolades include being named PGA of BC Player of the Year in 2017 and receiving the PGA of BC Teacher of the Year Award in 2012. He won the Vancouver Golf Tour Order of Merit in 2007 and was the PGA of Canada Assistants Champion in 2004 and 2006. Jonas also won the PGA of BC Championship in 2003 and was a multiple-time PGA of BC Player of the Year.

As a professional, Jonas secured victories in various tournaments, including the 2000 Quebec Tel Open, the 1999 Alliant Cup, the 1996 and 1997 Peru Open, and the 1990 Goodyear Classic. He finished ninth on the South African Tour Order of Merit in 1990 and fourth on the PGA Tour Canada Order of Merit in 1993. Jonas was also a dominant force on the Lower Mainland Assistants Tour, winning the Order of Merit in multiple years 2003, 2004, 2005, 2007, 2009, and 2010. In total, he has won over 100 professional events in Vancouver, British Columbia.

In addition to his playing career, Jonas served as an on-course TV reporter at the Canadian Open for TSN/CTV in 2004 and 2005, further showcasing his deep connection to the game. His contributions to golf as a player, coach, and mentor have left a lasting impact, particularly in British Columbia, where he continues to influence the next generation of golfers.

JOOSTE, MRS K UNION SOUTH AFRICA

Mrs. Jooste was a pioneering figure in South African women's golf, playing a crucial role in the establishment and development of key golf organizations. Her administrative efforts were instrumental in the foundation of the Transvaal Ladies' Golf Union (LGU) in 1912, alongside Gibb. She served as the First Honorary Secretary of the Transvaal LGU from 1912 to 1931 and held the position of President from 1917 to 1918.

In addition to her work with the Transvaal LGU, Mrs. Jooste was also deeply involved in the creation of the South African Ladies' Golf Union (SALGU). She began working towards its establishment in 1912, collaborating with Grindlay Ferris and others. That same year, Gibb, Ferris, and Jooste successfully formed the SALGU. Mrs. Jooste served as the First Honorary Secretary of SALGU from 1914 to 1918 and again from 1924 to 1925, later becoming the President from 1928 to 1931.

Her contributions extended to the Johannesburg Golf Club as well, where she was the Honorary Secretary in 1905. In 1910, she played a key role in affiliating the Johannesburg Golf Club with the British Ladies' Golf Union (LGU), further strengthening the ties between South African and British women's golf.

Mrs. Jooste's leadership and dedication were vital to the growth and organization of women's golf in South Africa, and her legacy continues to be felt in the institutions she helped establish and lead.

K

KAMTE, JAMES (1982) SOUTH AFRICA

James Bongani Kamte, widely known as "Cobra," is a trailblazing South African professional golfer who has made significant strides in both his home country and on the international stage. As an Ernie Els Foundation Member from 2000 to 2003, Kamte honed his skills before turning professional in 2003. Prior to this, he had a successful amateur career, representing Gauteng in the Under-23 division and later in the Gauteng Seniors side, achieving a ranking as the 5th best amateur in South Africa.

Kamte's professional career took off in 2007, a standout year for him on the Sunshine Tour. He finished second in two consecutive tournaments, the Samsung Royal Swazi Sun Open and the Vodacom Origins Tournament in Pretoria. His persistence paid off when he secured his first Sunshine Tour victory at the Seekers Travel Pro-Am tournament at the Dainfern Country Club in Johannesburg on 8 September 2007. He continued to build on this success, winning his fourth Sunshine Tour title at the BMG Classic in 2011.

On the international front, Kamte made history as the first black South African player since Vincent Tshabalala in 1976 to earn European Tour playing privileges. His best finish on the European Challenge Tour was a second-place finish at the Kenya Open in Nairobi, Kenya, along with a fourth-place finish at the Vodafone Challenge in Germany.

In January 2008, Kamte achieved a landmark victory by winning the Sunshine Tour's Dimension Data Pro-Am, becoming the first black South African golfer to win an event on the tour's summer swing. This victory further solidified his status as a leading figure in South African golf.

Kamte's success continued when he entered the Asian Tour qualifying school for 2009 and finished fourth. He quickly capitalized on this by winning the first event of the 2009 season, the Asian Tour International in Thailand, securing his place in events co-sanctioned by the Asian and European tours for the rest of the season.

Throughout his career, Kamte has accumulated five professional wins and numerous top finishes, making him one of the most successful black South African golfers in history. His achievements and dedication to the sport have paved the way for future generations of South African golfers, especially those from underrepresented backgrounds.

KAPLAN, RICHARD (1962) SOUTH AFRICA

Richard Dennis Kaplan had a distinguished career both as an amateur and a professional golfer, marked by significant achievements on the South African and international golfing stages. During the 1980s, Kaplan established himself as a formidable amateur player, earning four Springbok caps and winning notable titles, including the English Men's Open Amateur Stroke Play Championship (Brabazon Trophy) in 1986 and the Southern Transvaal Open Strokeplay in 1984.

Kaplan's transition to professional golf was equally successful. He earned his Springbok colours four more times as a professional and represented South Africa in the 1999 World Cup. His first victory on the Sunshine Tour came in 1995, and he went on to secure three more tour wins by 2000. Kaplan consistently performed well on the Sunshine Tour, finishing 9th on the Order of Merit in 1993, 1994, and 1995, marking him as one of the top players during that period.

Kaplan also competed on the Asian Tour, where he achieved success b the Order of Merit that year. Throughout his professional career, Kaplan accumulated a total of nine professional wins, cementing his legacy as a highly accomplished golfer from South Africa.

KARMIS, PETER (1981) SOUTH AFRICA, GREECE

Peter Karmis is a professional golfer with a notable career on the Sunshine Tour, where he made history in 2009 by becoming the first player to record a round of 59 on the par-72 Royal Swazi Spa Golf Course astonishing 13-under-par with 23 putts. Karmis has accumulated a total of 10 professional wins, with five of them coming on the Sunshine Tour. His victories on the tour include the Lombard Insurance Classic in 2007 and 2009, the Sun Sibaya Challenge in 2016 from Oliver Bekker, and two significant wins in 2017 at the Investec Royal Swazi Open and the Sun City Challenge.

In addition to his success on the Sunshine Tour, Karmis also competed on the Asian Tour from 2010 to 2012, where he secured a win at the Handa Singapore Classic in 2010 from Jbe Kruger. Karmis represented Greece in the 2018 World Cup, showcasing his international presence in the sport. His achievements highlight his consistency and skill across multiple tours and events.

KEARTLAND, BASIL UNION SOUTH AFRICA

Basil Keartland was a prominent figure in South African golf, making significant contributions both in administration and as an amateur player. His involvement with the South African Golf Union (SAGU) was extensive; he served as a member from 1959 to 1973, including terms as Vice-President from 1967 to 1971 and President from 1971 to 1974. During his tenure, he was also a National Selector and Convenor of the committee, and he played a pivotal role as Chairman of the SAGU Handicapping Committee. Keartland was instrumental in founding and chairing the SA Golf Foundation in the early 1960s and served as Senior SAGU Chairman in 1965 and 1966.

His influence extended to the Transvaal Golf Union, where he was a member for 18 years and served as President from 1961 to 1963. At the Royal Johannesburg Golf Club, he held various leadership roles, including President and Captain over two terms each.

As an amateur player, Keartland achieved notable success, captaining the Springbok team in 1958 and 1967 and leading the Transvaal team from 1948 to 1960. He won the South African Amateur Championship three times 1946, 1952, and 1957 and was a recipient of the Proudfoot Trophy. Additionally, he was a two-time Transvaal Amateur Champion and a runner-up in 1950. His legacy is marked by his leadership and contributions to the growth and organization of golf in South Africa.

KEMP, DEREK SOUTH AFRICA

Derek Kemp was a distinguished South African amateur golfer whose career spanned from the late 1950s to the early 1970s. His notable achievements include winning the South African Amateur Championship and the Proudfoot Trophy in 1967. He also secured the Freddie Tait Trophy at the SA Open in 1968. Kemp's other notable victories include the Western Province Amateur Championship in 1960 and the OFS Open Amateur Championship in 1962. Additionally, he triumphed in the Western Transvaal Open Amateur Championship in 1963.

Throughout his career, Kemp excelled in various regional and national competitions, including multiple wins at the Transvaal Amateur Championship in 1962 and 1963, and a second-place finish in 1970. His international achievements include a second-place finish in the Australian Amateur in 1963, where he was narrowly defeated by John Hayes, and a second-place finish in the Mozambique Championships in 1964. Kemp also achieved a second-place finish in the SA Stroke-Play Championship in 1971. He represented Western Province, Southern Transvaal, Transvaal, and South Africa in numerous tournaments, showcasing his talent and versatility on the golf course.

KEYTER, BRUCE UNION SOUTH AFRICA

Bruce Keyter had a distinguished career in golf, marked by significant achievements both as an amateur and a professional. As an amateur, he secured the Natal Open Championship in 1954 and the South African Amateur Championship in 1955. Transitioning to professional golf, Keyter's notable victories include the Transvaal Open Championship in 1956, where he notably defeated the renowned Bobby Locke for the first time in 20 years in South Africa. He also won the Natal Open Championship in 1957.

Keyter's success continued with the Southern African Masters Championship in 1963, where he shot 291 to win by three strokes over contenders like Terry Westbrook, Hugh Inggs, and Eric Moore. That same year, he was a runner-up in the South African Open, finishing two strokes behind Allan Henning.

His other significant accomplishments include winning the South Rhodesia Open in 1962 and 1963, with a runner-up finish in 1961, and the Mahonaland Open in 1958 and 1961. He also claimed victory in the Central African PGA Championship in 1962 and was a runner-up in the Grand Prix Series 2 in 1964. Keyter's career reflects a blend of regional dominance and competitive success on a broader stage.

KINGSLEY, C.W.M. (DIED 1947) UNION SOUTH AFRICA

Charles Kingsley had a profound impact on South African golf administration, contributing significantly over nearly five decades. He was a key figure in the establishment of the South African Golf Union (SAGU) in 1910 and held various positions within the organization, including Vice-President and President, and was an active member of the executive committee at different times.

Kingsley was heavily involved in organizing national tournaments, serving on the committee for the National Tournament (both Amateur and Open) on 30 occasions. At the Royal Cape Golf Club, he held multiple roles including Captain and Life Member, and was a Vice-President.

His influence extended to the Western Province Golf Union, where he was instrumental in its formation and served as its first President from 1910 to 1936. Kingsley also championed the idea of a golf museum in South Africa and had a deep interest in the history of the game.

His legacy was widely acknowledged, and his passing in 1947 was marked by a strong recognition of the significant contributions he made to the sport of golf.

KINGSTON, JAMES (1965) SOUTH AFRICA

James Hubert Kingston has had a distinguished career in golf, marked by notable achievements and victories across various tours.

In 2007, Kingston reached a significant milestone by topping the Sunshine Tour Order of Merit and securing his first European Tour win at the South African Airways Open, where he finished ahead of Oliver Wilson. This victory was pivotal in establishing his presence on the European Tour.

In February 2008, he won the Vodacom Championship on the Sunshine Tour, which helped him break into the top 100 of the Official World Golf Rankings for the first time. 2009 saw Kingston claim a playoff victory at the Mercedes-Benz Championship in Cologne, triumphing over Anders Hansen.

Kingston's success extends to the Asian Tour, where he has achieved four wins: the Thailand Open in 1998, the Maskyung Daks Open in 1999, the London Myanmar Open in 2000, and the Ericsson Classic in 2000.

On the Sunshine Tour, Kingston has accumulated ten victories, with two additional wins enhancing his impressive record. His accomplishments also include three wins on the European Senior Tour, with notable victories at the Senior Italian Open in 2021 and 2023, the Swiss Seniors Open in 2022, and the South Africa Senior Open in 2019.

KRUYSWIJK, JACQUES (1992) SOUTH AFRICA

Jacques Kruyswijk has carved out a notable career in professional golf with a series of achievements across both amateur and professional levels.

As an amateur, Kruyswijk made his mark by winning the Royal Silver Vase in 2011. He turned professional in January 2013 and quickly made an impact, securing his first professional victory on the Big Easy Tour after finishing 7th in the Sunshine Tour Q-School in 2013.

Kruyswijk's professional career saw significant progress in the 2016–17 Sunshine Tour season. He earned his maiden victory at the Lion of Africa Cape Town Open in November 2016 and followed up with a tie for 4th at the Joburg Open in February 2017, finishing 11th on the Order of Merit for the season.

The 2017–18 Sunshine Tour season continued his success, where he tied for 4th at the South African Open and again finished 11th on the Order of Merit. In 2020, Kruyswijk's best results included a 3rd-place finish at both the Eye of Africa PGA Championship and the Limpopo Championship.

By 2021, he had five top-10 finishes on the European Tour, retained his tour card, and won the Sunshine Tour Invitational at Centurion Country Club. This victory helped him break into the top-200 on the Official World Golf Ranking for the first time. Overall, Jacques Kruyswijk has accumulated two professional wins, marking a promising trajectory in his golfing career.

KRUGER, JAMES BARRY 'JBE' (1986) SOUTH AFRICA

Jbe' Kruger has enjoyed a successful golf career, winning 12 professional tournaments across various tours. On the Sunshine Tour, he claimed victories at the 2009 Zambia Open and the Zimbabwe Open in both 2010 and 2014. His prowess extends beyond South Africa, as he has triumphed internationally as well.

In February 2012, Kruger captured the Avantha Masters title, an event co-sanctioned by the European and Asian Tours, finishing ahead of notable players like Jorge Campillo and Marcel Siem. After a seven-year

victory drought, Kruger secured another international win at the Shinhan Donghae Open in September 2019, a tournament co-sanctioned by the Japan Golf Tour, Asian Tour, and Korean Tour.

His winning streak continued in July 2023, when he claimed victory at the Shigeo Nagashima Invitational Sega Sammy Cup on the Japan Golf Tour. In 2024, Kruger further cemented his reputation by winning the Mercuries Taiwan Open. With five Sunshine Tour wins and multiple international victories, Kruger is recognized for his consistent performances and ability to compete at a high level across multiple tours.

L

LASSEN, WERNER (1974) NAMIBIA

Werner Lassen is a prominent figure in Namibian golf, distinguished by his remarkable achievements. He holds the record for the most victories in the Bank Windhoek Namibian Open Golf Tournament, having won the event 10 times in 15 years as of May 2007. His latest victory in this tournament came after a sudden-death playoff against Andrew Dodds, and he surpassed the previous record held by Adri Basson, who had won the tournament five times.

In addition to his success in national tournaments, Lassen has represented Namibia on the international stage. He was a member of the Namibian national amateur golf team and competed in the 2006 Eisenhower Trophy amateur golf tournament held in Cape Town, South Africa. His contributions and achievements have made a significant impact on Namibian golf.

LAWRENCE, THRISTON (1996) SOUTH AFRICA

Thriston Lawrence has rapidly ascended in professional golf, achieving nine career victories and reaching a World Ranking of 62 in 2024. His amateur career was highlighted by wins at the South African Amateur Championship in 2013 and the Lytham Trophy, along with another South African Amateur Championship title in 2014. Turning professional, Lawrence's success continued with a notable win on the MENA Tour Order of Merit in 2015 and a victory at the Vodacom Origins of Golf at Stellenbosch on the Sunshine Tour in 2019. In 2021, he triumphed at the Joburg Open, a co-sanctioned event by the European Tour and Sunshine Tour.

Lawrence's impressive achievements include winning the Omega European Masters in August 2022, a victory secured in a playoff against Matt Wallace. He was recognized as the DP World Tour Rookie of the Year later that year and captured the Investec South African Open Championship in December, finishing just one shot ahead of Clément Sordet. In 2023, he demonstrated his competitive edge by overcoming a four-shot deficit to win the BMW International Open by one shot from Joost Luiten. His recent performances in 2024, including a 4th place at The Open and a 2nd place at the British Masters, have further solidified his reputation as a rising star in professional golf.

LEADBETTER, DAVID (1952) RHODESIA

David Leadbetter is a renowned golf instructor who has significantly influenced the sport through his innovative teaching methods and successful coaching career. Initially, Leadbetter played on the European and Southern African tours but shifted to golf instruction after experiencing

limited success as a player.

In the 1980s, Leadbetter, initially under the guidance of fellow Rhodesian Phil Ritson, gained widespread recognition for his work with Nick Faldo, whom he helped transform into a six-time Major champion by rebuilding his swing. This success led Leadbetter to establish the Leadbetter Golf Academies, headquartered at Champions Gate Golf Club in Davenport, Florida, with additional branches in North America, Europe, Asia, and Africa. His coaching career boasts an impressive record, including guiding players to 26 Major Championship titles and over 150 individual tournament victories. Notably, seven of his students have achieved the number one spot in the Official World Golf Ranking.

Leadbetter's roster of current and former students includes notable names such as Nick Price, Charles Howell III, Michelle Wie, Lydia Ko, and Byeong Hun An. Former students include legends like Nick Faldo, Greg Norman, and Ernie Els. In recognition of his impact on the sport, Leadbetter was ranked second on Golf Digest's 2005-2006 list of the "50 Greatest Teachers" in the U.S., just behind Butch Harmon. His lessons are highly sought after, with a price tag of $10,000 per day.

In addition to his coaching, Leadbetter has authored eight books on golf swings, with over two million copies sold. He has also developed training aids such as the SwingSetter and SwingSetter Pro. His influence extends into media, with appearances in video games like "David Leadbetter's Greens" and "My Personal Golf Trainer" for the Wii. Leadbetter's innovative approach and contributions to golf instruction have solidified his reputation as a leading figure in the field.

LEBBIE, JAMES (1958) SIERRA LEONE – CIVIL WAR

James Lebbie, often hailed as the "Tiger Woods of West Africa," is celebrated as one of the greatest golfers to emerge from the region, particularly in Sierra Leone. His impressive career boasts eight professional wins and significant contributions to golf in Africa.

Lebbie's career highlights include a notable victory at the 1992 Nigerian Open, where he triumphed over Paul Eales by four strokes. This win was distinguished by a skillful par-save and an eagle in the final round, showcasing his composure and expertise under pressure. He also secured wins at the Ghana Open in 1980 and the Sierra Leone Open multiple times in the late 1980s and early 1990s. Additionally, he won the Togo Open, although the specific year is not documented.

Before the Sierra Leone Civil War, Lebbie was a prominent figure in Sierra Leonean golf, playing at Freetown Golf Club, which features unique "browns" rather than traditional greens. He served as the Head Professional there until 1991. After the war, which led to the closure of the golf course, Lebbie relocated to the United States. He worked at Langston Golf Course in Washington, D.C., initially as a driving range manager but was later let go due to certification issues. As of 2016, he was working as a caddie at Congressional Country Club in Bethesda, Maryland. Despite his prestigious background, Lebbie preferred to remain low-profile, focusing on his current role rather than highlighting his past achievements.

Lebbie's career is a testament to his exceptional talent and dedication to golf, reflecting both his remarkable successes and the challenges he encountered throughout his journey.

LEEDS, MRS UNION SOUTH AFRICA

Mrs. Leeds made a lasting impact on women's golf administration over four decades. She served as the Honorary Secretary of the South African Ladies Golf Union (SALGU) starting in 1948 and then as President from 1948 to 1950. Her leadership extended to the Transvaal Ladies Golf Union (LGU), where she was President from 1927 to 1932. Additionally, she was the Captain of the Royal Johannesburg Golf Club in 1930. Mrs. Leeds was also a founding member and the first President of the Transvaal Senior Women's Golf Society, holding Life Membership and later Honorary Life Membership. Her dedication and leadership significantly advanced women's golf during her era.

LEEMHUIS, MICHAEL SOUTH AFRICA, USA

Michael Leemhuis is a highly accomplished leader in the world of club management and executive search, currently serving as the Chairman and Chief Executive Officer at ClubWorks. His career is marked by a deep expertise in managing elite private clubs and a robust background in executive recruitment, which he has brought to GGA Partners, enhancing their executive search services.

Over the past five years, Michael has been instrumental as a senior consultant, placing candidates in prestigious roles such as general manager, director of golf, and head golf professional at renowned clubs across the U.S., including Riviera Country Club, Brooklawn Country Club, Cherry Hills, Hazeltine, and Boca West. His extensive experience in managing top-tier private clubs and recruiting for them has positioned him as a key asset in delivering exceptional services to clients.

Before his role at ClubWorks, Michael held the position of President at Ocean Reef Club in Key Largo, Florida, one of the world's largest clubs. During his tenure, he managed significant investments and operations, overseeing a $110 million operation that included a hotel, airport, marina, and 17 food and beverage outlets. Prior to Ocean Reef, Michael was the CEO of Congressional Country Club in Washington, D.C., where he managed a $35 million annual operation and guided the club to the top of the Platinum Clubs of America ranking.

Michael's professional credentials are impressive. He is a certified PGA of America Professional, a PGA of South Africa Master Professional, and holds certifications as a Certified Club Manager and Certified Club Executive through the Club Management Association of America (CMAA). His education includes a Master's Degree in Sports Administration and Management from East Carolina University. His contributions to the field have earned him numerous accolades, including the CMAA Club Manager of the Year award, the Boardroom Magazine Leadership Award, and recognition as a CMAA Fellow.

Michael's journey began in South Africa, where he was educated at Pretoria Boys High School and Wits University in Johannesburg. He later pursued further studies at UCLA and earned his graduate degree at East Carolina University. His career spans diverse roles, including managing the Gary Player Country Club and Lost City Golf Course in South Africa, overseeing the Ellis Park Sports Stadium, and working with the PGA Tour on various events. His move to the United States saw him take on significant roles, including General Manager/Director of Golf at TPC at Avenel and later at Congressional Country Club, where he significantly impacted the club's status and success.

In his current role at ClubWorks, Michael continues to leverage his extensive experience and expertise to guide the organization and its clients, contributing to the continued excellence in club management and executive search services.

LEEN, MAURITZ SOUTH AFRICA

Mauritz Leen made significant contributions to golf in South Africa through various roles and initiatives. He served as the Tournament Director for the Sunshine Tour and was instrumental in founding the Winter Tour, which he managed from the late 1980s until 1995. Leen was also a key figure in the transformation of South African golf, playing a leading role in the unification talks during 1990-1991, which were critical for the sport's evolution in the country.

In addition to his administrative work, Leen authored a best-selling sports book, "ABC of Golf," in 1997 and created a popular weekly TV program that reached millions across seven European countries starting in 2003. He also developed the Platteland Golf Clinics, which were designed to promote and support golf at the grassroots level. His efforts have had a lasting impact on the sport, both in South Africa and internationally.

LE GRANGE, COBIE (1942) SOUTH AFRICA

Cobie Legrange was a prominent South African golfer in the 1960s and 1970s, recognized for his exceptional skills and notable achievements. His career highlights include a peak world ranking of 15 and 22 worldwide victories.

In 1964, Legrange had a standout year, finishing second in the French Open after a playoff with Roberto De Vicenzo and winning the Lake Karrinyup Bowl by one stroke. He also claimed victory at the Australian Wills Masters, defeating Jack Nicklaus and Bruce Devlin, and won the British Masters by a stroke. His success continued into 1965 with a wire-to-wire win at the Pringle of Scotland Tournament and a runner-up finish at the French Open.

Legrange's achievements in 1966 included winning the Western Province Open, the British Senior Services, and a runner-up finish at the South African Open. He continued to perform well in the late 1960s with wins at the Rhodesian Dunlop Open and the Bata Bush Babes tournament. In 1969, he won the Western Province Open again, had a T-11 finish at the Open Championship, and was runner-up at both the German Open and the R.T.V. International Trophy.

In the early 1970s, Legrange won the Holiday Inns Royal Swazi Sun Open in a playoff and the Schoeman Park Open. He also had a number of other notable victories, including multiple wins on the South African, British

PGA, and Rhodesian circuits.

Legrange was known for his long hitting and precision iron play, though his career experienced a decline in the mid-1970s due to a loss of confidence and a deliberate swing method. Despite this, he made significant contributions to the sport as a club professional, television commentator, golf course designer, and coach. He received the ProSport Media 5-Star Professional Award and the Master Professional Award in 2010 and was honored with an Honorary Life SA PGA Membership and induction into the Southern Africa Golf Hall of Fame.

LE ROUX, JANNIE UNION SOUTH AFRICA

Jannie Le Roux is a dominant figure in amateur golf during the late 1950s and early 1960s, made a substantial impact with his impressive record and contributions to the sport. His name is etched on the Inter-Provincial Trophy, with the Jannie le Roux floating trophy, awarded to the winner of the South African Inter-Provincial, highlighting his prominence in the sport.

His notable amateur achievements include winning the Cape Province Amateur twice (1953, 1957) and the WP Amateur multiple times (1952, 1957), along with several top finishes in the same tournament in other years. He claimed the South African Amateur title in 1961 and was a runner-up in 1954. He also secured victories in the Freddie Tait Trophy (1957, 1960) and the Proudfoot Trophy (1963). His consistent performances were reflected in his second-place finishes in various prestigious tournaments such as the Silver Vase (1955) and the Natal Amateur Stroke-Play (1963).

He achieved success in several regional and international tournaments, including winning the Transvaal Amateur 1955, 1956, 1959, the Mozambique Amateur 1955, 1958, and the Coronation Trophy in Kenya 1958. He was also part of the Commonwealth Eisenhower Trophy-winning team in 1959.

His record includes multiple victories in the Natal Amateur Stroke-Play 1960, 1961 and the Natal Amateur 1961, 1962, as well as the Swaziland Amateur 1961, 1962 and the Zululand Amateur 1962, 1963. Additionally, he earned Springbok Caps, representing South Africa in the sport seven times from 1957 to 1963.

His distinguished career and achievements have left a lasting legacy in amateur golf, solidifying his reputation as a key figure in the sport's history.

LEVENSON, GAVAN "STICKS" (1953) SOUTH AFRICA

Gavan Neil Levenson has had a distinguished and multifaceted career in golf, both as a player and coach. His journey began with impressive amateur success, including winning the South African Amateur Stroke Play Championship in 1975. In 1978, he added the French, Portuguese, and Rhodesian Open Amateur Championships to his list of victories, and two years prior, he represented South Africa at the Eisenhower Trophy, marking him as one of the country's top amateur golfers.

As a professional, Levenson's career was equally impressive. In 1979, he won the Belgian Open, defeating notable players like Bobby Cole and Nick Faldo by three strokes, and the Waterloo Open in the same year. His victory at the 1984 South African PGA Championship came with a convincing three-stroke win over Nick Price, and he topped the South African Order of Merit in 1983/84. In 1985, he won the prestigious South African Open and came close to victory multiple times, finishing second in 1978, 1979, and 1987. Levenson also found success on the international stage, with wins at the Open de Baleares and Majorcan Open in 1991.

In Europe, he continued his winning ways on the seniors circuit, claiming victory at the DGM Barbados Open in 2004, edging out Denis Durian and Carl Mason. On the PGA Tour, though he spent four years with limited success, he did achieve a notable T4 finish at the 1982 Greater Hartford Open.

Beyond his playing career, Levenson has had a significant impact as a coach and leader. He captained South Africa, Transvaal, and Southern Transvaal teams and became a key figure in developing future talents like James Kamte, Dylan Frittelli, and Charl Schwartzel. He also served as South Africa's Junior National Coach and earned nine Springbok caps. His contributions to the game were further recognized when he was named PGA Master Professional in 2008 and awarded PGA Teacher of the Year in 2002. Known for his unique swing, which earned him the nickname "Legs" due to his pronounced leg action, Gavan Levenson remains a respected figure in the world of golf.

LEWTHWAITE, LEJAN (1991) SOUTH AFRICA

Leján Lewthwaite's golf career began with a strong foundation during her amateur years, marked by her time at the Gavin Levenson Golf Academy. In 2011, she earned a full golf scholarship to Texas State University, where she quickly made an impact by winning the Johnny Imes Invitational, her first NCAA Division I collegiate tournament. This early success set the stage for her professional journey.

In 2016, Lewthwaite made the decision to turn professional, and just three years later, she claimed her first professional title at the South African Women's Masters in 2019. Her winning momentum continued in 2020, when she secured victories at both the SuperSport Ladies Challenge and the Dimension Data Ladies Pro-Am, further establishing herself as a force in women's golf. The following year, she achieved a notable T7 finish at the Ladies Italian Open, just three strokes off the lead.

With five professional wins to her name, Leján Lewthwaite's career highlights her steady rise through the ranks of women's golf, demonstrating both her skill and determination.

LIDDLE, BRETT (1970) SOUTH AFRICA

Brett Anthony Liddle has enjoyed a successful golf career, highlighted by his first professional win in 1995. That year proved to be a standout season for him, as he secured two victories, marking it as his best year on tour. Over the next few years, Liddle continued to perform strongly, adding five more wins to his record between 1995 and 2000. In total, he achieved nine professional victories, showcasing his consistency and skill throughout his career.

LINCOLN, BOBBY (1953) SOUTH AFRICA

Robert James "Bobby" Lincoln's professional golf career saw a steady rise, with his breakthrough win coming in 1985 at the Wild Coast Pro-Am, well into his thirties. Following this initial success, Lincoln consistently delivered strong performances, winning three tournaments in each of the subsequent three years, totaling 19 victories over his career. While none of these were major events, they highlighted his tenacity and skill on the tour.

Among his notable wins were the 1986 Johnnie Walker Air Mauritius Golf Classic, the 1987 Protea Assurance Classic where he triumphed over Fulton Allem, and the 1988 AECI Charity Classic, where he beat John Bland by two strokes. In 1992, Lincoln secured victory at the Tournament of Champions, besting a young Ernie Els. Later in his career, he teamed up with renowned golfers, winning the 2006 Nelson Mandela Invitational alongside Retief Goosen and the 2008 Gary Player Invitational with Garth Mulroy.

Lincoln also found success on the Senior Tour, notably winning the 2007 Jersey Seniors Classic by two strokes over Bill Longmuir. Beyond his playing career, he contributed to the golf community by serving on the Southern Africa Tour Players Committee for 15 years, from 1991 to 2006, demonstrating his commitment to the sport both on and off the course.

LITTLE, SALLY "SUNDAY SAL" (1951) SOUTH AFRICA, USA

Sally Little is widely regarded as the greatest South African woman golfer ever. Her illustrious career began with a strong amateur record, winning the Western Province Matchplay three times, the Transvaal Strokeplay three times, and claiming the South African Stroke and Match Championship in 1971. In 1970, she distinguished herself as the low individual and the only woman to break 300 in the World Amateur Team Championship. She also triumphed in the Portuguese East Africa (1969) and reached the semi-finals of the French Amateur (1970) before securing the British Team Trophy in 1971.

In 1971, Sally qualified for the US Tour, where she quickly made her mark despite participating in only seven events. She finished 51st on the money list and was named Rookie of the Year. With one of the best swings in women's golf, she consistently ranked in the top 50 over the next four years. However, Sally admitted that she initially struggled with the pressure of being in contention during this learning period. Her breakthrough came in 1976 when she claimed her first victory at the Women's International, famously holing a bunker shot on the final hole to secure a 1-shot victory over Jan Stephenson.

This win propelled Sally up the money list to 13th, and she continued to build on her success, winning tournaments in 1978, three in 1979, and two in 1980, including the prestigious US LPGA Championship. Her LPGA victory marked only the second time a non-American had won the title. Sally's success continued, with three wins in 1981 and four more in 1982, including a sensational 64 in the final round of the Dinah Shore. Her ability to deliver low scores on the final day earned her the nickname "Sunday Sal."

Sally consistently ranked in the top 10 from 1977 to 1982 and reached a career-high ranking of #2, accumulating 15 LPGA victories. She made a remarkable comeback after a two-year break from the circuit due to illness, winning the 1988 du Maurier Classic. In recognition of her achievements, she was awarded the 1989 Ben Hogan Award by the Golf Writers Association of America and was honored as one of the LPGA's top-50 players and teachers during the LPGA's 50th Anniversary in 2000.

Sally's legacy was further cemented when she was inducted into the inaugural Southern Africa Golf Hall of Fame in 2009, alongside golfing legends such as Gary Player, Bobby Locke, Ernie Els, and Nick Price. In 2016, she became the first female golfer from South Africa to be inducted into the South African Hall of Fame.

Throughout her career, Sally has received numerous accolades, including SA Sportsman of the Year (1970), US LPGA Rookie of the Year (1971), and recognition as the US LPGA's "Best Sand Player" in 1976. She was named SA Golf Star in 1979 and was nominated as SA Professional Golfer of the Year in 1980. She also represented the Rest of the World Seniors in competitions against the USA Seniors from 2002 to 2013, serving as captain in 2014 and 2015.

Today, Sally continues to make a difference through the Little Golf Development Trust, which she leads at her driving range. The trust focuses on coaching young underprivileged school girls, offering them both life skills and golf in the hopes of discovering the next "Sally Little."

Sally Little's impressive career and continued dedication to golf development have cemented her legacy as one of South Africa's greatest golfers.

LOCKE, ARTHUR D'ARCY "BOBBY" (1917–1987)
UNION SOUTH AFRICA

Arthur D'Arcy 'Bobby' Locke is remembered as one of the greatest golfers to ever play the game, with a record that cements his status among the legends of the sport. His career was filled with remarkable victories, including four Open Championships and a total of 15 PGA Tour events. In his homeland of South Africa, Locke was a dominant force, claiming over 50 major tournament wins, including the South African Open a staggering nine times—every time he entered the competition.

The debate over South Africa's best golfer often brings Locke's name into contention, though many believe Gary Player holds that title. However, Denis Hutchinson, a respected figure in the sport, considered Locke the best. Were it not for the interruption of World War II, Locke might have achieved even more remarkable feats, given his dominance between

1948 and 1951. During that period, Locke was virtually unbeatable and even banned from competing in the United States – an extraordinary punishment for being, quite simply, too good. His career took a tragic turn in 1960 when he lost the sight in one eye after a car accident.

One of Locke's defining moments came during the 1946-47 season when he faced Sam Snead in a 16-match series in South Africa. Locke's strategy was baffling to Snead. Instead of focusing on where the flag was, Locke played to land his ball on the green and sink the putt, a tactic that won him 12 of the 16 matches. Snead, one of the greatest golfers of all time, was so rattled by Locke's putting prowess that his own game faltered, and he fell from the top of the U.S. Tour for the first time in his career.

Locke had been encouraged by Walter Hagen to try his hand in the U.S. during the late 1930s. He finally made the trip in 1947, arriving in time for the U.S. Masters, where he finished a respectable 14th. Many American pros criticized his swing, claiming it was too long and lacked form, but Locke dismissed their comments with a wry remark, stating he used his right hand to cash his checks. Locke went on to win several tournaments, including the Carolina PGA and the Houston Invitational, placing third in the Texas Open. A key encounter came when he outplayed Ben Hogan at the Philadelphia Inquirer Open, where Locke took a swing of seven strokes to win the event.

The South African continued to dazzle the U.S. circuit, winning four out of five events, including the Goodall Round Robin and the Canadian Open. By the end of 1947, Locke had finished second on the money list, despite only playing part of the season. In 1948, he returned to claim even more victories, with his most significant achievement being a 16-stroke win at the Chicago Victory National Championship, tying the record for the largest margin in U.S. Tour history.

Locke's dominance was not universally appreciated. After his remarkable success, the U.S. PGA controversially banned him from their tournaments. Gene Sarazen called it "the most disgraceful action by any golf organization in the past 30 years." Locke, unfazed by the ban, found solace in the warm reception he received in Britain and Europe, where he continued to compete and win.

Locke's mastery of the game was built around his incredible putting. His discolored, light brown hickory-shafted putter became legendary, as did his unconventional technique, which involved spinning the ball in ways other golfers had never seen. He famously quipped, "You drive for show, but I putt for dough," encapsulating the essence of his game. His slow, methodical style on the greens often frustrated his American competitors, but Locke's results spoke for themselves. His putting ability was so precise that even long-time rivals like Snead and Hogan acknowledged his genius on the green.

Locke's career was studded with highlights, including his four victories in The Open Championship. His 1949 win was a crushing 12-stroke playoff victory over Harry Bradshaw, and in 1950, he set a championship record at Troon with a 279. He continued to perform at the highest level, coming close to further titles but finding himself outpaced by a young Peter Thompson. However, Locke had his revenge in 1957, when he made a final surge at St. Andrews to claim his fourth Open title, once again beating Thompson by three shots. His 1957 win was marked by controversy, as newsreel footage revealed he had failed to replace his ball properly after marking it on the 72nd green. Yet, the Championship committee, citing the "spirit of the game," upheld Locke's victory.

His ability to win in multiple countries and continents, including the 1955 Australian Open and the Transvaal Open in 1958, showcased his global dominance in the sport. Even after his career was cut short by the car accident that robbed him of his vision in one eye, Locke's place in golf history remained secure.

Bobby Locke was more than a winner; he was an innovator who revolutionized the way the game was played, especially in his approach to putting. His achievements earned him numerous accolades, including the

Harry Vardon Trophy three times, and he was inducted into the World Golf Hall of Fame in 1977, followed by the Southern Africa Golf Hall of Fame in 2009.

Locke's legacy lives on through the stories of his victories and his contributions to golf. His eccentric swing, unparalleled putting ability, and undeniable competitive spirit made him a true legend of the game, whose influence is still felt by golfers today.

LOMBARD, ZANDER (1995) SOUTH AFRICA

Zander Lombard is a prominent South African golfer with a strong track record in both amateur and professional golf. As a plus 5 amateur, Lombard achieved notable success, including several tournament victories across Africa and representing South Africa in the prestigious Eisenhower Trophy in both 2012 and 2014. His talent was further recognized when he finished as the runner-up to Bradley Neil 2/1 at The Amateur Championship in 2014.

Transitioning to professional golf, Lombard quickly made a name for himself. He earned a spot in the 2016 Open Championship following a commendable second-place finish at the Joburg Open. His skills were on full display in 2017 at the Rocco Forte Open in Sicily, where he narrowly missed out on victory, losing to Álvaro Quirós in a sudden-death playoff after the second hole.

Lombard continued to build on his success, winning the Vodacom Origins event on the Sunshine Tour in 2018. His consistent performance throughout the season earned him the top spot on the 2018-19 Sunshine Tour Order of Merit. To date, Lombard has secured nine professional wins, highlighting his status as a formidable competitor in the world of golf.

Zander Lombard has made significant strides in professional golf with a notable amateur background and a growing list of achievements. His consistent performances and victories, including his top finish in the Sunshine Tour Order of Merit, mark him as a prominent golfer.

LOUW, PETER SOUTH AFRICA – APARTHEID

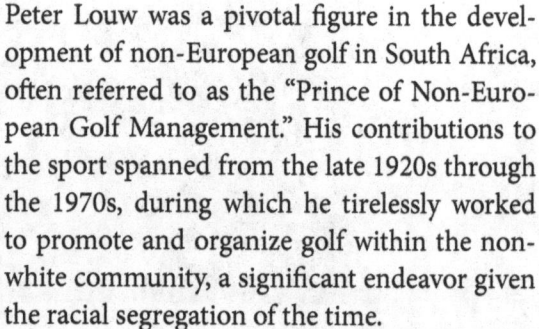

Peter Louw was a pivotal figure in the development of non-European golf in South Africa, often referred to as the "Prince of Non-European Golf Management." His contributions to the sport spanned from the late 1920s through the 1970s, during which he tirelessly worked to promote and organize golf within the non-white community, a significant endeavor given the racial segregation of the time.

As Vice-President of the South African Non-European Golf Association (SANEGA), Louw played a crucial role in organizing and formalizing golf clubs, particularly in the Cape Province. His efforts were not limited to local activities; he traveled extensively across the country and even abroad to advise on the formation and organization of golf clubs. Louw's commitment to spreading the "golfing gospel" among the non-white community was unparalleled, making him a cornerstone in the history of South African golf.

After World War II, under Louw's leadership, the SA Non-European Golf Association made significant strides. In 1948, Louw was instrumental in the establishment of the Association's headquarters in Bloemfontein. As vice-president, he was deeply involved in organizing the SA Non-European Open Championship, which became an annual event from 1949 onward. This championship was a beacon of hope and achievement for non-white golfers in a segregated society.

The challenges faced by the black golfing community during this time were immense. For instance, the 1956 SA Non-European Open was held on a makeshift nine-hole course on the Cape Flats, with unpredictable grass greens. Despite these conditions, the tournament showcased the talent and determination of players like A. (Polly) November, who won with a score of 305, and Simon Hlapo, who traveled from the Transvaal to compete.

A turning point in the history of the SA Non-European Open came in 1960, when a new 18-hole course was established at Wettonville, near the Wetton railway station in Cape Town. Remarkably, the Milnerton Golf Club, a white club, offered their course for the championship—marking the first time such an offer was made. This gesture was significant, as it symbolized a shift towards inclusivity in the sport.

The 1960 Championship at Milnerton was a memorable event, drawing over 800 spectators, many of whom were European. The tournament was won by Papwa Sewgolum, who braved a ferocious south-easterly wind to secure victory with scores of 80, 80, 74, and 74—a remarkable achievement under such challenging conditions.

Peter Louw's contributions to golf in South Africa were profound, yet his legacy is not widely known today. However, his impact on the game and his tireless efforts to promote inclusivity have been recognized with his induction into the Southern Africa Golf Hall of Fame. His work laid the foundation for future generations of golfers and played an essential role in the history of the sport in South Africa.

LOWRY, MRS (OWEN) KENYA

Mrs. Lowry was a formidable figure in Kenya's ladies' amateur golf scene, with a career that spanned multiple decades and was marked by numerous championships and accolades. Her dominance in the sport was evident through her repeated victories and consistent performance at the highest levels of competition.

Mrs. Lowry claimed the Kenya Ladies Championship title an impressive seven times, securing victories in 1952, 1955, 1957, 1958, 1959, and beyond. Her skill and determination on the course also led her to triumph in the European Championship twice, showcasing her abilities on a broader stage beyond the African continent.

In addition to her success in Kenya, Mrs. Lowry's prowess was evident even earlier in her career when she won the Northern Rhodesia Ladies Championship in 1938, further solidifying her status as one of the leading figures in women's golf during that era.

Despite facing tough competition, including a second-place finish in the Kenya Ladies Championship in 1953, Mrs. Lowry's record of achievements highlights her remarkable consistency and dominance in the sport, leaving a lasting legacy in the history of African women's golf with her impressive record and contributions to the sport.

M

MANIE, WILLIAM UNION SOUTH AFRICA – APARTHEID

William Manie was a talented golfer from South Africa who faced significant barriers due to the apartheid regime's racial policies, which barred him from competing in white-dominated tournaments in his home country. Determined to pursue his passion for golf on an international stage, Manie took a bold step by working his way overseas on a freighter to participate in the 1960 British Open. Unfortunately, he did not qualify for the tournament, but his journey was far from over.

Undeterred, Manie continued to compete in other tournaments across Europe. He made a notable impression at the 1960 Ballantine Tournament at Wentworth, where he shot an impressive 65 in the first round. His efforts also saw him participating in the 1960 Italian Open, where he finished 26th, the 1960 Portuguese Open, where he placed 30th, and the 1961 Spanish Open, where he again secured a 26th-place finish.

Given the oppressive apartheid policies in South Africa, Manie decided to remain in England, where he could continue his career in a more inclusive environment. He began his professional journey in England as the Assistant Professional at the Royal Winchester Golf Club in 1961. His skill and dedication eventually led him to become the Club Professional at Richmond Golf Club, a prestigious position that marked a significant achievement in his career.

Manie's story is a testament to his resilience and determination to overcome the racial barriers of his time, allowing him to pursue his passion for golf and succeed against the odds.

MANYAMA, THEOPHILUS 'THEO' (DIED 2023) SOUTH AFRICA

Theophilus 'Theo' Manyama, a South African golfer, faced significant barriers due to apartheid, which denied him the opportunity to compete on the South African circuit. Undeterred by these challenges, Manyama pivoted his focus to refereeing, where he forged an illustrious career as one of the most respected officials in the sport of golf.

His expertise and commitment led him to serve as the chief rules official, tournament director, and chief referee at some of the most prestigious events in the golfing world. His notable assignments included officiating at The Open Championship (19 times), The Masters (16 times), the US Open (9 times), the PGA Championship, The Players Championship, and numerous World Golf Championships, as well as events on both the US and European Tours.

In 2003, Manyama was appointed as the joint tournament director of the Presidents Cup, a significant achievement that underscored his authority and influence in the sport. His contributions were recognized when he received the Compleat Golf Magazine Award for his 'Lifetime contribution to the golf industry.'

Manyama's contributions to golf were further acknowledged in 2010 when he was inducted into the Southern Africa Golf Hall of Fame. That same year, he was honored with the Minister's Excellence Award at the South African Sports Awards, highlighting his impact beyond the golf course.

In 2015, Manyama achieved a rare 'Grand Slam' in officiating when he was invited to referee at The PGA Championship, completing his participation in all four major championships. His global recognition continued into 2016 when he served as a rules official at the Olympic Games in Rio de Janeiro, further cementing his legacy as a trailblazer in the sport.

Throughout his career, Theo Manyama's dedication, expertise, and trailblazing spirit broke barriers and set new standards in the world of golf officiating, making him a true legend in the sport.

MAQUBELA, ALFRED UNION SOUTH AFRICA – APARTHEID

The President of the South African Non-European Golf Association, Alfred Maqubela, receiving the Castle Breweries Floating Trophy for the Seniors "Teams of Two" event. Looking on is Peter Louw, vice-President of the Association.

After the passing of J. Jass, the first president of the South African Non-European Golf Union (SA N-E GU), Alfred Maqubela assumed the presidency, with Peter Louw serving as vice-president. Despite holding the title of president, Maqubela's role was largely ceremonial, as the real driving force behind the organization was Peter Louw, whose leadership and dedication propelled the union forward.

Under the auspices of the SA N-E GU, the "Golfers' Annual" was first published in conjunction with the SA Non-European Open and the General Meeting Association during the Easter of 1953/54. This marked a significant step in promoting and documenting the achievements and progress within the non-European golfing community in South Africa. The publication's Chief Editor was Mr. S. Mnisi, with Alfred Maqubela serving as a member of the Editorial Board, further contributing to the growth and recognition of non-European golfers.

In addition to his editorial contributions, Alfred Maqubela was also known for his generosity and support of the sport. In 1959, he sponsored the Kroonstad Open with a substantial contribution of 100 pounds—a significant amount at the time. This sponsorship played a crucial role in the tournament's success, which saw Cox Hlapo emerge as the winner, followed by David Motati and Ronnie Ditsebi.

Maqubela's commitment to the sport and the community was recognized when he was re-elected as president at the SA N-EGU's AGM in 1960. His leadership, both as a benefactor and a key figure in the union, helped to foster the development of non-European golf in South Africa during a challenging era.

MARJANE, AHMED MOROCCO

Morocco's Ahmed Marjane made history by becoming the first golfer from the Arab world to win a MENA Golf Tour event at the 2014 Ras Al Khaimah Classic. Entering the final round just one shot behind the leaders, Marjane shot a three-under-par 69, finishing with a total of eight-under-par 208 at Tower Links Golf Club. His performance outlasted the overnight leaders, who faded as the round progressed.

Marjane's victory is significant, marking the first time a MENA (Middle East and North Africa) national won the title after years of near misses, including several runner-up finishes by fellow Moroccan Faycal Serghini. Marjane, who turned professional in 2014 after winning the tour's Order of Merit as an amateur in 2011, expressed his excitement, saying, "Being the first from the MENA region to win a MENA Golf Tour tournament, I couldn't have asked for better."

His victory included four birdies and only one bogey, and he credited his strong play under pressure for the win. Marjane received a $9,000 winner's check, marking a significant milestone in his career. Meanwhile, the UAE's Ahmed Al Musharrekh, who shared the lead after two rounds, struggled in the final round, finishing in 23rd place after shooting a 77. Despite the setback, Al Musharrekh remained positive, viewing the tournament as motivation to improve his game.

MARITZ, LAURETTE 'LOLLY' (1964) SOUTH AFRICA

Laurette Maritz's illustrious golf career began after she met LPGA Tour player Sally Little in 1983, which led her to accept a golf scholarship to United States International University in San Diego. There, she earned All-American honors four times, highlighting her exceptional talent.

Maritz turned professional in 1988 and quickly made her mark on the Ladies European Tour (LET). She won her debut tournament, the Marbella Ladies Open, by three strokes over Dale Reid and Corinne Dibnah. Soon after, she claimed victory at the EMS Masters in Portugal in just her third start, securing the LET Rookie of the Year title.

Throughout her career, Maritz consistently performed at a high level. She was the runner-up at the TEC Players Championship at Patshull Park

Golf & Country Club in England in both 1989 and 1990. In 1990, she won her third LET title at the Laing Ladies Charity Classic at Stoke Poges in England and finished as runner-up in the Ladies German Open at Wörthsee Golf Club in Bavaria. Additional runner-up finishes included the 1991 Spanish Classic, the 2013 Ladies Norwegian Challenge, and the 1997 Open de France Dames, where she narrowly lost to Karen Lunn. In 2007, Maritz also tied for third at the Northern Ireland Ladies Open.

Maritz represented South Africa in the Women's World Cup of Golf from 2005 to 2008 and won numerous tournaments on the South African Tour, including three South African Women's Open titles, two South African Ladies Masters titles, and victories at the Pam Golding Ladies International and Telkom Women's Classic. In total, she amassed 10 professional wins during her career.

Her amateur career was equally impressive, with notable victories such as the Natal Amateur (1982), Transvaal Champion of Champions (1982), and the Belgium Amateur (1983). She also finished as a runner-up at the SA Stroke Play (1983) and Switzerland Amateur (1983) and placed third at the Australian Amateur (1983). Additionally, she won the Zurich Championship (1985) and the Chung Cheng Centennial Team Trophy (1987).

Maritz's achievements and awards are a testament to her skill and dedication. She won the 2005 Final Order of Merit on the Nedbank Women's Golf Tour and received the All-American Award from 1983 to 1987. In 1987, she was named the United States' Player of the Year, making her the top collegiate player in the USA. She won fourteen tournaments while attending university, including the Nancy Lopez Invitational and the University of Georgia Championship. Maritz was also inducted into the USA Hall of Fame for being the first player to be selected for the eight-player All-American Team for all four years of her university career.

Beyond her golfing accomplishments, Laurette Maritz has made significant contributions to charity. Over the past 16 years, she has been instrumental in the "Eyes4Zimbabwe" initiative, a golf-related project she started with her golf coach and manager, Reeve A. Nield. Through this project, they have provided free cataract surgery to thousands of people, restoring sight to those in need, including a patient as young as six months old. Maritz's dedication to helping others has made a lasting impact on the lives of many, further cementing her legacy beyond golf.

MARSHALL, ROBBIE SOUTH AFRICA

Robert Douglas Marshall ("Robbie") has been involved in the business of golf courses for more than 40 years since 1981, ultimately as Golf Data CC. He has developed more than 50 courses in South Africa either from a construction or maintenance aspect and built 7 Jack Nicklaus and 2 Ernie Els Courses in South Africa, comprising a third of the top 100 South African courses.

He won the Golf Digest "Best New Course" award on 6 occasions, and Golf Data courses have hosted the South African Open on more than 15 occasions. He has worked closely with numerous famous designers including Jack Nicklaus, Ernie Els, Greg Letsche, David Dale and Ronald Fream.

Golf Data Portfolio, inter alia, includes: Atlantic Beach; Bellville; Bosch Hoek; CCJ Mashie Course; Els Club at Copperleaf; Country Club Johannesburg; Dainfern; De Zalze; Durban Country Club; Glendower; Hazendal; Hermanus; Houghton; Humewood; KAUST; Killarny; Kyalami; Leopard Creek; Oubaai; Parkview; Pearl Valley; Pecanwood; Pezula; Randpark; Royal Johannesburg; Sabi River Sun; Serengeti; Simola; St Francis Links; Steenberg; Steyn City; Umthunzi Gardens; Umthunzi Valle; Wegewood; World of Golf; Zimbali.

MASHEGO, MOKGETENG JOHN (1951) SOUTH AFRICA – APARTHEID

Mokgeteng John Mashego made history as the first black player to win a tournament on the Southern African Tour after the removal of its whites-only rule. His landmark victory came at the 1991 Bushveld Classic, where he triumphed over Steve van Vuuren and Ian Palmer in a playoff.

Despite this significant achievement, Mashego did not secure another win on the Southern African Tour. The change in rules came too late for him to fully capitalize on his prime years on the tour. Nonetheless, he continued to perform strongly, finishing as a runner-up in several tournaments, including the Royal Swazi Sun Classic and the Cock of the North event, with his last notable finish in 2000-01.

In 2002, Mashego transitioned to the European Seniors Tour, where he continued to showcase his talent. His best finish on the European Seniors Tour was second place. Notable performances include a tied 8th place at the 2008 Russian Seniors Open and a third place in the Nelson Mandela Invitational alongside Andrew Coltart.

Mashego's pioneering success and enduring presence in the sport highlight his significant contribution to golf, both in Southern Africa and internationally.

MATKOVICH, PETER (1942) SOUTHERN RHODESIA

Peter Matkovich's journey in the world of golf began as a professional player from 1968 to 1973, but his transition from player to golf course designer would ultimately define his legacy. After his playing career, he took on a dual role at Umhlali Country Club, where he served as both the club professional and course superintendent for two decades. It was during this time that Matkovich's passion for golf course design began

to take shape. In 1992, he designed the 18-hole course at San Lameer Estate, an accomplishment that marked the start of his remarkable career in golf course architecture.

The 1990s saw Matkovich expand his design portfolio dramatically. His work was not confined to South Africa, though it flourished there; he ventured into international projects as well. He reimagined Zimbabwe's historic Chapman Golf Club, originally laid out in the 1920s, and contributed to the development of Leopard Rock. In Swaziland, Matkovich transformed the Royal Swazi's 18-hole course in Mbabane. One of his most notable collaborations came when he partnered with the legendary Nick Price to design Borrowdale Brooke Golf Course in Harare, showcasing his ability to work alongside greats of the game. While most of his projects were in Africa, he expanded his reach globally when he converted a short 7-hole course into a full 9-hole layout at Ga'ash Golf Club in Tel Aviv in 1998, his only non-African project of the time.

His work in South Africa during this period was equally prolific. Matkovich's expertise left a lasting impression across multiple provinces. He designed iconic courses in Gauteng like Silver Lakes and Centurion, while also contributing to courses in Kwazulu-Natal, including Prince's Grant and Kloof. The Western Cape was also a beneficiary of his talent, where Steenberg and Arabella became testaments to his design vision.

The turn of the millennium saw no slowdown in Matkovich's output. He continued to leave his mark with significant projects across South Africa, including Zebula and Elements in Limpopo, and later contributions in the Western Cape at Hermanus, De Zalze, Pinnacle Point, Simbithi, and Cotswold Downs. Internationally, Matkovich's influence grew even further. In 2005, he renovated the prestigious Muthaiga course in Nairobi, Kenya. Mauritius became a significant destination for his work as well; his designs there included Golf du Château, Avalon, and Mont Choisy, all of which stand as some of the island's most renowned courses. His efforts also reached Malawi, Namibia, Tanzania, and Zambia, bringing his total to an impressive 34 golf courses across several countries.

While Matkovich had an informal collaboration with Dale Hayes, another golfing legend, he formalized a partnership in 2016 with Louis Oosthuizen and his design associate, Louis van der Walt. This collaboration aimed to elevate Matkovich's design company and extend its global footprint.

Matkovich's talents were not confined to golf. In 1966, he was part of the Rhodesia golf team at the Eisenhower Trophy, representing his country in a prestigious international competition. A year later, he displayed his athletic versatility by playing rugby for the Rhodesian team against a touring French side in 1967. These achievements in both golf and rugby highlight Matkovich's well-rounded sporting prowess and his deep connection to the games he loved.

Through decades of dedication, Peter Matkovich's work in golf course design has left an indelible mark on both African and international golf landscapes. His designs reflect not only his technical expertise but his passion for crafting challenging and memorable golf experiences, ensuring his legacy in the world of golf endures for generations to come.

MCGUIGAN, DOUG (1970) SOUTH AFRICA

Douglas Gordon McGuigan has built an impressive career in golf, particularly on the Sunshine Tour, where his consistent performance has made him a respected figure. Between 2003 and 2017, McGuigan secured eight victories, demonstrating his skill and tenacity in a highly competitive field. His success on the Sunshine Tour reflects not just his ability to win but also his dedication to maintaining high standards over the years.

McGuigan's talents also extended beyond the local scene, with a notable highlight on the European Tour. In 2003, he finished as the runner-up in the prestigious Dunhill Championship, showcasing his ability to compete on the international stage. This achievement further solidified his reputation as a well-rounded and accomplished golfer, capable of excelling in both local and global competitions.

McGuigan's career stands as a testament to his hard work and talent, blending achievements from both the Sunshine Tour and the European Tour and leaving a mark on the golf world.

MCLARDY, ANDREW (1974) SOUTH AFRICA

Andrew Ronald McLardy has had a distinguished career in golf, marked by both amateur and professional successes. Before turning professional in 1997, McLardy represented South Africa twice in the Eisenhower Trophy, showcasing his skills on an international stage.

As a professional golfer, McLardy accumulated

five wins, with the pinnacle of his career being his victory at the 2004 Tour Championship. This win remains a highlight of his professional career and underscores his achievements on the Sunshine Tour. His career reflects a solid combination of amateur prowess and professional success.

McLardy's career is noted for a blend of strong amateur performance and significant professional accomplishments, particularly his Tour Championship victory.

MCNULTY, MARK 'SPARKLES' (1953) RHODESIA, IRELAND

Mark William McNulty's golf career spans several continents and tours, showcasing his remarkable talent and consistency. He first gained international attention when he represented Rhodesia (now Zimbabwe) at the 1974 Eisenhower Trophy in the Dominican Republic. Turning professional in 1977, McNulty secured his first notable victory at the Greater Manchester Open on the European Tour in 1979. His dominance soon extended to the Southern African Tour, where he captured his first win at the 1980 Holiday Inns Invitational in Swaziland and topped the South African Order of Merit for two consecutive seasons from 1980 to 1981.

McNulty became a prominent figure on the European Tour, claiming 16 titles, including a notable victory at the 1996 Volvo Masters. His ability to consistently perform at the highest levels was evident as he spent 83 weeks in the top 10 of the Official World Golf Ranking from 1987 to 1992. He finished in the top 10 of the European Order of Merit six times, with second-place finishes in both 1987 and 1990. One of his most memorable performances came at the 1990 Open Championship at St. Andrews, where he tied for second place alongside Payne Stewart, just behind Nick Faldo.

On the Sunshine Tour, McNulty was a dominant force. He won nine Sunshine Tour Order of Merit titles and secured seven victories in 1986, including the prestigious Million Dollar Challenge. His other notable wins in South Africa include the South African PGA Championship 1982, the South African Open 1987, and the South African Masters, which he won three times 1982, 1985, and 1987.

In 2004, after turning 50, McNulty joined the U.S.-based Champions Tour, where he quickly found success. His first full season saw him win three tournaments, including the Charles Schwab Cup Championship. Over the years, he accumulated seven wins on the Champions Tour, including victories at major events like the JELD-WEN Tradition in 2007 and the Liberty Mutual Legends of Golf in 2011.

McNulty also represented Zimbabwe on the international stage, competing in seven Alfred Dunhill Cups and eight World Cups. He and his partner, Nick Price, finished as runners-up in the 1993 World Cup, and McNulty repeated this achievement in 1994, partnering with Tony Johnstone. His total professional win count stands at 35 before joining the Senior Tour.

Outside of his playing career, McNulty is dedicated to nurturing young talent through the Mark McNulty Junior Golf Foundation. This nonprofit organization aims to use golf as a means of enhancing children's development both on and off the course, while also growing the game of golf in the region.

Mark McNulty's impressive career and contributions to golf, both as a player and a mentor, reflect his enduring passion and influence on the sport.

MERCER, JACQUIE (SMITH) SOUTH AFRICA

Jackie Mercer's career stands as a remarkable testament to exceptional skill and dedication in golf. Spanning more than 30 years, her achievements reflect both her prowess on the course and her significant contributions as a teacher and leader in the sport.

Mercer's tournament victories highlight her dominance and consistency. She won the Natal Ladies Title an impressive 18 times, illustrating her unrivaled skill in the region. Her success extended to national competitions, where she secured the South African Champion title four times 1948, 1963, 1974, and 1979, with her final win at the age of 50, underscoring her enduring competitive spirit.

On the international stage, Mercer's achievements included winning the British Team Trophy in 1966, which further demonstrated her global success and versatility. Her representation of South Africa as a Springbok Golfer from 1951 to 1981 reflects her long and distinguished service to her country.

Mercer's impact on the sport extended beyond her playing career. She turned professional and became a sought-after golf teacher, imparting her expertise and passion for the game to others. Her dedication to the development of golf is evident in her role as a co-founder of the South African Ladies Professional Golf Association (SALPGA), alongside Lisle Nel, and her subsequent presidency for four years.

Her leadership roles also included serving as a SALGU selector in 1970, contributing strategically to the growth of the game. She was instrumental in founding the National Junior Girls Championship, which has become a crucial event in nurturing young talent. Additionally, Mercer captained the Natal Ladies team for 20 years and led the South African Ladies team five times, showcasing her leadership and commitment to the sport.

Mercer's contributions were recognized through numerous awards and honors. She received the Sport Merit Award in 1975, honoring her achievements and impact on sports. In 1987, she was awarded honorary membership by the Women's PGA, acknowledging her significant contributions to golf. Her legacy was further cemented with her induction into the Southern Africa Golf Hall of Fame in 2013.

As an amateur player, Mercer's success was equally impressive. She won the SA Ladies Amateur title in 1948, 1963, 1974, and 1979, and was a runner-up in 1971 and 1975, with 16 semi-final appearances. Her victories in the Natal Ladies Amateur were numerous, with wins in 1949, 1950, 1952, 1953, 1956, 1963, 1965, 1972, 1975, 1977, 1979, and 1981, and runner-up finishes in several years. She also achieved notable wins in other stroke-play events, including the Natal Ladies Amateur Stroke-Play in 1979 and 1981 and the Transvaal Ladies Amateur Stroke-Play in 1966.

Jackie Mercer's impressive career and her role in shaping the game of golf, both as a player and a teacher, ensure her place as a significant figure in the sport's history. Her contributions have left a lasting legacy, celebrated by her induction into the Southern Africa Golf Hall of Fame and the naming of a leading amateur trophy in her honor.

MIDGLEY, CECIL NYASALAND

Cecil Midgley's golf career is a testament to his profound influence and enduring legacy in the sport, particularly within the Nyasaland and Rhodesian golf communities. His contributions extend beyond his achievements as an amateur golfer to include significant administrative roles that shaped the development of golf in the region.

Midgley's involvement in golf administration was both long-lasting and impactful. He served on the Nyasaland Executive Committee from 1931 to 1955, a period during which he played a pivotal role in the development and management of golf in the area. His leadership continued as he took on the role of President of the Nyasaland Golf Association from 1957, further influencing the sport's direction and growth beyond his initial executive service.

As an amateur golfer, Midgley's competitive achievements were notable. He finished as runner-up in the Federation Amateur Championship in 1927, showcasing his skill and competitive edge. His reputation as a formidable player was further established by his runner-up finish in the Southern Rhodesia Amateur Championship in 1929. Perhaps most impressively, Midgley won the Nyasaland Amateur Championship seven times between 1931 and 1956, demonstrating his dominance and consistent performance in local tournaments.

Cecil Midgley's legacy is marked by his dedicated service to golf administration and his impressive achievements on the course. His contributions have left a lasting impact on the sport in both Nyasaland and Southern Rhodesia, cementing his place as a significant figure in the history of golf in the region.

MOGOERANE, RICHARD 'BOIKIE' UNION SOUTH AFRICA – APARTHEID

2010 Bantu Holomisa, Richard Mogoerane, Vincent Tshabalala

Richard Mogoerane stands out as a significant figure in South African golf history, celebrated for both his impressive playing career and his influential contributions to the sport's development and administration.

On the course, Mogoerane achieved notable success with 12 professional victories, underscoring his skill and consistency. His achievements in the South African Non-European Championship include wins in 1973 and 1976, as well as runner-up finishes in 1972 and third-place finishes in 1967 and 1970. His dominance was further evident in the Orange Free State Non-European Open, where he secured 10 victories between 1968 and 1981, cementing his reputation as a leading player in the region.

Beyond his playing career, Mogoerane made substantial contributions to golf's growth and governance. In 1981, he established a junior golf development program in Soweto, aimed at nurturing young talent and promoting the sport in underrepresented areas. His efforts were instrumental in the negotiations that led to the unification of golf administration in 1992, which played a crucial role in integrating and enhancing the governance of the sport in South Africa.

Mogoerane's legacy was formally recognized in 2010 when he was inducted into the Southern Africa Golf Hall of Fame, honoring his significant impact both on and off the golf course. His career is a testament to his exceptional achievements as a player and his lasting influence on the development and unification of golf in South Africa.

MOORE, ERIC UNION SOUTH AFRICA

Eric Moore was a distinguished professional golfer throughout the 1950s, competing both in his homeland of South Africa and abroad in Europe. Despite the limited details of his overall playing record, Moore's career was marked by several notable achievements, cementing his reputation as a top contender in the competitive South African golf scene of his time.

One of Moore's most significant performances came in 1947, when he finished as the runner-up in the South African Open, narrowly missing the title by just one stroke to Ronnie Glennie. Two years later, in 1949, Moore once again found himself in contention, finishing three strokes behind the winner, Sid Brews. Although the elusive Open title slipped through his grasp, Moore continued to demonstrate his skill and consistency over the years.

His competitive spirit shone again in 1963 when he was runner-up to Bruce Keyter in the South African Masters, trailing by three strokes. In addition to his near misses in these prestigious tournaments, Moore secured victory in the 1947 Natal Open, showcasing his ability to close out wins when the opportunity arose.

Throughout his career, Moore was no stranger to intense competition. He placed second in the Western Province Open twice, first in 1959 to Harold Henning, and then again in 1963, when Bobby Verwey edged him out. Despite these second-place finishes, Moore's career remained a testament to his enduring presence in the South African golf scene, where he consistently competed against some of the era's most talented players.

MOORE, TICH (1976) SOUTH AFRICA

Trevor Richard 'Titch' Moore's journey in golf is a testament to his remarkable talent and dedication both on and off the course.

As a young golfer, Titch Moore made an immediate impact on the global stage with his performance in the 1993 World Under 17 Championship.

His skills quickly became apparent, and he went on to win several regional tournaments, including the Western Province, Transvaal, and Eastern Province Amateur Championships. These victories underscored his versatility and competitive edge, establishing him as a rising star in amateur golf.

By 1995, Titch had solidified his reputation further with a notable victory at the World International Master. His success continued into 1996 when he triumphed in the South African International Amateur Championship, one of the country's premier amateur events. This win, along with his strong performances in the South African Amateur Stroke Play Championship, highlighted his impressive prowess in the sport.

Transitioning to professional golf, Titch Moore's career continued to flourish. Over the years, he accumulated thirteen professional victories, reflecting his skill and consistency. On the Sunshine Tour, he made a significant mark with a best finish of 4th in the 2004–05 Order of Merit. His professional achievements include notable wins such as the Cock o' North in 2000, the Vodacom Origins of Golf Final in 2007, the PGA Championship in 2014, and the Royal Swazi Open in 2016.

In addition to his Sunshine Tour successes, Titch also made his mark on the Challenge Tour with a significant win at the 2003 Skandia PGA Open. His talent extended across the Atlantic to the United States, where he secured victories on mini-tours, showcasing his adaptability and skill across different golf circuits.

Throughout his career, Titch has demonstrated remarkable competitiveness, as evidenced by his three runner-up finishes in playoff events. These close calls highlight his ability to perform under pressure and his enduring presence in the sport.

Overall, Titch Moore's career is a blend of impressive amateur achievements and a successful professional journey, marked by notable victories and a consistent presence across multiple tours. His story is one of dedication, skill, and perseverance, solidifying his place in the annals of golf history.

MOSES, LETICIA & AMELIA SOUTH AFRICA

The story of the Moses sisters, Amelia and Letitia, unfolds as a powerful testament to resilience and ambition against the backdrop of apartheid South Africa. Their journey is marked by a blend of personal dedication, familial support, and notable achievements in the world of golf.

From a young age, Amelia and Letitia Moses were guided by their father, Oliver, whose vision and relentless support shaped their path. Oliver instilled in them a rigorous discipline that was crucial for success in a challenging era. His dream was for his daughters to excel both academically and professionally in golf. To this end, the sisters adhered to a demanding routine: three hours of practice daily after school, and eight hours on weekends. Their training regimen was intense, including regular 10 km runs on Tuesdays and Thursdays, and frequent participation in local events under Oliver's watchful eye.

The sisters' dedication soon bore fruit. Both Amelia and Letitia achieved several victories in club championships, highlighting their burgeoning talent. Their prowess on the course was further demonstrated when they represented the Transvaal A Team, where their combined skills made them a formidable duo. In the South African Matchplay Championship, Amelia faced Letitia in a gripping semi-final match, emerging victorious for the first time. However, Amelia's triumph was bittersweet, as she fell short in the final the following day, reflecting the emotional highs and lows inherent in competitive sports.

Their talent soon gained international recognition. Amelia had the honor of representing South Africa at the World Junior Championships in Belgium, following in her sister's footsteps. Letitia had participated in the same event the previous year. Amelia also won the South African Under-23 Championship in the same year Letitia moved to the United States, marking a significant milestone in her rising golf career.

Education played a crucial role in their journey. Letitia attended the University of Missouri-Columbia from August 1995 to December 1999, becoming the first African to play on its golf team. Her success at the university opened doors for Amelia, who earned a full golf scholarship to the same institution in 1997. Amelia graduated with a marketing degree in May 2001, following her sister's trailblazing example.

Upon returning to South Africa, Letitia continued to make her mark in the golf world. She played on the professional tour, managed a golf course, and represented South Africa in the Ladies World Cup. Her achievements earned her recognition as the SA female amateur 'Athlete of the Year' in 1995, and she won multiple amateur titles throughout her career.

Amelia, after her time on the developmental tour in the US, transitioned to a different role, contributing to the sport through education. She began teaching at a local school, continuing her involvement in golf from a different perspective.

The legacy of the Moses sisters is a powerful narrative of overcoming adversity and achieving excellence. Their story, shaped by their hard work, their father's sacrifices, and their contributions to golf, embodies the spirit of determination and talent triumphing over challenges.

MOTATI, DAVID UNION SOUTH AFRICA – APARTHEID

David 'Bobby Locke' Motati's journey through the world of golf is a compelling narrative of talent and perseverance against the backdrop of apartheid South Africa. His career, marked by impressive achievements, stands as a testament to his skill and resilience during a time when racial segregation imposed significant challenges.

Motati's golfing career began to shine brightly in the late 1950s. He

Ismail Chowglay, Vincent Tshabalala, David Motati, Papwa Sewgolum

captured the South African Non-European Open title in 1958 and again in 1966, demonstrating his ability to excel in high-stakes competitions. His prowess was evident as he finished as the runner-up in the same tournament in 1959, solidifying his reputation as a formidable competitor.

In 1959, Motati also triumphed in the OFS Non-European Open and the Free State Non-European Championship, further showcasing his dominance in regional events. He continued to make his mark with a notable victory in the Transvaal Non-European Matchplay in 1961, a testament to his exceptional skills in match play formats.

Despite the prevailing restrictions of the time, Motati's performances were consistently strong. He was the runner-up in the Orange Free State Special Strokeplay in 1964 and finished as the runner-up again in the Transvaal Non-European Open the same year. His dedication to the sport and his ability to perform at a high level in various tournaments were indicative of his exceptional talent.

Motati's career continued to be highlighted by his third-place finish in the Western Province Non-European Open in 1967, demonstrating his enduring skill and commitment to golf. His achievements, while constrained by the systemic barriers of apartheid, remain a powerful reminder of his remarkable contributions to the sport.

David 'Bobby Locke' Motati's legacy is celebrated for his accomplishments in the face of adversity. His victories and consistent performances reflect his dedication to golf and his ability to excel despite the significant challenges of his era.

MULLER, GRANT (1970) SOUTH AFRICA

Grant Muller's golf career is a testament to his skill and dedication, particularly within the competitive realm of the Sunshine Tour. His achievements on the tour underscore his consistency and prowess in the sport.

Muller's professional journey was highlighted by a notable victory at the Vodacom Series: Kwazulu-Natal in 1997. This win marked the beginning of a successful period in his career, demonstrating his ability to perform under pressure and achieve top results.

Another significant milestone came in 2010 when Muller clinched the Lombard Insurance Classic. This win further cemented his reputation as a formidable competitor on the Sunshine Tour and showcased his enduring talent over the years.

In total, Grant Muller amassed five professional wins throughout his career, each reflecting his dedication and competitive spirit. His success on the Sunshine Tour not only highlights his individual skill but also his contributions to South African golf.

MULROY, GARTH DAVID (1978) SOUTH AFRICA

Garth David Mulroy's golf career is marked by a series of impressive achievements and a versatile presence across multiple tours.

Starting with a strong amateur foundation, Mulroy attended North Carolina State University, where he earned NCAA Division I All-American honors, setting the stage for a successful professional career.

Turning professional in 2002, Mulroy quickly made his mark across various tours. On the Nationwide Tour, now known as the Korn Ferry Tour, he achieved notable victories, including the South Georgia Classic in 2009, where he secured a narrow win by a single stroke over Chris

Tidland. He followed this with another victory at the BMW Charity Pro-Am in 2011.

His time on the Sunshine Tour also showcased his talent. In 2007, he finished tied for third in the South African Airways Open, and in 2008, he won two minor tournaments and ended the season second on the Order of Merit behind Richard Sterne.

Mulroy's career reached a significant milestone on the European Tour in 2011 when he won the Alfred Dunhill Championship. This victory highlighted his skill and adaptability on a global stage.

Notably, in 2009, Mulroy's success on the Korn Ferry Tour earned him a spot on the PGA Tour for the 2010 season. His ability to perform consistently across different tours and conditions underscores his versatility and accomplishments in the sport.

MURIDZO-CHITENGWA, LEWIS SOUTHERN RHODESIA – DISCRIMINATED

Lewis Muridzo-Chitengwa's journey in golf is a compelling narrative of resilience and trailblazing achievements in a sport historically marred by racial barriers.

Lewis's introduction to golf began in 1958, amidst the challenging conditions of makeshift courses in Highfield, Zimbabwe, where he and his peers fashioned their own putting greens. This humble start laid the foundation for a groundbreaking career. By 1959, he played a pivotal role in establishing Gleneagles Golf Club in Rhodesia, a significant milestone as it was the only course where people of all races could gain membership at that time.

Lewis Muridzo, his wife Faith and their daughters

A landmark in his career came in 1977 when he became the first black member of a traditionally "white" golf club, Salisbury South, now known as Harare South. Just three years later, he marked another milestone by winning the club championship at Salisbury South, underscoring his growing prominence in the sport.

In 1985, Lewis made history as Zimbabwe's first black professional golfer, a significant achievement in a country where the sport was still overcoming racial segregation. His professional career was notable for its breadth, spanning the Asian Tour, European Tour, and Safari Tour. Among his victories were the Castle and African Distillers Championship and the Coca-Cola Trophy. His competitive spirit was also evident in his 2nd place finish at the Mashonaland Amateur in 1976 and his debut as the first black Rhodesian to compete in the Rhodesian Open in 1974.

Beyond his playing career, Lewis made a profound impact as a coach and mentor. He worked with renowned golfers such as Nick Price, Vijay Singh, Ben Follet-Smith, Brendon de Jonge, and Simon Chigorimbo-Murungweni, shaping the careers of many. His coaching also extended to developing over 80 junior golfers who received golf scholarships in the US. His own son, Lewis Chitengwa, emerged as a notable talent, winning the Orange Bowl in 1992 and the South Africa Amateur in 1993 before his untimely passing.

Lewis's dedication to the sport continued for over 57 years, influencing countless young talents through his coaching. His legacy extends to his family, with his daughter, Rhodah Muridzo, achieving success as the Zimbabwe Ladies Champion.

Lewis Muridzo-Chitengwa's story is a testament to overcoming adversity, breaking barriers, and leaving a lasting impact on the world of golf, both in Zimbabwe and beyond.

MURIDZO, RHODAH ZIMBABWE

Rhodah Muridzo's journey in golf exemplifies a seamless transition from a remarkable playing career to a significant coaching role, reflecting her deep commitment to the sport in Zimbabwe.

In 2005, Rhodah made a strong impact in Zimbabwean golf by winning both the Zimbabwe National MatchPlay and StrokePlay Championships, showcasing her exceptional skills and determination. Her talent was further recognized on the regional stage when she finished as the runner-up at the Kenya Ladies Open, demonstrating her competitiveness across borders. Representing Zimbabwe in various regional tournaments, she further cemented her reputation as a prominent player.

Her professional journey began in 2009 when she turned professional, marking a new chapter in her career. Embracing her role as a mentor, she was appointed Zimbabwe National Lady's Coach, where she has dedicated herself to nurturing and developing the next generation of female golfers in Zimbabwe. Rhodah's contributions as a coach are instrumental in advancing the sport and inspiring future talent.

Rhodah Muridzo's career is a testament to her enduring influence in Zimbabwean golf, both on and off the course.

MURRAY, DR C.M. UNION SOUTH AFRICA

Dr. Murray's legacy in South African golf is profound and multifaceted, reflecting his pioneering efforts in both turf research and golf course architecture. His contributions were instrumental in shaping the game as it is known in South Africa today.

In 1907, Dr. Murray made a significant impact by convincing the Royal Cape Golf Club to transition from artificial greens to natural grass greens. This move was groundbreaking at the time and was based on his own experiments and research. His advocacy for grass greens extended beyond a single club, as he led the South African Golf Union (SAGU) to mandate that only courses with grass greens could host South African Championships. This decision marked a turning point in the quality and maintenance of golf courses across the country.

As the first South African golf course architect, Dr. Murray established himself as a leading figure in the design and development of golf courses. His early designs, including those for George Golf Club, Clovelly Country Club, and Royal Cape Golf Club, set high standards for golf course architecture in South Africa. These courses remain influential examples of his work.

Dr. Murray's commitment to the sport extended to his publications and educational contributions. In 1926, he published a 12-page booklet titled "Green-Keeping in South Africa," which became an essential resource for golf clubs across the country. He also contributed regularly to South African Golf, sharing his expertise on grass maintenance and advancements in golf course management.

In 1939, Dr. Murray played a crucial role in establishing the South African Turf Research Fund, which supported the upkeep of the Frankenwald Research Station in Johannesburg. His expertise was sought after globally, as he provided valuable advice on grass cultivation and golf course management to experts around the world.

Dr. Murray's contributions to golf in South Africa laid the groundwork for modern course maintenance and architecture, ensuring that the sport could thrive in the country and setting a standard for excellence that continues to influence the game today.

MUTHIYA, MADALITSO (1983) ZAMBIA

Madalitso Muthiya's career in golf is a testament to his groundbreaking achievements and trailblazing path, both in Africa and on the international stage.

Muthiya's journey in golf began with notable junior success. In 1999, he triumphed in the 16-18 year age group at the Nolan Henke/Patty Berg Junior Masters held in Fort Myers, Florida. This early victory marked him as a rising talent in the sport.

Turning professional in 2005, Muthiya embarked on a diverse career across various tours. His breakthrough came in 2006 when he finished as the runner-up at the Zambia Open, a significant achievement that led to his entry into the Canadian Tour later that year. The following year, he made history by becoming the first Zambian and black African golfer to compete in the U.S. Open, impressively starting his round with an eagle on the first hole.

Muthiya's professional career saw him achieving notable success on several tours. On the Nationwide Tour in 2010, he achieved his best finish with a tie for 7th place at the Mylan Classic. His accomplishments on the Sunshine Tour were particularly historic. In July 2016, he secured his first title at the Vodacom Origins of Golf Tour event, making him the first Zambian and only the fourth black African golfer to win on this tour.

In 2019, Muthiya continued to make strides by winning the Castle Lite Uganda Open, further solidifying his status as a prominent golfer in the region.

Muthiya's career not only highlights his individual achievements but also reflects his significant role in advancing the presence and recognition of Zambian and African golfers on the global stage. His milestones and pioneering efforts continue to inspire future generations in the sport.

N

NAIDOO, "STAR" UNION SOUTH AFRICA – DISCRIMINATED

'Star' Naidoo stands out as a figure of remarkable achievement and dedication in the world of golf, particularly in an era fraught with the challenges of apartheid-era South Africa. His legacy is marked by both his prowess as a golfer and his esteemed career as a caddy.

As a golfer, Naidoo demonstrated exceptional skill despite the constraints of segregation that limited access to courses. He played on bush courses due to these restrictions but still achieved a notable plus-2 handicap, showcasing his high level of expertise. One of his most impressive feats occurred in 1935, when he scored a remarkable 73 with a 2-iron on a course with a par of 76, illustrating his exceptional talent and adaptability.

Naidoo's caddying career was equally distinguished. He served as a caddy at Royal Durban Golf Club for an impressive 48 years, during which he became a highly respected figure in the golf community. His role included caddying for prominent players such as Bobby Locke during the 1936 Natal Open, reflecting his significant presence and the high regard in which he was held. His reputation as the doyen of caddies was a testament to his extensive experience and the respect he garnered from golfers and peers alike.

Naidoo's story is a testament to his dedication to the sport of golf and his ability to excel despite the racial barriers of his time. His achievements and contributions have left an indelible mark on the sport, highlighting his exceptional skills and enduring influence in the golfing world.

NELSON, LOUIS (DIED 1973) SOUTH AFRICA – APARTHEID

Louis Nelson was a remarkable figure in South African golf, his career marked by significant achievements and complex challenges. Rising from humble beginnings as a caddy, Nelson's early years were spent navigating the segregated world of golf, a sport deeply divided by apartheid-era restrictions. His rise through the ranks of the Liquor and Catering union, where he became a prominent trade union leader, set the stage for his later contributions to the sport.

Nelson's influence grew as he took on the role of manager for Papwa Sewgolum, a pioneering golfer who defied the racial barriers of his time. Under Nelson's management, Sewgolum made history, with Nelson playing a crucial role in the golfer's career. He helped Sewgolum secure a position as the professional at Springfield Golf Course, an opportunity that marked a significant achievement in an era when such positions were rare for non-white golfers. Nelson's efforts extended beyond South Africa, facilitating Sewgolum's international exposure with a notable trip to the UK and Europe in 1960. His persistence led to a groundbreaking court ruling, allowing Sewgolum to participate in predominantly white tournaments, starting with the 1961 SA Open.

Nelson's contributions were not limited to his role as a manager. He was instrumental in forming the Natal Non-European Golf Association, reflecting his commitment to creating opportunities for non-white golfers. As chairman of the 'Papwa Trust Fund,' he raised £1,000 to support Sewgolum's international ambitions, demonstrating his dedication to advancing the careers of talented players despite systemic obstacles.

His leadership extended to political and golf administration roles. Nelson served as President of the Durban Golf Club and held significant positions in the Natal (N-E) Golf Union and the South African (N-E) Golf Association. His political voice, however, faced challenges, particularly in persuading Sewgolum to publicly oppose apartheid.

Despite his achievements, Nelson's career was marred by controversies. His leadership style led to conflicts with Sewgolum over the organization and financial aspects of non-white tournaments. These tensions culminated in a public dispute and the eventual termination of Sewgolum's coaching position. In July 1970, Nelson faced suspension from the Durban Golf Club due to issues with management and record-keeping, marking a significant decline in his career after a decade of influential leadership.

Louis Nelson's death in 1973 brought an end to the era of the Tournament Professional Association (TPA) tournaments, reflecting the end of a chapter in South African golf. His legacy is a complex tapestry of groundbreaking achievements and contentious conflicts, highlighting both his role in advancing the sport for non-white players and the challenges that ultimately overshadowed his contributions.

NORRIS, SHAUN (1982) SOUTH AFRICA

Shaun Patrick Norris's career in professional golf is distinguished by his success across various international tours and notable achievements. His journey in the sport has been marked by consistent excellence and a series of significant victories.

Norris first garnered attention on the international stage when he represented South Africa at the 2007 Eisenhower Trophy, showcasing his

potential early in his career. His professional career has been highlighted by a total of 13 wins across different tours.

On the Japan Tour, Norris has been particularly successful, with six victories to his name. Notable among these wins are the Japan Golf Tour Championship Mori Building Cup Shishido Hills in 2017 and the Japan Open Golf Championship in 2021, underscoring his prowess on this competitive circuit.

In addition to his achievements in Japan, Norris has also excelled on the Sunshine Tour, where he has claimed three victories. These include the Africa Open in 2008 and the Nashua Masters in 2011, reflecting his strong performance in South Africa.

His success extends to the Asian Tour, where he has accumulated five wins, further demonstrating his versatility and skill across different golfing environments.

Norris's career reached a new milestone with his victory on the European Tour. In March 2022, he won the Steyn City Championship, securing his first European Tour title with impressive rounds of 64 and 62, finishing three shots ahead of Dean Burmester. Adding to his accolades, Norris claimed the Sunshine Tour Order of Merit for the 2021–22 season, solidifying his standing as one of the top players on the tour. This was followed by a victory at Japan's 2024 Golf Nippon Series JT Cup.

Shaun Norris's career highlights reflect his ability to perform consistently across multiple tours, showcasing his skill, versatility and dedication.

O

OLANDER, CLARENCE UNION SOUTH AFRICA

Clarence Olander's career in golf is a testament to his remarkable skill and dedication, leaving a lasting impact on the sport in South Africa. His achievements are both historic and impressive, showcasing his prowess on the golf course.

In 1936, Olander achieved a rare and illustrious feat by winning the South African Amateur and the South African Open Championships back-to-back. This accomplishment was particularly notable for its demanding schedule: over an 11-day period, he played through two medal rounds and multiple stages of the SA Amateur, followed by a grueling 72-hole SA Open Championship. After ending the Open Championship in a tie with J. Robertson, Olander endured a 36-hole playoff the following day, making it his 17th round in just 11 days. His triumph in this marathon effort solidified his place as one of the sport's greats.

Olander's career highlights include multiple victories in prestigious tournaments. He won the SA Amateur Championship three times (1932, 1934, and 1936) and was a runner-up twice (1930 and 1937). He also claimed the Freddie Tait Trophy in 1932 and 1939, an accolade reserved for the best amateur golfer. His dominance extended to the Border Amateur, where he won a remarkable ten times between 1927 and 1936. Additionally, he excelled in the Eastern Province Amateur, securing victories in 1931, 1932, 1933, 1934, and 1947, and in the Eastern Province & Border tournaments in 1946 and 1947. His win in the Eastern Province Open in 1956, followed by a second-place finish in 1957, further highlights his enduring skill.

Olander's contributions extended to team play as well. He was selected for the South African national team, known as the Springboks, on multiple occasions 1937, 1945, 1947, 1954, and 1955, demonstrating his standing in the sport on an international level.

Despite the challenges posed by World War II and the emergence of new golfing talent such as Bobby Locke, Olander remained a dominant force in South African golf. His consistent performance and exceptional skill earned him recognition as one of the top amateurs of his time. Olander's legacy is marked by his enduring achievements and contributions, establishing him as a key figure in the history of South African golf.

OKELLO, JACOB (1968) KENYA

Jacob Okello is a revered figure in Kenyan golf, best known for his record-setting appearances at the Kenya Open and for delivering the best-ever round at Muthaiga Golf Club with an 11-under-par 61. Okello's journey to stardom wasn't easy, but it was certainly inspiring. By the time he was 28, he had already secured back-to-back wins in the Kenya Open as an amateur in 1992 and 1993, before turning professional in 1996. His defining moment came in 1998, at Muthaiga Golf Club in Nairobi, where Okello etched his name into the annals of Kenyan sports history.

The 1998 Barclays Kenya Open was a landmark event for Okello. He was leading the field with just four holes to play, and the crowd could feel the excitement building. Okello, representing a nation with high hopes of seeing a local winner, played with the weight of a country's dreams on his shoulders. However, a double bogey at the par-three 15th hole threatened to derail his challenge. Despite the setback, he regrouped and finished the tournament tied at 12 under par with Argentina's Ricardo Gonzalez, forcing a dramatic sudden-death playoff.

As the sun began to set on Muthaiga Golf Club, the stage was set for a thrilling finish. After two play-off holes, it came down to the par-three 13th, where Okello faltered with a bogey, handing the title to Gonzalez.

Though Okello fell just short of victory, his second-place finish remains the best result by a Kenyan in the Kenya Open to date. His performance also earned him a full season on the Challenge Tour the following year, marking him as a player to watch.

The near-miss didn't define Okello's career, but rather it motivated him. He continued to compete at the highest levels of Kenyan and international golf, finishing in the top five at the Kenya Open in both 2006 and 2007, further cementing his legacy as one of the country's finest golfers.

As the Kenya Open celebrated its 50th anniversary in 2018, Okello, who had represented Kenya in 20 editions of the tournament, reflected on his career. "I came really close in 1998," he recalled. "It is very difficult to make it as a pro here in Kenya, but we need to support our local players to help them reach the next level."

Okello's contributions to Kenyan golf extend beyond the fairways. Since 2003, he has served as the manager of the Ngong Racecourse Golf Club in Nairobi, where he continues to nurture and mentor young golfers.

Jacob Okello's story is one of determination, passion, and resilience. He has inspired generations of golfers in Kenya and across Africa, proving that with hard work and belief, greatness is achievable. Today, at 52, Okello remains a central figure in Kenyan golf, continuing to break barriers and set records, while hoping that one day a Kenyan will finally lift the Kenya Open trophy—a dream he came so close to achieving.

ONITA, SADI (DIED 2004) UGANDA

Sadi Onito stands as a legendary figure in Ugandan golf, celebrated for his extraordinary achievements and distinctive presence on the course. His unparalleled success in the Tusker Malt Uganda Golf Amateurs Open is a testament to his skill and dedication. Over the years, Onito secured the title an astounding 12 times, with victories spanning from 1976 to 1996. This remarkable feat not only solidified his place as the most decorated golfer in the history of the Uganda Open but also underscored his dominance in the sport.

Onito's journey from a caddie in 1972 to becoming one of Uganda's finest golfers is a story of resilience and dedication. His transition

 from carrying clubs to claiming victories exemplifies his commitment to the game and his exceptional talent. Known for his consistent performance, Onito's ability to excel in both high-stakes games and less favorable conditions made him a formidable competitor. His characteristic playing style ensured that he was often at the top of the leaderboard, and even when he didn't win, he consistently secured strong finishes.

His personal traits further cemented his legacy. Onito was renowned for his humility, positive attitude, and eagerness to mentor and encourage others. He was always supportive and never spoke harshly, qualities that endeared him to both his peers and fans. His vibrant style, often marked by his choice of red or yellow trousers, made him a recognizable and colorful presence on the golf course. This distinctive attire became a hallmark of his identity and contributed to his iconic status in the sport.

Onito's impact extended beyond his performances. Former golfer Payne Stewart once remarked on Onito's ability to make difficult shots seem effortless and his colorful contribution to the game. Stewart's tribute highlights how Onito's legacy is not only defined by his impressive achievements but also by his unique and memorable presence.

Sadi Onito's career is a rich tapestry of extraordinary success, sportsmanship, and enduring influence. His achievements and distinctive style have left an indelible mark on golf, continuing to inspire and resonate within the sport long after his time on the course.

OOSTHUIZEN, ANDRIES (1954) SOUTH AFRICA

Andries Oosthuizen's golfing career is marked by notable achievements and several close calls that showcase his talent and competitive spirit.

In 1973, Oosthuizen made a significant mark by winning the South African Amateur, where he overcame Coen Dreyer with a 3 & 2 victory in the final. This triumph was a prelude to a promising professional career. Later that year, he finished as the runner-up at the South African Tour's Qualifying School, falling just short to George Harvey, and turned professional.

Oosthuizen's early professional years were highlighted by his performances on the European Tour from 1974 to 1977. In 1974, he was in contention at the General Motors Open, where he was tied with the legendary Gary Player after three rounds but ultimately lost by one stroke after Player's birdie-birdie finish. The same year, Oosthuizen was the runner-up at the ICL International, losing in a playoff to Vin Baker, who secured the win with a birdie on the first hole. He also tied for third at the Penfold Tournament, behind Tommy Horton.

The peak of Oosthuizen's career came in 1975, which was arguably his best season. He was a runner-up in the Piccadilly Medal, narrowly losing to Bob Shearer at the 19th hole. During the 1975 Open Championship, he began with strong rounds of 69, 69, and 70, and was tied for fifth after three rounds. However, despite starting the final day just four strokes behind the leader Bobby Cole, Oosthuizen finished tied for 12th after a final round of 78. That year, he also achieved his best finish on the European Tour Order of Merit, ending 14th.

The late 1970s were marked by several near-misses for Oosthuizen. In November 1976, he was the runner-up at the Victoria Falls Classic in Rhodesia, losing in a playoff to Nick Job. In 1979, he faced another heartbreak at the Holiday Inns Open in Swaziland, where he was runner-up to John Bland after a five-hole playoff.

Oosthuizen also contributed to South African golf on the team stage, representing his country in the Datsun International in 1976 and being part of the winning team.

Oosthuizen's career is a testament to his skill and competitiveness. His close finishes against prominent golfers and his role in significant tournaments reflect his talent and resilience. His contributions to the sport, particularly his performances on the European Tour and in team events, have left a lasting impact on South African golf.

OOSTHUIZEN, LOUIS (1982) SOUTH AFRICA

Lodewicus Theodorus 'Louis' Oosthuizen, affectionately nicknamed 'Shrek,' has built an illustrious career in professional golf, renowned for his skill and consistency. With 26 professional victories, his career is highlighted by notable wins across both the Sunshine Tour and the European Tour, as well as impressive performances in major championships.

Oosthuizen's success on the Sunshine Tour includes victories at the 2004 Vodacom Origins of Golf Tour event at Arabella and the 2007 Dimension Data Pro-Am. He also triumphed at the Telkom PGA Championship in both 2007 and 2008.

On the European Tour, Oosthuizen has achieved considerable success, including his win at the 2010 Open de Andalucia de Golf, where he shot a final round 63. His performance that year also included winning the Masters Par 3 Contest. He continued his success with wins at the Africa Open in 2011 and 2012 (where he defended his title), the Volvo Golf Champions in 2013 and 2014 (retaining the title in 2014).

One of the highlights of Oosthuizen's career is his victory at the 2010 Open Championship. He dominated the tournament, winning by seven strokes with a total score of 272, the second-lowest in the history of St Andrews. His commanding performance included a crucial eagle on the 9th hole and a steady final round of 71.

Oosthuizen has also had several notable runner-up finishes in major championships. He was the runner-up at the 2012 Masters Tournament, losing in a sudden-death playoff to Bubba Watson, despite making an albatross on the 2nd hole. He finished tied for second at the 2015 Open Championship, the 2017 PGA Championship, and the 2021 PGA Championship, adding a fifth and sixth runner-up finish to his major record. He also finished second at the 2021 U.S. Open at Torrey Pines Golf Course.

His career highlights include achieving a highest Official World Golf Ranking of 4th in January 2013. As an amateur, Oosthuizen won several titles, including the 2000 World Junior Championship and various amateur championships in 2001 and 2002. He also represented South Africa in the Eisenhower Trophy and played in the World Cup and Presidents Cup multiple times.

In June 2022, Oosthuizen joined LIV Golf, marking a significant shift in his career that affected his participation in PGA Tour events. Notably, he came close to victory in the 2023 LIV Golf Tucson, finishing in a playoff.

Early in his career, Oosthuizen received support from the Ernie Els Foundation, which helped him establish himself in the professional ranks. His focus techniques, including using a red spot on his glove and consulting a sports psychologist, have been part of his approach to maintaining peak performance.

Louis Oosthuizen's career is characterized by significant victories, consistent high-level performances, and a series of near-misses in major championships, reflecting his exceptional skill and dedication to the game of golf.

P

PACE, LEE-ANNE (1981) SOUTH AFRICA

Lee-Anne Pace has enjoyed a highly successful professional golf career, marked by numerous victories and accolades. Since turning professional, she has amassed 26 wins, making her one of the most accomplished players on the Ladies European Tour (LET) and beyond.

Pace's breakthrough year came in 2010, where she achieved an incredible five victories, including wins at the Deutsche Bank Ladies Swiss Open, the S4C Wales Ladies Championship of Europe, the Finnair Masters, the Sanya Ladies Open, and the Suzhou Taihu Ladies Open. Her stellar performance that season earned her the top spot on the Order of Merit ahead of Laura Davies, and the prestigious LET Player of the Year award.

Continuing her success, Pace had another remarkable season in 2013. She claimed her sixth LET victory at the Turkish Airlines Ladies Open in May, followed by another win in July at the Open De España Femenino. She capped off the year with a playoff victory at the Sanya Ladies Open, securing her eighth LET win and a second LET Player of the Year title.

In October 2014, Pace achieved a significant milestone by winning her ninth LET event at the Cell C South African Women's Open in her home country, following a dramatic final-round comeback. A week later, she won her first LPGA Tour event at the Blue Bay LPGA in China, further solidifying her status as a top player.

Pace's dominance on home soil continued as she won her fourth national open title at the Investec South African Women's Open Championship at Westlake Golf Club. In challenging conditions, she carded a level-par 72 in the final round, fending off young German Leonie Harm by one stroke to secure the victory. This win added to her legacy, making her the first player to achieve three consecutive victories in the SA Women's Open.

Her historic hat-trick was completed with a commanding seven-stroke victory over Ashleigh Buhai at San Lameer Country Club. By doing so, Pace etched her name in South African golf history, becoming the first player to win three consecutive national championships. Reflecting on her achievement, Pace expressed immense pride in owning "a little piece of golf history" in her homeland.

Pace's commitment to supporting the Sunshine Ladies Tour is evident as she adjusted her LPGA Tour schedule to compete in the SA Women's Open. Her dedication paid off, as she claimed her third victory in the event, tying the record held by Mandy Adamson. Looking ahead, Pace is already thinking about returning to San Lameer to pursue a fourth title.

While Pace was the star of the day, young amateur Woo Ju Son also made a strong impression, finishing in the top 10 and earning the Jackie Mercer Trophy as the leading amateur.

Pace's remarkable career and her ongoing success on both the LET and LPGA Tours have cemented her legacy as one of South Africa's greatest golfers.

PAPPAS, BRENDAN (1970) SOUTH AFRICA, GREECE

Brendan Pappas, the youngest of four brothers—Craigen, Sean, and Deane—has made his mark in professional golf with a solid career that includes three professional wins. On the Nationwide Tour, Pappas secured two runner-up finishes and gained significant recognition.

His most notable achievement on the PGA Tour came in 2003 when he finished 2nd at the Southern Farm Bureau Classic. A few years later, in 2006, Pappas earned his first victory in the United States, winning the Rex Hospital Open on the Nationwide Tour.

Since 2009, Pappas has been competing full-time on the Nationwide Tour, where he continued to demonstrate his skills. In 2011, he added an unofficial win to his record by triumphing in a tournament in Colombia.

Throughout his career, Brendan Pappas has accumulated a total of three professional wins, establishing himself as a consistent and competitive player in the golfing world.

PAPPAS, DEAN (1967) SOUTH AFRICA, GREECE

Deane Pappas, is a successful professional golfer known for his achievements on both the Sunshine Tour and the Buy.com Tour (now the Web.com Tour). He is the second youngest of four brothers, three of whom became professional golfers. Deane was a three-time All-American at the University of Arkansas, where he played alongside John Daly.

In 1988, Deane, along with his brother Sean, represented Greece at the Eisenhower Trophy held at Ullna Golf Club in Stockholm, Sweden. After turning professional in 1992, he joined the Sunshine Tour in 1994. His first victory on the tour came in 2001 at the prestigious South African PGA Championship, followed by a second win in 2009 at the Dimension Data Pro-Am.

Deane also had a successful run in the United States between 1996 and 2007, winning two tournaments on the Buy.com Tour – one in 2000 and another in 2001. Despite playing three seasons on the PGA Tour, he was unable to retain his card. However, in 2001, Deane and his younger brother Brendan made history by becoming the first brothers to graduate simultaneously to the PGA Tour by finishing in the top 15 on the Buy.com Tour money list.

PAPPAS, SEAN (1966–2015) SOUTH AFRICA, GREECE

The Pappas brothers, due to the sporting boycott of South Africa during the apartheid era, represented Greece in several international golf competitions. Dean and Sean Pappas played in the European Amateur Team Championship in 1985 and the Eisenhower Trophy in 1984, 1986, and 1988.

Dean Pappas also made history by shooting a 59 in the first round of the Hartland Classic, a T.C. Jordan Tour event in Bowling Green, Kentucky. Despite this remarkable achievement, his early professional career was challenging, leading him to return to South Africa for the 1993 season. In South Africa, Dean found more success, winning five times on the Sunshine Tour between 1993 and 2000.

Over his career, Dean Pappas played in more than 230 events in South Africa, securing over 30 top-10 finishes and winning one-third of his playoff appearances. A notable highlight of his career was an albatross in December 1999 at the Vodacom Players Championship on the 3rd hole at the Royal Cape Golf Club during the 3rd round.

After a brief return to the United States from 1994-95, where he won two mini-tour events on the NGA Hooters Tour in 1994, Dean continued to build on his success. In total, he accumulated seven professional wins.

In 2010, Sean Pappas transitioned into a new role as the resident Club Professional at The Ranch Resort Executive Golf Course and Academy, where he has continued to contribute to the sport.

PARHAM, FIONA (WATERS) FEDERATION, RHODESIA

Fiona Waters, who later became known as Fiona Parham after marriage, was a dominant figure in ladies' golf during her time. She was the Rhodesian Ladies Champion for six consecutive years, from 1926 to 1931, showcasing her remarkable consistency and skill. After a brief hiatus from the top spot, she continued her success, finishing as runner-up in the Rhodesian Ladies Championship in 1938 and 1939. In addition to her national success, Fiona also claimed victory in the Manicaland Ladies Championship seven times, beginning in 1938, further cementing her legacy as one of the leading female golfers of her era.

PELTZ, BETTY (BENTEL) UNION SOUTH AFRICA

Betty Peltz had an outstanding amateur golf career, marked by numerous victories and accolades. She won the South African Ladies Amateur titles in 1936 and 1949, and she was the runner-up in 1952. Her success extended internationally with a victory at the Swiss Ladies Open in 1947. Betty also dominated the Transvaal Ladies Amateur, winning in 1937, 1946, 1950, 1951, and 1955, and finishing as the runner-up several times between 1948 and 1961.

In addition to these achievements, she placed 2nd in the 1949 Natal Ladies and Eastern Transvaal Championships, and in the Free State Championships in 1952 and 1954. She also secured a 2nd place finish in the Silver Vase in 1959, and in the OFS, Kimberley & Basutoland Championships in 1953.

Betty Peltz's dominance was further demonstrated by her 29 club championships. She made history as the first woman in the Transvaal to achieve a +1 handicap. A recognized Springbok in 1951, she played in the Wirth Cup eight times between 1932 and 1962, solidifying her legacy as one of South Africa's most accomplished amateur golfers.

PLAYER, GARY JAMES (1935) SOUTH AFRICA

Gary Player's career stands as a testament to unparalleled success and global influence in the world of golf. Known for his remarkable achievements, Player's legacy is highlighted by nine major championship victories. These include three Open Championships in 1959, 1968, and 1974, three Masters titles in 1961, 1974, and 1978, two PGA Championships in 1962 and 1972, and the 1965 U.S. Open.

Player's career is closely linked with that of Jack Nicklaus and Arnold Palmer, forming a triumvirate that significantly popularized golf during

the late 1950s through the 1970s. The intense competition among these three legends, especially in major tournaments, played a crucial role in elevating the game's global profile.

Player's illustrious career is filled with remarkable feats, including his victory at the 1978 Masters. It was an incredible victory for the 42-year old. He hadn't won in four years in the United States, and heading into the final round he trailed Hubert Green by seven shots. However, aided by a spectacular 30 on the back nine the South African star carded a final round 64 to claim his third green jacket. "I shot 30 on the back nine and I rimmed the hole three times," said Player. "I thought to myself it was a good thing those putts didn't go in because if you shoot 27 round Augusta they'll never invite you back," he joked.

His achievements extend beyond the majors, with 13 victories in the South African Open, seven in the Australian Open, and three wins in the World Series of Golf. .He is famously known for his quote: "The more I practice, the luckier I get," which encapsulates his relentless work ethic and dedication.

By the age of 29, Player had achieved the career Grand Slam, becoming only the third golfer to win all four major tournaments, a feat previously accomplished by Ben Hogan and Gene Sarazen, and later matched by Jack Nicklaus and Tiger Woods. His career, spanning six continents and seven decades, saw him amass an astounding 167 professional tournament victories, cementing his place among the sport's elite.

Player's impact on golf transcended his own accomplishments. As part of the legendary "Big Three" alongside Arnold Palmer and Jack Nicklaus, he played a pivotal role in popularizing golf worldwide during the 1960s and 70s. This trio's influence helped elevate the sport's profile and accessibility during the television era, contributing significantly to its global popularity.

In 1974, Player was inducted into the World Golf Hall of Fame, a recognition that underscored his remarkable career. Over the years, he continued to earn accolades, including being named South Africa's Sportsman of the Century in 2000 and receiving the U.S. Presidential Medal of Freedom in 2021. His contributions also extended into golf course design, where he became a respected architect, working on over 400 projects across five continents.

1986 brought him success in a senior major win in the PGA Seniors' Championship. Player added a second senior major in 1987 when he won the US Senior Open. 1988 proved to be a very big year for the Black Knight as he claimed three senior major titles. He won his first British Senior Open and took his second victories in both the US Senior Open and the PGA Seniors' Championship. He repeated his success in the British Senior Open in 1989. 1990 brought Player a 'three-peat' as he won his third British Senior Open in succession, while he also won the PGA Seniors' Championship for the third time. It was the last of his nine senior majors, to go with his nine major championships place him third on the all-time list.

Off the course, Player's philanthropic efforts have had a profound impact. Through the Player Foundation, he has raised over $60 million to support education for underprivileged children worldwide, reflecting his commitment to giving back to those in need.

Despite his monumental successes, Player's career was not without controversy. Early in his life, he endorsed apartheid policies in South Africa, which led to significant backlash. However, he later renounced these views, describing apartheid as a "cancerous disease" and acknowledging the misinformation that had influenced his earlier stance. This evolution in his thinking highlighted his willingness to adapt and grow in response to changing social realities.

Nicknamed "The Black Knight," "Mr. Fitness," and the "International Ambassador of Golf," Player was renowned for his physical fitness and mental toughness. His commitment to a healthy lifestyle, which included avoiding smoking, alcohol, and caffeine, and adhering to a rigorous fitness regime, set him apart from his peers. Known for his powerful short game and accuracy with short irons, Player's bunker play was considered among the best in golf history. Despite some technical imperfections in his swing, his resilience and will to win made him one of the sport's most formidable competitors.

Gary Player's legacy is a blend of extraordinary skill, determination, and global influence. His story is one of remarkable achievements, unmatched discipline, and a profound commitment to the sport, securing his place as one of the greatest golfers of all time.

Player has surpassed Jack Nicklaus by 63 wins. His signature all-black attire earned him the nickname "Black Knight," and he is one of only five golfers to achieve the coveted career Grand Slam, capturing all four major championships: the Masters, U.S. Open, The Open Championship, and PGA Championship.

Beyond his Grand Slam achievements, Player's record includes 13 wins at the South African Open, seven at the Australian Open, and five World Match Play Championship titles. His longevity in the sport is remarkable, as he continued to compete at a high level well into his senior years, accumulating multiple senior tournament victories.

Player's impact extends beyond his accomplishments. His rivalries with Jack Nicklaus and Arnold Palmer were instrumental in elevating golf's global popularity. The fierce competition between the trio in the 1960s and 1970s became a defining aspect of the sport. In 2012, Player was honoured to join Nicklaus and Palmer as an honorary starter at the Masters, celebrating their collective contributions to golf.

In addition to his playing career, Player made significant strides in golf course design through his firm, Player Design. With over 400 projects in 41 countries, including courses like the Gary Player Country Club and Leopard Creek, his influence on the sport's growth is considerable.

Despite his remarkable career, Player's early support of apartheid policies in South Africa cast a shadow over his legacy. In 1966, his endorsement of Hendrik Verwoerd's apartheid regime led to protests and backlash. However, Player later disavowed apartheid, describing it as a "cancerous disease" and acknowledging his previous misjudgments.

Off the course, Player's philanthropic efforts through the Player Foundation have raised over $60 million to support education for underprivileged children. His commitment to fitness and positive thinking set new standards in professional sport and mental toughness. His commitment to a healthy lifestyle, which included avoiding smoking, alcohol, and caffeine, and adhering to a rigorous fitness regime, set him apart from his peers. In 2013, Player made headlines as the oldest athlete ever to pose nude for ESPN The Magazine's Body Issue, advocating for lifelong health and wellness.

Throughout his life, Player has received numerous honors, including induction into the World Golf Hall of Fame in 1974, the Presidential Medal of Freedom in 2021, and the Laureus Lifetime Achievement Award in 2003. He was also the first golfer to be featured on a country's postal stamp and received the Payne Stewart Award in 2006 for exemplifying character and charity. Gary Player's influence on golf, both as a competitor and ambassador, remains profound.

Despite some controversies, such as the withdrawal of a charity invitation due to business ties in Burma, Player's legacy as a golfing legend remains firmly established. His career and achievements underscore his status as a global icon in the sport of golf.

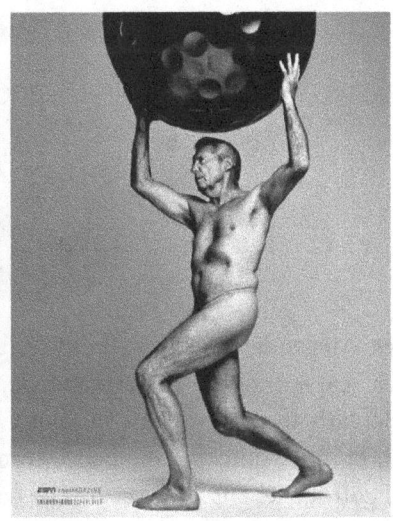

PORTEUS, HAYDN (1994) SOUTH AFRICA

Haydn Porteous is a South African professional golfer who has achieved notable success both as an amateur and a professional. As an amateur, he won several prestigious tournaments in South Africa, including back-to-back victories at the South African Stroke Play Championship in 2012 and 2013. His impressive performances made him the top-ranked South African amateur before he turned professional in 2013.

Porteous quickly made his mark in the professional ranks, securing his first major victory on the Challenge Tour at the 2015 Barclays Kenya Open. His breakthrough on the European Tour came in January 2016, when he won the Joburg Open, a tournament co-sanctioned by the Sunshine Tour, with a two-stroke victory. He continued to build on his success, claiming another European Tour title at the 2017 D+D Real Czech Masters.

In total, Haydn Porteous has secured five professional wins, including his triumphs at the 2016 Joburg Open, 2017 D+D Real Czech Masters, and the 2015 Barclays Kenya Open. His victories highlight his talent and potential as one of South Africa's leading golfers.

PRENTICE, JIMMY (1885–1915) CAPE COLONY, SCOTLAND

James Alexander Webster Prentice, a distinguished Scottish amateur golfer, carved out a remarkable legacy in the early 20th century, particularly during his time in South Africa. Moving to South Africa in 1905, Prentice quickly established himself as a formidable player on the local golf scene. His prowess on the course was evident from the outset.

In 1907, he secured a runner-up position in the South African Amateur Championship, signaling his arrival as a serious competitor.

The following year, 1908, Prentice demonstrated his skill by winning the Amateur Championship, where he also finished an impressive 5th overall in a combined Open and Amateur event. His success continued in 1909 when he retained the Amateur Championship title and emerged as the leading amateur, finishing 4th overall. The trend of strong performances persisted in 1910, with Prentice finishing 5th overall and securing the position of the second amateur.

In 1911, Prentice achieved another milestone by winning the Amateur Championship for the third time and finishing 4th in the Open Championship, where he was the leading amateur. His achievements were a testament to his consistency and skill in the game.

Returning to the UK in 1912, Prentice's excellence on the course did not wane. He won the Transvaal Amateur and competed in the Amateur Championship at Royal North Devon Golf Club, reaching the last-16 round. His impressive form continued as he triumphed in both the Cruden Bay Amateur Tournament and the Peterhead Amateur Tournament, besting his brother Thomas in both competitions.

The pinnacle of Prentice's career came in 1913 when he achieved a historic triumph by winning both the Open and Amateur Championships in the same event. Finishing with a score of 304, he was 10 strokes ahead of the next amateur and surpassed all the professionals, marking his greatest achievement.

Despite a less successful performance in 1914, where he finished 4th in the Amateur Championship and struggled in the Open, Prentice's impact on golf remained significant. His contributions extended beyond his playing career. He was a strong advocate for junior golf, with young golfers referred to as Prentice Golfers in his honour. He also left a bequest to support the development of junior golf, ensuring his legacy would benefit future generations.

Tragically, Prentice's life was cut short during World War I. He was wounded at Hooge near Ypres and passed away in the hospital the following day. His contributions to the sport were recognised posthumously, and in 2009, he was inducted into the inaugural Southern Africa Golf Hall of Fame.

James Alexander Webster Prentice's legacy endures through his remarkable achievements in amateur golf and his lasting impact on junior development. His name continues to be celebrated in the world of golf, a testament to his skill, dedication, and influence on the sport.

PRICE, NICK (1957) ZIMBABWE

Nick Price's journey into the world of golf began in a rather unassuming manner. His older brother, Tim, introduced him to the game with a left-handed 5-iron, a gesture that would set the stage for a remarkable career.

On his first trip to the U.S. as a 17-year-old, he won the Junior World Championship in San Diego, defeating a strong field. He turned pro in 1977, first making waves on the Southern African and European PGA Tours, winning four tournaments by 1982. However, that same year, he finished a disappointing second in the Open Championship to Tom Watson after leading the third round.

Turning professional in 1977, Price first made his mark on the Southern African and European PGA Tours. By 1982, he had already claimed four victories, but that year's Open Championship was a bittersweet milestone. Despite leading after three rounds, he fell short in the final round, finishing second behind Tom Watson.

His breakthrough on the PGA Tour came in 1983 when he achieved a wire-to-wire victory at the World Series of Golf, outlasting Jack Nicklaus. However, a period of struggle followed. Price's fortunes turned around when he refined his swing with coach David Leadbetter, leading to significant success. In 1991, he won the Byron Nelson Classic and the Canadian Open, setting the stage for his dominance in the early 1990s.

Price's first major victory came in 1992 at the PGA Championship, marking the start of a stellar period in his career. The following year, he won four PGA Tour events, including THE PLAYERS Championship, and was named PGA TOUR Player of the Year. The year 1994 was particularly extraordinary for Price; he won six tournaments, including the British Open and the PGA Championship, and reached the world No. 1 ranking, holding the position for an impressive 43 consecutive weeks.

Throughout the 1990s, Price was unparalleled in his achievements, securing 15 PGA Tour titles and 12 international victories. He was one of only seven players since 1945 to capture consecutive majors, joining the ranks of legends like Hogan, Nicklaus, and Palmer. His sportsmanship and grace earned him the Payne Stewart Award and the Bob Jones Award.

Price's influence extended beyond his playing career. Representing Zimbabwe in various international team competitions, including the Presidents Cup and the World Cup, he also made significant contributions to golf course design through his company, Nick Price Golf Course Design. He launched his own line of signature golf apparel and continued to compete on the Champions Tour, where he won four events, including the 2009 Outback Steakhouse Pro-Am.

In addition to his playing accolades, Price received numerous honors, including induction into the World Golf Hall of Fame in 2003, the Vardon Trophy in 1993 and 1997, and the Bob Jones Award in 2005. His contributions to the sport were further recognized with the Old Tom Morris Award in 2011 and his induction into the inaugural Southern Africa Golf Hall of Fame.

Price's legacy is defined by his exceptional skill, resilience, and significant contributions to golf. His career highlights include major championships, numerous victories, and a reputation as one of the sport's most respected and personable figures.

PROUDFOOT, DOUG CAPE COLONY

Douglas Proudfoot, a towering figure in South African golf from the late 19th and early 20th centuries, is celebrated for his unparalleled achievements in amateur golf. His dominance on the course was evident as he captured the South African Amateur Championship an extraordinary eight times between 1893 and 1902. This period of triumph was briefly interrupted by the Anglo-Boer War, during which the championship was not held in 1900 and 1901, but Proudfoot resumed his winning ways in 1902 with a victory in King Williams Town.

Proudfoot's exceptional skill was recognized early on, and after winning the championship in 1893, 1894, and 1895, the trophy became his permanent possession. To honor his achievements, the Union Steamship Co. provided a new floating trophy for the competition, ensuring that the tradition of excellence would continue.

Remarkably, Proudfoot achieved all this without formal coaching. He developed his game by closely observing the leading players of his time. According to Jon Ings, Proudfoot's iron play was "a joy to witness, ever crisp and clean," and his short pitch and run were unmatched by anyone of his era.

In addition to his South African Amateur victories, Proudfoot also excelled in other prestigious tournaments. He won the Natal Amateur Championship eight times, spanning from 1900 to 1914, and claimed the Transvaal Amateur title in 1895. His other notable victories included the Royal Durban Amateur Championship in 1906 and the Silver Salver.

Proudfoot's impact on the sport extends beyond his tournament wins. He bequeathed the Proudfoot Trophy for the South African Amateur qualifying rounds, ensuring his name would continue to be associated with golfing excellence. Furthermore, an annual golf festival in Graaff-Reinet was named in his honor, celebrating his contributions to the sport.

In 2009, Proudfoot's remarkable career and contributions were immortalized with his induction into the inaugural Southern Africa Golf Hall of Fame, alongside other legends such as Locke, Player, Price, and Els. His legacy, marked by his dominance on the golf course and his self-taught mastery of the game, solidifies his status as one of South African golf's greatest pioneers.

R

RETO, PAULA (1990) SOUTH AFRICA

Paula Reto has built a distinguished career in professional golf, marked by notable achievements on both the LPGA Tour and the South African Ladies Sunshine Tour. Her journey began with a solid foundation in collegiate golf, where she was a standout member of the Purdue Boilermakers. Reto's collegiate career was highlighted by her role in the team's victory at the 2010 NCAA National Championship, and she garnered individual accolades, including the Mary Fossum Award for the lowest stroke average in the Big Ten Conference in 2013. Additionally, she was named a First-Team All-Big Ten Conference selection three times and earned First-Team All-American honors in 2013.

Transitioning to the professional scene, Reto's career has been marked by consistent performances and significant milestones. On the LPGA Tour, she achieved a career-defining moment with her win at the 2022 CP Women's Open. Her performance, with scores of 62-69-67-67 for a total of -19, set a tournament record with an opening round of 62. This victory not only highlighted her competitive edge but also underscored her ability to perform under pressure. The 2022 season was a standout year for Reto, as she played in 27 events, made 19 cuts, and earned $808,130. Her season included four top-10 finishes, with her win at the CP Women's Open being the most significant.

In 2023, Reto continued to make an impact by participating in 27 events, making 13 cuts, and earning $179,827. She recorded two top-10 finishes, including a T6 at the Hilton Grand Vacation Tournament of Champions. Her performance in the 2016 Rio Olympics, where she finished tied for 16th, further showcased her ability to compete on a global stage.

Reto's achievements extend to the South African Ladies Sunshine Tour, where she won the 2022 SuperSport Ladies Challenge. Her career highlights reflect her adaptability and resilience, traits that have been crucial in her continued success in diverse competitive environments. Notably, Reto has also excelled in various amateur tournaments, including back-to-back wins at the Dixie Amateur in 2011 and 2012 and reaching the quarterfinals of the 2012 U.S. Women's Amateur Championship.

Beyond her professional achievements, Reto's personal interests and influences play a significant role in her career. Standing at 5'6", she began playing golf at the age of 16 and credits her father as a major influence on her career. Reto enjoys working out, kayaking, and spending time with friends and family. Her journey from a promising amateur to a record-setting professional exemplifies her perseverance and passion for the game.

RICE, ANDREW SOUTH AFRICA, USA

Andrew Rice's journey from playing junior golf in South Africa to becoming a top golf instructor in the U.S. is quite impressive. His background, coupled with his coaching expertise and published work, showcases a deep commitment to the game and to helping golfers improve their performance.

Andrew Rice is a Golf Digest 50 Top Teacher in America and #1 coach in Georgia. Growing up in South Africa, Andrew spent time studying and playing junior events with and against legends like Ernie Els and Retief Goosen. In 1987 he came to the U.S. on a college golf scholarship to play at the University of Central Florida.

Andrew started playing competitive golf with the ambition to play professionally however he wanted more consistency in his life, thus the move to instruction. He got his big break at David Leadbetter's academy and during those 5 years he went through a learning period to become a "high quality" instructor.

Across his impressive 25 year coaching career, Andrew has helped over 50,000 older amateurs gain distance without sacrificing consistency. He is also an author of the golf instructional book "It's all about impact" which has sold over 10,000 copies and received testimonials from the likes of Ian Poulter, Nick Price, Ian Woosnam, Ian Baker-Finch, and Conrad Ray.

RITCHIE, JUAN CARLO 'J.C.' (1994) SOUTH AFRICA

J.C. Ritchie's career has been quite impressive, with multiple wins and notable performances on both the European and Sunshine Tours where he has won (16) times .

His first win on the Sunshine Tour was at Royal Harare Golf Club in the 2017 Zimbabwe Open where he beat Trevor Fisher Jnr at the second hole of a playoff. He was third in the 2018 BMW SA Open and also finished third in the 2017-18 Sunshine Tour Order of Merit. In August 2018 he won the Sun Carnival City Challenge. In March 2019, partnered with Jaco Prinsloo, he won the Sunshine Tour Team Championship and the following week won the Limpopo Championship at the first hole of a playoff with Steve Surry. The following month he won the Zanaco Masters in Zambia, again at the first hole of a playoff against Rhys Enoch. He had two further wins in early 2020, retaining the Team Championship and the Limpopo Championship in successive weeks.

In May 2021, Ritchie won the Bain's Whisky Cape Town Open, beating Jacques Blaauw in a sudden-death playoff. He successfully defended this title in February 2022, winning by one shot ahead of Christopher Mivis. The following week, he won the Jonsson Workwear Open, winning by six shots, again ahead of Mivis.

RITSON, PHILLIP (PHIL) UNION SOUTH AFRICA, USA

Phil Ritson's career stands as a testament to his profound impact on the world of golf, blending his personal achievements as a player with an exceptional dedication to coaching and golf education. In the 1950s and

1960s, Ritson earned a name for himself on the golf course with victories such as the WP Open in 1952 and the South African PGA in 1953. His talent was further recognized when he was awarded Springbok Honours in 1953, affirming his status as one of the leading golfers of his era.

However, Ritson's influence stretched far beyond his playing career. Ranked among the top five golf coaches globally, he became renowned for his rigorous coaching methods, shaping the careers of many of the sport's greatest players, including David Leadbetter, Gary Player, Curtis Strange, and Seve Ballesteros. His teaching legacy extended to players across demographics, as he worked with both white and black golfers, showcasing his commitment to the inclusivity of the sport.

Ritson often stated his preference for teaching over playing, famously declaring, "I'd rather stand on the tee helping students, than play golf." This passion for instruction led him to the United States in 1975, where he accepted an invitation from the Walt Disney Group. By 1977, he had taken on the role of Chairman of the Disney Classic and Golf Director at Walt Disney World in Orlando, Florida. His work at Disney cemented his reputation as one of the top educators in golf, and he was sought out by the sport's elite for his expertise.

In the 1980s, Ritson ventured into golf course design, creating notable courses such as Golden Ocala in Florida. In 1997, he founded the Orange County National Golf Center and Lodge, solidifying his status as a visionary in both instruction and course design. In recognition of his lasting contributions to the sport, GOLF Magazine awarded him "EMERITUS STATUS: Top 100 Teacher For Life" in 2007, honoring his significant influence on golf education.

Ritson's legacy was further immortalized in December 2010 when he was inducted into the Southern Africa Golf Hall of Fame. His dedication to making golf accessible and enjoyable for players of all levels, along with his belief in the sport's universal appeal, remains central to his enduring impact. As Ritson once said, "Golf has a common bond, a universal language that crosses all boundaries," capturing his lifelong commitment to enriching lives through the game of golf.

ROESTOFF, ASHLEY TREVOR (1963) SOUTH AFRICA

Ashley Trevor Roestoff, a prominent figure in South African golf, began his professional journey on the Sunshine Tour in 1992. His career was marked by a series of victories, starting with his first title at the Fish River Sun Classic in 1992. Roestoff's success extended beyond the South African borders as he made a significant impact on the European Challenge Tour. Notably, he achieved a win at the Tusker Kenya Open and had a strong performance in the 2001 season, finishing 26th on the final standings. His expertise is now shared through his role as a teaching professional at Parkview Golf Course and Jackal's Creek Golf Estate, where he continues to influence and mentor aspiring golfers.

ROLFE, A UNION SOUTH AFRICA

A. Rolfe, a notable figure in early South African amateur golf, achieved considerable success throughout his career. His victories included wins at the W.P. Amateur in 1926 and 1930, the Natal Amateur in 1930, 1931, and 1933, and the Mozambique Amateur in 1932. Rolfe's achievements across various regional tournaments underscored his prominence and skill in the amateur golf scene during his era.

ROOS, JAKE (1980) SOUTH AFRICA

Jake Roos has made a mark in both South Africa and international golf with a string of impressive victories. His career highlights include winning the Suncoast Classic in 2008 and the Nedbank Affinity Cup in 2009. Roos's prowess was further demonstrated in 2012 when he triumphed in multiple events, including the Platinum Classic and the Lombard Insurance Classic, both of which were decided in playoffs. His win at the Lion of Africa Cape Town Open in a four-man playoff and subsequent victories, such as the Golden Pilsener Zimbabwe Open in 2013 and the Barclays Kenya Open in 2014, reflect his consistent performance across multiple tours. Roos's career also saw success on the Challenge Tour, where he secured his European Tour card for 2015. His overall tally of 16 professional wins, including titles on the Golden State Tour, highlights his enduring success and influence in the world of golf.

ROWE, LYLE (1987) SOUTH AFRICA

Lyle Rowe has made a notable impact in the world of professional golf with several significant victories that highlight his skill and consistency. In 2014, he captured the Zambia Sugar Open, triumphing by four strokes over Neil Schietekat. Two years later, in 2016, Rowe further solidified his reputation by winning the Zimbabwe Open, finishing two strokes ahead of Dylan Frittelli. Across his career, Rowe has accumulated a total of five professional wins, with three of these victories coming on the Sunshine Tour, showcasing his prowess on the regional circuit.

RUPERT, JOHANN SOUTH AFRICA

Rupert's influence on sports, particularly golf, is both profound and multifaceted. In 1990, he founded the Laureus Sport for Good Foundation, a remarkable initiative that supports 65 global projects aimed at addressing social issues through sports, with a focus on benefiting underprivileged children. His commitment to advancing sports science is also evident from his role as a co-founder of the Sports Science Institute, alongside Morne du Plessis and Tim Noakes. This institute is dedicated to enhancing sports science and development, underscoring Rupert's dedication to improving athletic performance and knowledge.

In the realm of golf, Rupert's contributions are especially noteworthy. He played a pivotal role in the development of Leopard Creek Golf Club, a prestigious course designed by Gary Player in Mpumalanga, South Africa. The course is highly esteemed, ranked among the top three in South Africa and number 25 outside the U.S. by Golf Digest. Rupert's leadership extends beyond course development; he has served as Chairman of both the South African PGA Tour and the South African Golf Development Board, significantly influencing the growth and management of golf in South Africa.

His remarkable contributions to sports and golf have been recognised with inductions into the South African Sports Hall of Fame in 2007 and the Southern African Golf Hall of Fame in 2009. These honours underscore Rupert's significant role in advancing both sports and golf, highlighting his lasting impact on the field.

S

SABBATINI, RORY (1976) SOUTH AFRICA, SLOVAKIA

Rory's career highlights are impressive, and his Olympic achievement is a notable addition.Intense and aggressive on the course "Sabbatini's Goal Is to Win Tournaments, Not Friends", and easy-going everywhere else., .

Rory Mario Trevor Sabbatini won (9) professional tournaments, six times on the PGA Tour between 2000 and 2011, and was runner-up in the 2007 Masters. He spent 21 weeks in the world top 10 in late 2007 and early 2008, with a high of 8th.

As an amateur represented South Africa in the 1994 Eisenhower Trophy, and joined the PGA Tour in 1999. During the first decade of the 2000s, Sabbatini had five PGA Tour wins; he finished 2006 placed 12th on the money list. In September 2007, he reached the top 10 of the world rankings for the first time, He spent 21 weeks in the top-10.

Having lost the 2004 Buick Open in a play-off, Sabbatini tied for second at the 2007 Masters Tournament and the 2007 WGC-Bridgestone Invitational. He won the Par 3 Contest at the 2008 Masters Tournament. Sabbatini has represented South Africa in the World Cup six times and won the event with Trevor Immelman in 2003, and for the International Team in the Presidents Cup in 2007.

In May 2009 Sabbatini captured his fifth PGA Tour title by winning the HP Byron Nelson Championship by two strokes over Brian Davis. He broke the tournament record for scoring with a score of 269 (−19), beating the previous record of 270 (−18).

In March 2011 Sabbatini won his sixth PGA Tour Title at The Honda Classic with a one-stroke victory over South Korea›s Yang Yong-eun. Sabbatini entered the final round with a five-stroke lead over the rest of the field, helped by a course record-equalling 64 on day two. He started his final round solidly with an early birdie at the 3rd hole, however as the round progressed, he made bogeys at the 9th and 14th, meaning that Yang was able to cut that lead to just one, with a spectacular tee shot on the par-three 15th that landed 18 inches past the pin. On the next hole though, Sabbatini holed a clutch birdie putt to tighten his grip on the title and played out the 17th and 18th in even-par to hold on for a one-stroke victory.

Other results include finishing 3rd US Open and in the PGA. On the PGA he won the 2000 Air Canada, 2003 FBR Capital Open, 2006 Nissan Open, 2007 Crown Plaza Invitational, and a 2nd 2007 Wachavia Championship. On 15 December 2019, Sabbatini won the QBE Shootout with partner Kevin Tway. Sabbatini qualified to represent Slovakia at the 2020 Summer Olympics and won the silver medal.

Controversy: In the final round of the 2005 Booz Allen Classic, frustrated by the slow pace of play by his partner, Ben Crane, Sabbatini finished the 17th hole and walked over to the next tee, leaving Crane behind to complete the hole by himself. He received heavy criticism, and some sympathy, and later apologised for the incident.

SAUERMAN, PETER SOUTH AFRICA

Peter Sauerman's work has indeed been pivotal in preserving and celebrating South African golf history. His extensive involvement in both the historical and administrative aspects of the sport has left a lasting legacy.

South Africa owes a great debt for the contribution Peter Sauerman has made as a historian of South African golf, having taken over, in a sense, from RG Fall. His latest book is the history of SA golf, whilst he played a significant part in selecting potential Golf Hall of Fame inductees, and the setting up of the Southern Africa Golf Museum where as a collector, his magnificent golf collection formed the backbone of the museum. "My most important 'work' is the contribution I have made and continue to make in the preservation of the history of the game in Southern Africa."

Sauerman also played a part as an administrator. At George GC he served on the golf club committee and also played for Southern Cape in 1968, 1969 and 1970. Thereafter he served on the committee at Royal Cape in 1973 and went on to be captain on two occasions, 1977/8 and 1983/4. A WP Selector 1975, and president of the WPGU 1989-90, and also on to the executive of the SAGU, where he served six years. He was also magazine owner, publisher and editor 1986 SA Golf magazine for two years. He also designed a golf course situated on the Algarve in Portugal near the village of Espiche.

SCHIETEKET, NEIL (1987) SOUTH AFRICA

Neil Schietekat's professional golf career has been marked by impressive achievements. He first made headlines with his victory at the Vodacom Origins of Golf in 2018, a win he repeated with an encore performance in 2023. His prowess on the course continued to shine as he clinched another significant win at the Zimbabwe Open in 2024, further solidifying his reputation as a formidable golfer.

SCHUTTE, WARREN SOUTH AFRICA

In 1992 Warren Schutte became the first of 3 South Africans to win the USGA APL (U.S. Amateur Public Links Championship) and two other South Africans, Tim Clark and Trevor Immelman. He also reached the Round of 16 at the U.S. Amateur. He also won the Junior Worlds, San Diego in 1986. His forte was a good short game.

Presently he is a teaching pro at Moon Valley CC, Phoenix where he works almost exclusively with youngsters.

SCHWARTZEL, CHARL (1984) SOUTH AFRICA

Charl Adriaan Schwartzel, a distinguished figure in professional golf, currently competes in the LIV Golf Invitational Series. His career highlights include winning the Masters Tournament in 2011, becoming the third South African to secure this prestigious major title after Gary Player and Trevor Immelman. Schwartzel achieved a career-high world ranking of number six in 2012 and has accumulated 16 professional victories, including two on the PGA Tour.

Schwartzel's impressive junior and amateur career saw him secure wins at the 2002 Indian Amateur and the English Open Stroke Play Championships (Brabazon Trophy). He also represented South Africa in the 2002 Eisenhower Trophy. He was named Sunshine Tour Rookie of the Year for 2002-03 and topped the Sunshine Tour Order of Merit for three consecutive years: 2004-05, 2005-06, and 2007.

In 2005, Schwartzel won the Dunhill Championship, co-sanctioned by the European Tour, and went on to claim first place on the Sunshine Tour's Order of Merit in 2004-05. He repeated this achievement in 2005-06 and 2007. In April 2007, he won the Open de España, outlasting Jyoti Randhawa with an eagle on the 16th hole. His European Tour successes continued with a victory at the Madrid Masters in 2008 and two consecutive tournament wins in 2010.

Schwartzel's 2011 season was particularly noteworthy. He retained his Joburg Open title and, in a dramatic final round at the Masters, overcame a four-stroke deficit with a round of 66. His performance included four consecutive birdies to secure the Green Jacket and his first major championship. He also had strong finishes in other majors that year, including a tie for 9th at the U.S. Open and a tie for 12th at the PGA Championship.

In 2012, Schwartzel won the Thailand Golf Championship on the Asian Tour and followed it up with a victory at the Alfred Dunhill Championship in South Africa. He defended his Alfred Dunhill Championship title in 2013, marking his ninth European Tour win. He added his second PGA Tour victory with a win at the Valspar Championship in 2016, decided by a sudden-death playoff.

Schwartzel's recent successes include winning the inaugural LIV Golf Invitational London in June 2022, where he also led his team to victory in the team portion of the event. He has competed in multiple Presidents Cups (2011, 2013, 2015, 2017) and the World Cup (2011), with notable finishes in other majors such as 3rd at The Masters in 2017, 7th at the U.S. Open in 2015, 3rd at The Open Championship in 2020, and 2nd at the Players Championship in 2018. Schwartzel's dramatic final round at the 2011 Masters, featuring four consecutive birdies, remains a standout moment in his career.

SEWGOLUM, SEWSUNKER 'PAPWA' (1928-1978) UNION SOUTH AFRICA - APARTHEID

Papwa Sewgolum's story is one of remarkable perseverance and achievement in the face of adversity. A pioneering South African golfer of ethnic Indian origin, Sewgolum began his journey in the sport as a caddie. His early years were characterized by an unconventional grip, with his left hand positioned below his right, a technique that set him apart. At just 16 years old, he clinched victory at the Natal Indian Open in 1945, and his talent was  further demonstrated when he shot a stunning 59 during a 1957 caddy tournament at Beachwood.

Sewgolum's achievements extended well beyond South Africa. He made history as the first non-white golfer to win a European National Championship by claiming the Dutch Open title in 1959. Remarkably, he repeated this victory in 1960 and 1964, becoming the only golfer to do so. His 1959 win was particularly significant, as it was only his second appearance in a tournament held on a 'white' golf course.

In 1963, Sewgolum achieved another groundbreaking milestone by winning the Natal Open, becoming the first non-white golfer to win a South African circuit event. His performance at the 1963 Open Championship, where he finished 13th, further highlighted his prowess on the international stage. The following year, in 1965, Sewgolum narrowly missed out on victory at the Natal Open in a dramatic final-day duel with Gary Player. Despite a tense finish, where Sewgolum made a par on the last hole and Player's putt for eagle lipped out, Sewgolum emerged victorious. That same year, he also triumphed in the Grand Prix Series.

However, Sewgolum's career was not without its challenges. Political and racial barriers severely impacted his professional life. After achieving considerable success, he faced bans from South African tournaments and had his passport withdrawn, hindering his ability to compete internationally. Despite these setbacks, Sewgolum's resilience shone through. He was eventually reinstated and participated in the 1970 Rest of the World vs. Britain match.

Throughout his career, Sewgolum amassed at least 78 tournament victories, including 11 Open tournaments, 18 lesser South African events, and 10 SA Non-European Open titles (nine in ten years). His achievements earned him recognition as the South African Non-European Sportsman of the Year in 1959 and 1963/64. He also finished third in the South African Order of Merit in 1964/65, despite being barred from participating in two events.

Sewgolum's legacy has been honoured posthumously. In 2004, he was awarded the Order of Ikhamanga in Silver, and in 2009, he was inducted into the inaugural Southern Africa Golf Hall of Fame alongside golf legends such as Gary Player, Bobby Locke, and Ernie Els. The Papwa Sewgolum Municipal Golf Course was named in his honor in 2010, and he received the South African Sports Trust Award in 2017. Papwa Sewgolum's pioneering spirit and exceptional contributions to golf continue to inspire and celebrate his enduring impact on the sport.

SHEAN, KELLI 'KELLOGS' (1987) SOUTH AFRICA

Kelli Shean Rackley's journey in golf is marked by exceptional achievements both as a player and a coach. Her early career was distinguished by a series of impressive performances. In 2005, she made a name for herself as an amateur with several notable accomplishments. She finished second in the Spirit International Team Championships, alongside Ashleigh Simon, and also as a runner-up in the World Division of the same event. Her success continued with a runner-up position in the South African Amateur Stroke Play Championships and a victory in the South African Amateur Match Play Championships. Additionally, she secured the Order of Merit for the Ernie Els Junior Tour, highlighted by two wins, three runners-up, and one third-place finish.

The following year, 2006, was a remarkable period for Rackley. She excelled in international and local tournaments, winning the World Amateur Team Championships and the Gauteng Open Match Play Championships. Her dominance was evident in the Southern Cape Open Championships, and she set records with an impressive 11-shot victory at the Kwa-Zulu Natal Open Championships and a 12-shot win at the Western Province Open Championships.

Rackley's talent earned her a golf scholarship to the University of Arkansas in 2007, where she continued to build on her success. Her college career saw her secure her first collegiate win at the Marilynn Smith Sunflower Invitational in Kansas in 2009, finishing an impressive seven under par.

Today, Kelli Shean Rackley is not only celebrated for her playing career but also for her contributions as a coach. She runs her own academy, "More Than a Game Golf Academy," where she continues to inspire and mentor aspiring golfers, sharing her extensive knowledge and experience in the sport. Her journey from a talented amateur to a successful coach highlights her significant impact on the game of golf.

SHEARD, ALISON (1951) SOUTH AFRICA

Alison Sheard is a distinguished South African golfer whose career spans both amateur and professional levels, marked by significant achievements and contributions to the sport.

In her amateur career, Alison Sheard dominated South African women's golf from 1974 to 1979. During this period, she clinched the South African Ladies Championship three times consecutively, from 1976 to 1978. She also excelled in the South African Strokeplay Championship, winning it in 1974, 1975, 1976, 1978, and 1979. Her prowess was further evidenced by a notable runner-up finish to Cathy Panton at the 1976 British Ladies Amateur.

Transitioning to her professional career, Sheard made a mark on the Ladies European Tour (LET), where she secured four victories between 1979 and 1985. Her notable wins include the Carlsberg Welsh Classic and the McEwans Welsh Classic in 1979, the same year she claimed one of her most significant triumphs at the Ladies British Open, today a Major tournament. She continued to perform well on the LET, with a victory at the Spanish Open in 1985. Her impressive form in 1979 also earned her the title of leading money-winner on the British circuit. Sheard's consistent performances were evident as she finished 9th in the British Open in 1982 and tied for 12th in 1986.

On the LPGA Tour, Sheard competed from 1980, consistently finishing inside the top 100 during her initial years. Her best performances included tying for 19th at the 1980 LPGA Championship, tying for 23rd at the 1980 U.S. Women's Open, and achieving a 10th place at the 1981 Peter Jackson Classic. She also tied for 7th at the 1983 West Virginia LPGA Classic.

In addition to her tournament successes, Alison Sheard was awarded the Sports Merit Award in 1976 and was named a Springbok golfer in 1975,

1977, and 1979. Her contributions to the sport were further recognized when she was inducted into the Southern Africa Golf Hall of Fame by Sally Little in 2010.

Today, Alison Sheard continues to influence the sport through her role at the Alison Sheard Golf Academy, where she focuses on coaching and mentorship. Her legacy in golf is underscored by her remarkable achievements and her ongoing dedication to nurturing future generations of golfers.

SMIT, MONIQUE (1991) SOUTH AFRICA

Monique Smit is a prominent South African golfer whose career showcases remarkable achievements both as an amateur and a professional.

As an amateur, Smit made her mark early on. In 2005, she secured four titles on the Ernie Els Junior Tour, demonstrating her potential. She continued to excel, winning the Gus Ackermann Championship in both 2010 and 2011 and claiming the Western Province Stroke Play Championship in 2008 and 2011. Her talent was evident on the international stage as well; she represented South Africa at the 2008 Espirito Santo Trophy and was the individual winner of the 2008 All Africa Challenge Trophy. Her international successes extended to victories on three continents, including the Jakarta World Junior Championship and the Gosh Leinster Championship in Ireland.

Turning professional in 2012, Monique Smit joined the Ladies European Tour (LET) and began to make her mark in the professional arena. In 2014, she had a standout year on the Sunshine Ladies Tour, winning the Dimension Data Ladies Pro-Am with a record-setting round of 63 at Oubaai Golf Club, and triumphing in the SuperSport Ladies Challenge against Lee-Anne Pace. She also finished as the runner-up at the Zambia Ladies Open.

Smit's career faced a significant setback when she took a four-year break from the tour due to injury. However, she made a strong comeback in 2020. She was a runner-up at the Investec South African Women's Open, narrowly missing out on victory to Alice Hewson, but bounced back by winning the Joburg Ladies Open. Her performance that year earned her the Sunshine Ladies Tour Order of Merit title.

Monique Smit's career highlights are marked by her consistent performance, resilience, and significant contributions to women's golf, establishing her as a notable figure in the sport.

SOLE, MEL SOUTH AFRICA, USA

Mel Sole is a distinguished golf instructor and former South African PGA Tour player renowned for his extensive contributions to the sport. His career spans over three decades, during which he has earned widespread recognition for his teaching and coaching achievements.

Sole's career in golf instruction began with early mentorship under Phil Ritson, a highly respected figure in golf coaching. Ritson considered Sole to be "possibly the best teacher I've ever come across," a testament to his early promise in the field. In 1981, Sole started coaching Junior Golf Teams, producing two national champions and several other promising young golfers, establishing himself as a skilled and influential coach.

In 1984, he expanded his impact by opening the Canadian Golf Academy in Toronto, an innovative indoor/outdoor teaching facility. This move marked the beginning of a series of milestones in his career. By 1988, he joined the Phil Ritson Golf School in Myrtle Beach, and in 1991, he took sole ownership of the school. The institution was renamed the Phil Ritson-Mel Sole Golf School in 1997 and later became the Mel Sole Golf School in 2013.

Sole's teaching philosophy is well-regarded for its emphasis on the mental aspects of golf, an approach that has helped many golfers improve their game. His contributions to golf instruction have been recognized by Golf Magazine, which has consistently ranked him among the "Top Teachers in North America" in their biennial review since 2003. His golf school has been acknowledged as "one of the Top 25 Golf Schools in America" every year since 1999.

In addition to his practical coaching, Sole has also made significant contributions to golf literature and media. He has served as a teaching editor for GOLF TIPS Magazine and authored "Golf Step-by-Step," a guide that reflects his expertise and innovative teaching methods. His lessons and insights have been featured in prominent publications such as Golf Digest and GOLF Magazine.

Mel Sole's innovative approach to golf instruction and his dedication to the sport have left a lasting impact both nationally and internationally, solidifying his reputation as a leading figure in the world of golf coaching.

SOLOMON, HARRY UNION SOUTH AFRICA

Harry Solomon rendered invaluable service to Western Province golf from 1923 to 1956. Served as the Honourary Secretary of Metropolitan Golf Club for 37 years. Held the position of Honourary Secretary of the Western Province Golf Union (WPGU) for 28 years.

Harry Solomon Cup: A prestigious floating trophy awarded in honor of Harry Solomon, presented by JM Logan. The Harry Solomon Cup is competed for annually in recognition of Solomon's significant contributions to golf in the Western Province.

STENT, WILLIAM C. UNION SOUTH AFRICA

William Stent was a distinguished figure in South African amateur golf, known for his impressive achievements and consistent performance. His golf career was marked by several notable victories and commendable finishes in major tournaments, reflecting his skill and dedication to the sport.

Stent's success at the South African Amateur was particularly remarkable. He clinched the title in 1922 and 1923, establishing himself as a formidable competitor. His competitive spirit was evident in 1927 when he was the runner-up, and he also earned a third-place finish in 1926, demonstrating his ability to remain at the top of the game.

In the Western Province Amateur, Stent's dominance was even more pronounced. He secured victories in 1911, 1912, 1921, and 1922, showcasing his talent across several years. His consistent performance was further highlighted by multiple runner-up finishes between 1910 and 1929, including near misses in 1910, 1913, 1914, 1919, 1920, 1923, 1924, 1928, and 1929. His persistence and skill were again evident in 1930, when he earned a third-place finish, solidifying his status as a key player in the tournament's history.

The Royal Cape Championship was another arena where Stent made his mark. He achieved victory five times, a testament to his prowess on the course. His competitive nature was evident through his eight runner-up finishes, underscoring his ability to consistently challenge for the title.

William Stent's career in amateur golf is remembered for its impressive achievements and significant contributions to the sport. His legacy lives on as a prominent figure in South African golf history, celebrated for his remarkable successes and enduring impact on the game.

STERNE, RICHARD (1981) SOUTH AFRICA

Richard Sterne's journey in golf began with notable promise during his amateur years. In 1999, he showcased his talent by finishing as the runner-up in the Boys' 15–17 Division at the World Junior Golf Championships. His amateur career was highlighted by significant victories, including the South African Junior Strokeplay and Matchplay Championship, the South African Amateur, the Southern Cross in 2000, and the South African Amateur Strokeplay Championship in 2001.

Turning professional, Sterne's career gained momentum quickly. He secured his first European Tour victory at the Open de Madrid in 2004, marking the beginning of a successful stint on the tour. His exceptional form continued in 2007, where he achieved notable successes: winning the Celtic Manor Wales Open, finishing second at the Johnnie Walker Classic, third at the BMW PGA Championship, and fourth at the Barclays Scottish Open. By the end of the year, he was ranked 14th in the Order of Merit, underscoring his rise in the golfing world.

The year 2008 was another milestone for Sterne. He won the Joburg Open, which was co-sanctioned by the Sunshine Tour, and added two more European Tour victories in South Africa. His consistent performance earned him the Sunshine Tour Order of Merit title.

Despite a career setback due to injury, which kept him from competing in most of 2010 and 2011, Sterne made a strong comeback in 2013. He won the Joburg Open for the second time, triumphing by seven strokes over Charl Schwartzel, and ended a four-year winless streak. His impressive year continued with a second-place finish at the Dubai Desert Classic and strong showings at various tournaments, including second at the Alstom Open de France, ninth at the WGC-Bridgestone Invitational, 13th at the Omega European Masters, and 14th at the DP World Tour Championship, Dubai.

In 2014, Sterne continued to make his mark with a fourth-place finish at the WGC-Cadillac Championship and 17th at the WGC-Accenture Match Play Championship. He also performed well in the PGA Championship and qualified for the Web.com Tour Finals, where he finished second at the Nationwide Children's Hospital Championship.

Throughout his career, Richard Sterne has amassed a total of nine professional wins, demonstrating his skill and resilience on the golf course. His journey reflects a blend of early promise, professional success, and remarkable comebacks.

STEWART, ARTHUR UNION SOUTH AFRICA

Arthur Stewart's golfing career is marked by significant achievements and a deep involvement in the sport. His journey began in the early 1950s, when he made a strong impact as an amateur golfer. In 1954, Stewart showcased his talent by winning the Orange Free State Championship and the Maccauvlei Match Play Championship, while also finishing as the runner-up at the W. Transvaal Closed Championship.

The following year, 1955, Stewart's prowess was further highlighted by his victory at the South African Amateur Championship. This win was particularly notable as he defeated Peter Vorster in an epic 41-hole match. He also reached the semi-finals of the South African Amateur that same year.

In 1956, he added another title to his name by winning the Eastern Transvaal Championship. The year 1957 was a pinnacle in his career, as he clinched the South African Open Championship with a score of 281, overcoming notable golfers such as Gary Player, Bobby Locke, and Dai Rees. This victory was a testament to his skill and established him as a formidable player on the national stage. Stewart also represented South Africa as a Springbok in 1957, a recognition of his high level of performance.

Continuing his impressive run, Stewart won the Western Transvaal Closed Championship and the South African Open Championship again in 1958. His success in 1959 included a win at the East Rand Amateur Championship, and in 1961, he secured the Western Transvaal Match Play Championship.

Stewart's career was not limited to domestic achievements. In 1968, he won the Mozambique Amateur Championship, and he was a runner-up in the same event in 1969 and 1973. The year 1971 saw him as a runner-up at the Maccauvlei Match Play Championship.

In his senior years, Stewart continued to excel. In 1976, he won the Transvaal Senior Championship, and from 1977 to 1980, he achieved the South African Seniors Championship in consecutive years, demonstrating his enduring skill and competitiveness.

Throughout his career, Stewart represented Western Transvaal from 1954 to 1973 and was honored to play as a Springbok for South Africa in 1957 and 1958. His career highlight remains his victory at the South African Open Championship, a testament to his remarkable talent and contributions to the sport of golf.

STONE, BRANDON (1993) SOUTH AFRICA

Brandon Stone began his professional journey in 2013 after a standout year at the University of Texas, where he secured three victories in college golf. His transition to professional golf was marked by a series of notable achievements. In 2015, he made an impressive debut with a runner-up finish at the Barclays Kenya Open and the GANT Open. He also earned his first professional win at the Sunshine Tour's Lion of Africa Cape Town Open.

His success continued to build in 2016, when he clinched the South African Open by two strokes, defeating Christiaan Bezuidenhout. The following year, 2017, he demonstrated his skills by winning the Alfred Dunhill Championship with a total score of 267, finishing six strokes ahead of Richard Sterne.

In 2018, Stone reached a significant milestone by winning the Aberdeen Standard Investments Scottish Open at Gullane. His final-round 60 set a European Tour record, though he narrowly missed a birdie putt on the last hole that would have given him a 59.

His recent achievements include winning the Limpopo Championship in 2021 after a thrilling four-man playoff, where he made a birdie at the first extra hole. Throughout his career, he has accumulated a total of five professional wins and achieved a highest world ranking of 67.

STRYDOM, OCKERT 'OCKIE' (1985) SOUTH AFRICA

Ockie Strydom's professional career has seen notable successes and a journey filled with perseverance. In 2019, he won the Vodacom Origins of Golf, setting the stage for future accomplishments. His career breakthrough came in December 2022 when he claimed his maiden European Tour win at the Alfred Dunhill Championship. During this victory, he set a course record in the third round, following a string of 19 second-place finishes.

Continuing his impressive run, Strydom won the Singapore Classic on the European Tour in 2023, shooting a final-round 63 to secure a narrow victory over Sami Välimäki. In addition to his European Tour successes, he has accumulated nine victories on the IGT Pro Tour, a secondary South African tour. Despite three playoff losses on the Sunshine Tour, Strydom has established himself with a total of 14 professional victories.

SUDDARDS, DAVID (1954) SOUTH AFRICA

David Suddards made a significant impact on the amateur golf scene, garnering attention for his remarkable achievements and his close encounters with the game's top players. His breakthrough moment came in 1976 during the South African Open at Durban Country Club, where, as a 22-year-old amateur, he led by two shots deep into the third round. Although he ultimately finished in a tie for second place, his performance against the legendary Gary Player put him firmly in the media spotlight.

Over the next few years, Suddards continued to excel in various tournaments. He achieved runner-up status in the British Amateur in 1979 and repeated this feat in 1980. His domestic success was equally impressive. He won the South African Strokeplay Championship in both 1978 and 1979, and later clinched the South African Amateur Championship in 1981, with additional runner-up finishes in 1980 and 1983.

He was a dominant force in the Natal Championships, securing the Champion of Champions title five times from 1977 to 1984 and finishing as a runner-up on several occasions. His victories also extended to other significant amateur tournaments, including the Natal Amateur, which he won in 1978, 1979, 1980, and 1982, and the Natal Amateur Stroke-Play Championship, where he took the title in 1975, 1980, and 1984.

In 1976, he triumphed in the Rhodesian Amateur with a remarkable score of 273. He also earned accolades such as the Freddie Tait Trophy in 1977, 1980, and 1982, and the Cape Province Amateur in 1979. Despite his impressive record, including notable second-place finishes in various tournaments, his true strength lay in his short game and bunker play. Known for his exceptional skill around the greens, he was described as small in stature but large in heart, epitomizing the true spirit of amateur golf.

His record of 18 Springbok caps, spanning a decade, stands as a testament to his enduring presence and influence in the sport. As he once remarked, had he hit the ball just a bit farther in the '70s, he might have turned professional. Nonetheless, his amateur career is marked by remarkable achievements and a deep passion for the game.

SUDDARDS, KEVIN SOUTH AFRICA

Kevin Suddards enjoyed a distinguished amateur golf career, particularly notable during the early 1970s. His performance on the course earned him a place among South Africa's top amateur golfers and garnered him several prestigious accolades.

In 1970, Kevin's golf prowess was evident as he won the South African Junior Championship, the Transvaal Amateur, the Eastern Transvaal Amateur, and the Natal Amateur, showcasing his dominance in the amateur circuit. His success continued into 1971, where he clinched the South African Amateur Stroke Play Championship and was the runner-up in the South African Amateur Match Play Championship. He also secured victory in the Natal Amateur Stroke Play, cementing his reputation as a formidable competitor.

Kevin's remarkable form continued into 1972, highlighted by his win at the Freddie Tait Trophy and another victory in the Transvaal Amateur. His performance at the Eisenhower Trophy, where he finished in third place, further demonstrated his skill and competitiveness on an international stage.

In 1973, Kevin added to his list of accomplishments by winning the Freddie Tait Trophy for the second time. Over his career, he earned three Springbok caps in 1971, 1972, and 1973, representing South Africa with distinction. Kevin Suddards' career is remembered for his significant contributions to South African amateur golf and his consistent high-level performance during a pivotal period in his career.

SUNDELSON, NEVILLE "ROCK" SOUTH AFRICA

Neville 'Rock' Sundelson's amateur golf career is a remarkable yet often underappreciated chapter in the sport's history. Spanning from 1967 to 1974, his achievements on the course established him as a formidable player both locally and internationally, and his later role as a World of Golf Coach cemented his influence in the golfing world.

In 1967, Sundelson made a strong impression by winning the Somerset West Open, the Transvaal Amateur, and the Eastern Rand Championship. His dominance was evident as he continued to excel, securing the runner-up position in the Transvaal Amateur in 1969.

The early 1970s marked the pinnacle of Sundelson's amateur career. In 1971, he triumphed in the North Transvaal Silver Salver and claimed the prestigious English Amateur Brabazon Trophy, demonstrating his capability on an international stage. His success continued into 1972 when he won the South African Amateur, further showcasing his skill and consistency.

In 1973, Sundelson's career reached new heights. He won the Rhodesian Amateur and played a pivotal role in South Africa's victory at the World Team Championship alongside Andries Oosthuizen. His partnership with Oosthuizen and Murray also earned him the Huberto Alemida Trophy, underscoring his collaborative success on the international circuit.

Sundelson's final notable achievements came in 1974 when he won the South African Amateur Stroke Play Championship and the Freddie Tait Trophy. He also achieved a commendable 6th place finish at the

SA Masters. His contributions to the sport were further acknowledged through his four Springbok caps from 1971 to 1974.

Neville 'Rock' Sundelson's exceptional amateur career, characterized by numerous victories and consistent performances, has left a lasting legacy in the golfing world, despite being relatively unknown among today's younger golfers. His achievements during this period reflect a remarkable talent and dedication to the sport.

SWANEPOEL, CHRIS (1984) SOUTH AFRICA

Swanepoel's career on the Sunshine Tour has been marked by notable successes and dramatic moments. Among his achievements, his four professional victories highlight his skill and consistency on the tour.

One of the standout moments in his career came in April 2012 when he secured a thrilling victory at the Golden Pilsener Zimbabwe Open. In a tense playoff, he emerged victorious against Trevor Fisher, showcasing his resilience and ability to perform under pressure.

In addition to his wins, Swanepoel has experienced the heartache of playoff losses on two occasions. These near-wins are a testament to his competitive spirit and close finishes, emphasizing the fine margins that define professional golf.

Overall, Swanepoel's tenure on the Sunshine Tour reflects a successful and competitive career, marked by both significant victories and challenging playoff encounters.

SWARTZ, S UNION SOUTH AFRICA – DISCRIMINATED

Swartz's achievements in golf are remarkable not only for their sporting significance but also for the context in which they occurred. As the first non-European to win the South African Non-European Open, he made a profound impact on the game, despite the challenges posed by the racial segregation of his time.

Swartz won the unofficial South African Non-European Open an impressive six times between 1942 and 1947. This series of victories underscored his dominance in the tournament, even though he was restricted by colonial policies that limited his access to white golf courses and tournaments. The official South African Non-European Open was established only in 1949, making Swartz's early successes even more notable.

With a handicap of +2, Swartz's skills on the course were exceptional. His repeated triumphs in the SA Non-European Open not only highlight his golfing talent but also his ability to excel under significant restrictions. His career stands as a testament to his perseverance and excellence in the sport despite the racial barriers of his era.

SYMONS, DAVE SOUTH AFRICA

Dave Symons, a prominent figure in South African golf, left an indelible mark on the sport through his remarkable achievements and steadfast dedication. His career spanned from 1959 to 1980, during which he earned 15 Springbok caps between 1963 and 1973—a record second only to that of Neville Sundelson.

Symons' amateur career was characterized by numerous victories and notable performances. In 1959, he clinched the Natal Amateur, Transvaal Amateur, and E Transvaal Amateur titles, setting the stage for a career filled with triumphs. His success continued with wins at the Transvaal Amateur in 1960, 1961, and 1964, and he also excelled in the Transvaal Amateur Stroke-Play, securing victories in 1961 and 1964.

He was particularly successful in the Silver Vase, capturing the title in 1960, 1961, 1969, 1972, and 1980. His dominance extended to the N Transvaal Amateur, where he won multiple times from 1959 to 1968. Symons also made significant contributions to team events and represented South Africa with distinction.

In addition to his national successes, Symons competed internationally, reaching the semi-finals of the British Amateur in 1966 and finishing as the runner-up in the Rhodesia Amateur in 1963. His victories in the Oppenheimer Trophy, N Transvaal Silver Vase, and Maccauvlei Amateur, along with his win at the Tournament of Champions in 1969, further cemented his legacy.

Symons' career was recognized posthumously with his induction into the Southern Africa Golf Hall of Fame in 2015, an honor accepted by his daughter. This accolade highlights his enduring impact on the sport and his standing as a distinguished player in South African golf history.

T

TAIT, LT. FREDDIE GUTHRIE (1870-1900) SCOTLAND, ANGLO-BOER WAR

Freddie Guthrie Tait was a remarkable figure in both golf and military history. A Scottish amateur golfer with an impressive track record, Tait made his mark in the late 19th century with a string of notable achievements. He won the Amateur Championship twice, in 1896 and 1898, dominating both tournaments with commanding performances. His prowess on the golf course was evident not just in these victories but also in his numerous tournament wins, tallying at least 28. Tait's skill was further demonstrated by his strong showings in the Open Championship, where he tied for third place in 1896 and 1897 and earned the distinction of leading amateur on six occasions.

Despite his golf career's brilliance, Tait's life was tragically cut short by war. Having rejoined the Black Watch regiment, he served valiantly during the Second Boer War. On February 7, 1900, Tait was killed in action at Koodoosberg, South Africa, a poignant end to a life marked by excellence both on the golf course and in military service. He was laid to rest at Koodoosberg, leaving behind a legacy that intertwines his dual passions of golf and service.

In recognition of his contributions and to honor his memory, the Freddie Tait Cup was established in 1928. This prestigious trophy is awarded to the leading amateur at the South African Open Championship, contingent on the golfer making the 36-hole cut. The cup features the R&A Club die and crest, alongside the Army Golfing Society's medal die, and was funded by surplus money from a British Amateur Tour to South Africa. The inaugural Freddie Tait Cup was awarded to Bernard Wynne at Royal Cape in 1929, continuing Tait's legacy in the world of golf.

TAYLOR, REG UNION SOUTH AFRICA

Reg Taylor's career was marked by a multitude of significant achievements and victories in both domestic and international amateur golf, cementing his reputation as South Africa's greatest amateur golfer.

Reg Taylor was South Africa's greatest amateur golfer. A Springbok 1954, 1957, 1958, 1959, 1960, 1962, 1963, 1964, he won the SA Open 1954, 2nd 1955, and the South African Amateur 1956, 2nd 1968, also the Belgian and German amateurs in 1958, the Canadian amateur in 1962, and the 1970 French Amateur's among many others, when Taylor made a golfing comeback after five years, he defeated Didier Charmat of France 7/6, and won the French amateur championship. In 2009 he was inducted into the inaugural Southern Africa Golf Hall of Fame along with all the greats like Player, Locke, Els, Price.

His Amateur victories were numerous. Here are just a few additional successes: Commonwealth Eisenhower Trophy 1959; Transvaal Amateur Stroke-Play 1960, 1963, 1971, 2nd 1955; W. Transvaal Amateur 1952, 1962; E. Rand Amateur 1955, 2nd 1962; Natal Amateur 1956, 1957; Maccauvlei Amateur 1955, 1961, 1962, 2nd 1960; Transvaal Amateur 1962, 1963, 2nd 1959; Freddie Tait Trophy 1955, 1963, 1972, 1976; Mozambique Amateur 1960, 1961, 1962, 1966, 2nd 1959, 1968; S.W.D. Amateur 1959; OFS Amateur 1960; Transvaal Silver Vase 1963, 2nd 1961, 1971; as well as the SA Senior Amateur 1984, 1986, 1987, 1988, 1989, 1990.

TEBBUTT, GILLIAN (WHITFIELD) (1954) SOUTH AFRICA

Gillian Tebbutt's impressive career spans over several decades, highlighting her remarkable achievements and contributions to South African golf both as a player and a coach. Her long-standing success at the club level and her leadership role with the South African team underscore her significant impact on the sport.

It's been an amazing ride for one of South Africa's most accomplished amateurs, Gillian Tebbutt, who has won her Club Championship for 43 times. She represented South Africa 1981 – 2006 and Western Province 1972-2009. In 1999 Tebbutt was appointed the coach of the South African golf team, and in 2013 she was inducted into the Southern Africa Golf Hall of Fame. Her record includes the South Africa Womens Strokeplay 1984, 1988, 1990, 1991, 1995, 1996, 2nd 1983, 2000, 2001; and the All Africa Challenge Trophy in 1992.

TERBLANCHE, DES SOUTH AFRICA

Terblanche's career highlights include significant victories both locally on the Sunshine Tour and internationally on the Asian PGA Tour. His early achievements as a Junior Springbok and in the Junior World Championship set the stage for a successful professional career spanning nearly two decades.

Terblanche a Junior Springbok 1980 – 83, won the Junior World Championship in 1983. In 1985 he won the SA under 23, and in all he has 17 professional wins. His 14 wins on the Sunshine Tour came 1989 – 2007. On the Asian PGA Tour he has three victories being the 1997 Sabah Masters; 1997 Volvo Asian Matchplay; and the 2000 Thailand Open.

THOMAS, FRANK SOUTH AFRICA, USA

Frank Thomas' contributions to golf, from technological advancements to educational resources, have significantly impacted the game. His work continues to influence golfers and the industry alike.

Frank Thomas is the inventor of the graphite golf shaft. Thomas, long-time Technical Director of the United States Golf Association is one of its unsung heroes and a popular contributor to Golf Digest and the Golf Channel. He was Technical Director of the USGA for 26 years, and was responsible for the testing of, and ruling on, the acceptability of every new club and ball.

His personal achievements are, to say the least, impressive. He went to work at Shakespeare Sporting Goods in 1965, and it was at Shakespeare that he invented the graphite shaft. He also introduced the Stimpmeter

 to the game, a device for measuring the speed of the green, and he directed the development of today's Golf Handicap and Information Network (GHIN),

During his 26 years at the USGA, Thomas examined, tested, and ruled on more than 6,000 items submitted for USGA approval – clubs, putters and balls. The decisions he made during those years affected everyone who plays the game.

On his retirement from the USGA in 2001 Thomas founded Frankly Golf, "a consulting and equipment company devoted to growing the game by 0lending his considerable expertise to players, teaching pros, and equipment manufacturers alike."

"Frankly Golf has three different divisions," Thomas says. "There's Frankly Consulting, the Frankly Golf Institute, and Frankly Golf Equipment. I also write a monthly column for Golf Digest and a weekly Q&A on GolfDigest.com., developed an online putting course so PGA and LPGA golf professionals can become Certified Putting Instructors (CPI's). I decided to apply what I know to making my own putter, Thomas says." The first Frankly putter, the F-16, introduced some unique technology. Alignment is easy because Thomas incorporated a line that goes from the putter head all the way up the shaft. It also has a flanged blade which allows it to move easily through the fringe. The head of the putter is encased in tenite, a plastic made from wood rather than petroleum, this is a renewable material and environmentally friendly. "But we also decided to do something no one else does," he says. "Every putter comes with a guide that explains the fundamentals of good putting, and exercises for working on both the stroke and the psychology of putting. it begins when someone buys a putter. Each one has a serial number that serves as a password for our owners' Web site."

Frankly's newest product is somewhat controversial The new putter is machined from a single block of aluminum. Its design incorporates two heavy tungsten weights positioned low and several inches to the rear of the face giving it "perfect balance and an optimum Moment of inertia." Thomas's new putter is forgiving and gives the ball a positive roll immediately upon impact. The controversy arises not from the practicalities of the putter, or the way it performs, but from its looks. "I came up with design in a few hours one evening. When I showed the drawings to one of our draftsmen," Thomas says, 'Frank, it looks like a frog'. So, in the end, we decided to call it simply, 'The Frog.'

TINDALL, JEAN SOUTH AFRICA

Jean Tindall's impressive amateur career and repeated selections for the Springboks highlight her significant contributions to South African golf. She was selected multiple times for the Springboks 1957, 1959, and other. He amateur successes include SA Ladies Amateur 1961; Transvaal Ladies Amateur 1959, 1960, 1961, 1963; and the Natal Ladies Amateur 2nd six times

TOMLINSON, GABY (1910) SOUTHERN RHODESIA, RHODESIA

In 1974, Gaby Tomlinson, a small, grey-haired grandmother, made history by becoming the first woman in Rhodesia to receive the Quail's Trophy. This prestigious award, presented by the all-male Rhodesia Golf Union, was a fitting tribute to Tomlinson's remarkable contributions to the sport of golf and her storied career. Despite never claiming the title of a world-beater, Tomlinson's achievements in Southern Africa were nothing short of extraordinary, spanning three decades of impressive play.

Tomlinson's journey in golf began relatively late, at the age of thirty, but she quickly established herself as a dominant force. Within just four years of picking up her first club, she captured the Rhodesian championship. Over the next two decades, she amassed a collection of titles that demonstrated her exceptional talent and dedication. By 1978, when she moved to South Africa at the age of sixty-eight, her list of accomplishments was extensive. She had won the Rhodesian title an astonishing thirteen times and claimed every provincial title multiple times: Mashonaland fifteen times, Matabeleland seven times, Manicaland thirteen times, and Midlands twice.

At Royal Salisbury, Tomlinson reigned supreme, capturing the club championship eighteen times in twenty years, and at Chapman Club, she was champion twenty-two times in twenty-four years. Her competitive edge was evident in her performances at the South African match play championships, where she reached the final twice, only to be defeated by her close friend and rival, Rita Easton. Despite these setbacks, including her inability to secure official Rhodesian colors due to political issues and the fact that she never played in a Springbok team, Tomlinson's achievements remained remarkable.

Before her golfing career, Tomlinson had already made a name for herself in other sports. She played hockey for Rhodesia in the 1930 and 1933 South African inter-provincial tournaments and was the Rhodesian doubles tennis champion in 1936. Her transition to golf, guided by professional Dick Morley, saw her win the Rhodesian title for the first time in 1948. Her final national title came twenty years later, at fifty-eight, and she claimed her last provincial title at the age of sixty-eight.

Tomlinson's legacy extends beyond her playing career. She served as president of the Rhodesia Ladies' Golf Union for over a decade, contributed to the Mashonaland Ladies Golf Association, and captained the ladies' section at Royal Salisbury. Her extensive collection of cups, medals, and trophies reflects a career filled with triumphs, and her competitive spirit and dedication to golf have left an indelible mark on the sport's history in Rhodesia. Gaby Tomlinson's name will forever be associated with excellence and commitment in Southern African golf recognised by being selected for induction into the Southern Africa Golf Hall of Fame.

TORRENS, LT. GENERAL SIR HENRY D'OYLEY (1833–1889)
UNITED KINGDOM

Lieutenant-General Sir Henry D'Oyley Torrens was a distinguished British Army officer and colonial governor, remembered for his contributions to golf in both South Africa and Malta. Born in Meerut, India, he later became the Governor of Cape Colony in 1886 and the Governor of Malta in 1888.

A passionate golfer, Torrens was instrumental in the establishment of two historic golf clubs: the Royal Cape Golf Club in 1886 and the Royal Malta Golf Club in 1888. His role in founding these clubs left a lasting legacy on the golfing communities of both regions.

The Royal Cape Golf Course, situated on the slopes of Table Mountain in the Western Cape, is one of South Africa's most historic courses, boasting over 100 years of golf. Shortly after Torrens arrived in Cape Town in 1885, he gathered local citizens to establish the Cape Golf Club. They laid out a 9-hole course on Waterloo Green in Wynberg (later moved to Rondebosch Common), and held their first monthly medal contest in 1886. A photograph commemorating this historic event, with Torrens driving off, still hangs in the clubhouse today. The General himself won the inaugural contest with a gross score of 94.

TRELOAR, KEN NORTHERN RHODESIA, FEDERATION

Gordon Bunting and Ken Treloar

Ken Treloar's illustrious golfing career stands as a testament to his skill and dedication to the sport. A left-handed golfer from Northern Rhodesia, Treloar's remarkable achievements from 1945 to 1957 showcase his dominance in amateur golf. His prowess earned him the nomination for Sportsman of the Year in 1956, and he was a key figure in various teams, including the 1957 and 1960 Federation teams, as well as the 1958

Central African Team. He earned numerous caps for Northern Rhodesia from 1948, highlighting his long-standing commitment to the sport.

Treloar's amateur record is both extensive and impressive. He reached the semi-finals of the South African Amateur in 1952 and secured a notable 16th place in the 1952 South African Open. His success extended to international tournaments, with semi-final appearances in the Craw's Nest Tassie at Carnoustie in 1954. His achievements in the Federation Amateur were particularly noteworthy, with victories in 1948, 1951, 1957, 1958, and 1960, and a second-place finish in 1955. He also excelled in Southern Rhodesia tournaments, winning the South Rhodesia Amateur in 1948, 1951, and 1960, and clinching the South Rhodesia Open in 1964.

Treloar's dominance continued in Northern Rhodesia, where he won the title in 1946, 1947, 1948, 1950, 1952, and 1959, with additional second-place finishes in 1945, 1951, 1954, 1956, and 1966. His victories in the Central African Amateur (1961, 1962, 1964) and the Belgian Congo Amateur (1958) further illustrate his exceptional talent. Treloar also won the Mashonaland Amateur in 1953 and was victorious in the Copperbelt Amateur on multiple occasions. His competitive edge was evident in his performances at the Champion of Champions (1965, 1966), and he earned notable finishes in events like the Cock o' North and the Katanga Amateur.

Treloar's skill was particularly evident in his match play against touring teams. In 1947, he defeated Glennie, and in 1955, he bested B. Locke with impressive rounds of 67. Treloar, alongside his partner Bradfield, triumphed over Dai Rees and K. Bousfield, and later secured victories in 1957 and 1959 against strong opposition including Springboks and international players like Gary Player and Henning. His performance in the 1960 Federation team, which finished 8th in the Eisenhower Trophy, further solidified his reputation as a top golfer.

Following his relocation to Cape Town, Treloar set the amateur course record at Clovelly with a remarkable 65. In 1967, he was selected for the Western Province Team, where he partnered with Gordon Bunting in the Inter-Provincial competition. His contributions to Southern African golf were recognized with his induction into the Southern Africa Golf Hall of Fame under a new category.

Ken Treloar's legacy is marked by his exceptional achievements in amateur golf, his impressive record against top international players, and his significant contributions to the sport. His career highlights reflect a dedication and skill that have left an enduring impact on Southern African golf.

TSHABALALA, VINCENT (1942-2017) UNION SOUTH AFRICA – APARTHEID

Vincent Vesele Tshabalala's career is a remarkable story of talent, perseverance, and resilience in the face of racial adversity. Designated as "Coloured" under the Apartheid racial classification scheme, Tshabalala was barred from participating in the Southern African Tour during the 1970s and 1980s, a time when he was at the peak of his golfing prowess. Despite these barriers, his skill and determination allowed him to make a significant impact both locally and internationally.

In 1976, Tshabalala achieved a landmark victory at the French Open, a triumph that was particularly notable given the political climate of the time. Playing with a caddy-cart he pulled himself, Tshabalala finished the tournament with a stunning performance, overcoming a three-stroke deficit to Salvador Balbuena with a final round of 67, totaling 16-under and winning by two strokes. This victory was a testament to his exceptional ability and tenacity.

The following month, Tshabalala faced a critical decision when he was selected to represent South Africa alongside Gary Player in the World Cup. He chose to decline the selection, citing political motivations behind the offer and the lack of genuine merit in the choice, as he had not qualified for selection. This decision led to Brian Henning, chairman of the SA PGA, rejecting Tshabalala's entry to the South African Open, a move that catalyzed Tshabalala to establish the Bantu Golf Union.

His career, unfortunately, suffered a setback due to an injury, limiting his competitive play. However, Tshabalala made a notable comeback in the senior ranks, finishing in the top 20 on the European Senior Tour Order of Merit four times during the 1990s. His career achievements include 17 professional wins and multiple second-place finishes. His notable victories include the South African Non-European Open in 1965, 1971, 1977, and 1983, as well as the Western Province Non-European Open in 1963, and the Natal Non-European Open in 1971 and 1972.

In addition to his domestic successes, Tshabalala managed to compete in some 'white' tournaments later in his career. He placed 5th in the 1976 South African Masters, 7th in the Sumrie-Bournemouth Better-Ball, and 8th in the Rhodesian Dunlop Masters. He also participated in The Open in 1977 and finished 56th. His performance continued to be strong as a senior, with notable finishes including 3rd in the J&B All African Classic in 1994 and 2nd in the 1997 Kenya Open at the age of 55.

Tshabalala's leadership extended beyond the golf course. In 1990, he served as captain of the South African Professional Golfers' Association (SAPGA) and played a crucial role in uniting the SAPGA and the Tournament Players Association (TPA). His advocacy for racial equality in golf was bold and significant, challenging the status quo and fighting for the rights of black golfers.

Despite the obstacles and challenges he faced, Vincent Tshabalala's contributions to golf and his role in advancing the rights of black golfers remain a pivotal part of Southern African golf history. His achievements, both on and off the course, earned him a well-deserved induction into the Southern Africa Golf Hall of Fame in 2010, cementing his legacy as a trailblazer and a champion of equality in the sport.

TURNER, BRIAN RHODESIA

Brian Turner made significant contributions to amateur golf in Rhodesia and South Africa, showcasing his talent across multiple tournaments and earning recognition as a top amateur golfer. His involvement in prestigious teams and consistent performances highlight his distinguished career.

Brian Turner was another golfer who had an excellent amateur career during Rhodesia's golden era. His achievements included being 1966 Eisenhower trophy – reserve; 1968 Eisenhower Cup team; 1970 Eisenhower Cup team – cancelled; Rhodesia 1972, 1973, 1978. After relocating to South Africa he was 1974 Springbok team – reserve

His amateur record reads: Nu Way Open 1967; 1968 Rhodesian Amateur; Matabeleland Amateur 1968; Rhodesia Dunlop Masters 1969 1972 leading amateur; 1972 SA Amateur 1972, 74 Quarter-finals; Natal Champion of Champions 1976, 2nd 1972 1977; Transvaal Amateur Stroke-Play 1973; South Coast Amateur 1974 Natal Amateur 1974, 1975; Natal Stroke Play 1978, 1979; Zululand 1978; and the N Coast Stroke Play 1982

V

VAN ASWEGEN, TYRONE (1982) SOUTH AFRICA

Tyrone Frank van Aswegen played in college at Oklahoma City University from 2000 to 2004, where he was a three-time NAIA All-American, led OCU to four NAIA team championships, and won seven times, including the 2002 individual national title and was inducted into the NAIA Hall of Fame.

He turned pro in 2004 after graduation, and began playing on the Sunshine Tour where he won twice in 2008, and finished a career-best seventh on the Order of Merit in 2009. After three seasons on the Web.com Tour, van Aswegen earned his PGA Tour card for the first time at the inaugural 2013 Web.com Tour Finals.

His best finish on the PGA Tour was a T-3 at the 2015 Frys.com Open. His best finish on the Web.com Tour was a T-3 at the 2009 Soboba Classic. In all he had three professional wins. He lost three playoffs.

Tyrone van Aswegen had a notable career with significant achievements both as an amateur and professional golfer. His success on the Sunshine Tour and Web.com Tour, combined with his strong performance on the PGA Tour, highlights his skill and dedication to the sport.

VAN DEN BERG, ULRICH (1975) SOUTH AFRICA

Ulrich van den Berg had a successful amateur career which peaked in 1997 when he won the South African Amateur Strokeplay Championship, the Transvaal Amateur, and the Western Province Strokeplay Championship. He turned professional in 1999 and joined the Sunshine Tour where he has several tournament victories on the tour, all on the less lucrative "Winter Swing". He had 7 professional wins and 3 playoff losses.

Ulrich van den Berg's career is marked by a strong amateur record and consistent performance on the Sunshine Tour, particularly during the less prominent winter season.

VAN DER WALT, TJAART (1974) SOUTH AFRICA

Vincent van der Walt's journey through professional golf is a testament to his skill, perseverance, and dedication to the sport. His story began with a significant opportunity when he received a golf scholarship to study at Central Alabama Community College in the United States. This educational experience was a crucial stepping stone in his career, setting the stage for his future successes.

Turning professional in 1996, van der Walt immediately made his mark by joining the Sunshine Tour in South Africa. His dedication to the game quickly became apparent, and in 2004, he expanded his horizons by joining the PGA Tour. His time on the PGA Tour was highlighted by a notable performance in 2005 when he came close to victory at the Buick Championship, ultimately losing in a playoff to Brad Faxon.

After his stint on the PGA Tour, van der Walt shifted his focus to the Nationwide Tour in 2007, where he continued to demonstrate his golfing prowess. His consistent performances included recording a third runner-up finish before returning to South Africa. His career took a new turn in 2011 when he qualified for the Asian Tour. On the Asian Tour, he achieved significant milestones, including a runner-up finish at the ISPS Handa Singapore Classic and earning the title of Asian Tour Rookie of the Year.

Van der Walt's achievements continued to grow as he competed on the European Tour, where he finished as the runner-up at the Africa Open in early 2012, narrowly missing out on victory to Louis Oosthuizen. His perseverance and skill were ultimately rewarded in 2013 when he won the Lion of Africa Cape Town Open on the Sunshine Tour. This victory was particularly significant, marking his first professional win after seventeen years of competing at the highest levels.

In addition to his achievements on the golf course, van der Walt has made notable contributions to the sport through his role in the management side of the industry. In 2017, he co-founded AnchorUp Sports, an exclusive talent management agency for top golfers. As the managing director of the company, he has continued to influence the golf world, working with some of the sport's most elite players.

Van der Walt's career is characterized by a series of impressive runner-up finishes across various tours, including the Sunshine Tour, Nationwide Tour, PGA Tour, European Tour, and Asian Tour. His long-awaited victory in 2013 was a testament to his enduring talent and determination. Through his achievements on the course and his role in talent management, van der Walt has left an indelible mark on the world of golf.

VAN RENSBURG, NICO (1966) SOUTH AFRICA

Nicholas Marthinus van Rensburg has won six times on the Sunshine Tour between 1989 and 2005, three times on the Asian PGA Tour, and a total of 9 professional wins. He won his first Sunshine Tour event in 1989 and has played consistently on tour ever since. He maintained a steady presence on the Sunshine Tour throughout his career.

VAN ROOYEN, ERIK (1990) SOUTH AFRICA

Frederik van Rooyen currently plays on the PGA Tour, where he has won twice on the PGA Tour, as well as once on the European Tour, with 7 professional wins.

As an amateur he won the 2012 Minnesota State Amateur. The following year Van Rooyen turned professional. He has played on the Sunshine Tour since turning professional and had his first win on the tour in early 2017, the Eye of Africa PGA Championship, making a birdie at the first extra hole in a three-man playoff. During 2017 he played on the 2017 Challenge Tour where he had his second professional win, the Hainan Open. A number of other good finishes, including fourth place in the Kazakhstan Open and a tie for third in the season-ending NBO Golf Classic Grand Final, put van Rooyen third in the Challenge Tour Race to Oman rankings, earning a card for the 2018 European Tour season.

In December 2017, he won the Eye of Africa PGA Championship, and he was runner-up in the Joburg Open, three strokes behind Shubhankar Sharma. He led the 2018 Dubai Duty Free Irish Open by four strokes after three rounds, but a final round 74 dropped him into a tie for 4th place.

Van Rooyen made a good start to 2019, finishing joint runner-up in the Commercial Bank Qatar Masters and the Hassan II Golf Trophy, and also had a top-10 finish in the 2019 PGA Championship, then he won his first European Tour title at the Scandinavian Invitation outside Gothenburg, Sweden. He sank a 12 feet birdie putt on the finishing par 5 72nd hole, to win by a stroke with a new tournament record 261 on the par 70 course. After he tied for third at the WGC-Mexico Championship in February 2020, he advanced to a career best 40th on the Official World Golf Ranking.

In August 2021, he won his first PGA Tour event at the Barracuda Championship, breaking the tournament scoring record by shooting a total of 50 points (modified stableford) over four rounds. In November 2023, he won the 2023 World Wide Technology Championship for his first PGA Tour win in over two years. He made a putt for an eagle on the par-5 18th hole on Sunday to win. In the last round, van Rooyen played the back nine in 8-under 28 as part of a 9-under 63, two strokes ahead of Matt Kuchar and Camilo Villegas.

VAN TONDER, DANIEL (1991) SOUTH AFRICA

Daniel van Tonder's career in professional golf is marked by notable achievements and a consistent display of skill across both the Sunshine Tour and the European Tour. Turning professional in 2011, van Tonder quickly made an impression by earning the Sunshine Tour's Rookie of the Year title in 2012. This early recognition set the stage for what would become a distinguished career.

On the Sunshine Tour, van Tonder's talent was evident from the start. In 2014, he secured two significant victories, winning the Investec Royal Swazi Open and the Vodacom Origins of Golf at Euphoria. These wins demonstrated his ability to compete at a high level and laid the foundation for further success. His prowess continued into 2019 when he claimed the Mopani Redpath Greendoor Logistics Zambia Open, further establishing his reputation on the tour.

The year 2020 was particularly remarkable for van Tonder, as he achieved an impressive four tournament victories on the Sunshine Tour within just a three-month span. This period of dominance highlighted his exceptional form and competitiveness in the sport.

Van Tonder's success extended beyond the Sunshine Tour when he joined the European Tour. In March 2021, he celebrated his first European Tour victory at the Kenya Savannah Classic. A memorable birdie putt on the final hole secured his place in a playoff, where he emerged victorious against Jazz Janewattananond. This win marked a significant milestone in his career and showcased his ability to perform under pressure.

His strong performances continued into April 2021, where he narrowly missed out on another victory, losing in a four-man playoff for the Limpopo Championship. However, he rebounded with a major triumph later that year. In December 2021, van Tonder won the prestigious SA Open Championship, the Sunshine Tour's flagship event, with a final-round 65 that secured a narrow one-shot victory over Oliver Bekker.

Throughout his career, van Tonder has amassed a total of ten professional wins, underscoring his consistent excellence and competitiveness. His achievements across both the Sunshine Tour and the European Tour highlight his skill and dedication to the sport, establishing him as a prominent figure in professional golf.

VAN VUUREN, STEVE (1959) SOUTH AFRICA

Stephen Daniel van Vuuren enjoyed a successful career in professional golf, with notable achievements on the Sunshine Tour and beyond. He turned professional in 1981 and soon began to make his mark in the golfing world. By 1995, van Vuuren was making waves on the SA Winter Tour, where he clinched the Order of Merit title, showcasing his skill and consistency.

His affiliation with the Sunshine Tour began in 1993, setting the stage for some of his most remarkable achievements. The 1995-96 season was a standout period in his career. During this season, van Vuuren secured four victories, demonstrating his exceptional form and competitive edge. His impressive performance throughout the year also earned him a commendable 7th place on the Order of Merit.

Overall, van Vuuren amassed a total of six wins on the Sunshine Tour, contributing to a total of twelve professional victories throughout his career. His accomplishments, particularly during the standout 1995-96 season, highlight his significant skill and competitiveness in professional golf.

VAN ZYL, JACO (1979) SOUTH AFRICA

Jaco Phillipus van Zyl has built an impressive career in professional golf, marked by a blend of significant achievements on both the Sunshine Tour and the European Tour. His journey began with notable amateur success, including winning the South African Amateur Championship in 2000, which set the stage for his professional endeavours.

Turning professional in 2001, van Zyl quickly made his mark on the Sunshine Tour. He secured his first win at the Platinum Classic in 2005, and his career took off from there. In 2009, he enjoyed a standout season, capturing the Telkom PGA Championship among his three victories that year, and finishing 4th on the Order of Merit. The following year, 2010, saw him add four more Sunshine Tour victories to his tally, showcasing his dominance on the tour.

Van Zyl also achieved notable success on the European Tour. His 2011 season was marked by five top-10 finishes, including a narrow playoff loss at the Trophée Hassan II to David Horsey. His performance continued to impress, culminating in a runner-up finish at the Turkish Airlines Open in November 2015, where he was just one shot shy of victory behind Victor Dubuisson. By February 2016, he had reached the top 50 in the Official World Golf Ranking, a testament to his rising stature in the sport.

A highlight of his European Tour career came in January 2017 when he lost in a sudden-death playoff at the Commercial Bank Qatar Masters to Wang Jeung-hun. Despite the close call, van Zyl's career continued to shine.

In September 2022, van Zyl achieved a significant milestone by winning the Gary & Vivienne Player Challenge, his first victory in over six years, finishing two shots ahead of Hennie Otto. This win added to his impressive tally of 16 professional victories.

Overall, van Zyl's career is characterised by consistent performance on the Sunshine Tour, notable achievements on the European Tour, and a resilient comeback, demonstrating his enduring skill and competitiveness in professional golf.

VAUGHAN, BRADFORD (1975) SOUTH AFRICA

Bradford Vaughan's golf career is distinguished by notable achievements and a versatile performance across different tours. His journey in golf began with significant success in the amateur ranks. Vaughan claimed the South African Amateur Championship in 1994, showcasing his talent early on. Additionally, he represented South Africa in the Eisenhower Trophy, further establishing his presence in the golfing world.

Turning professional in 1995, Vaughan quickly made an impact on the Sunshine Tour. He secured eight tournament victories throughout his career, demonstrating consistent excellence and competitiveness on the tour. His success on the Sunshine Tour was complemented by his participation in various European Tour events. Vaughan competed on the Challenge Tour and played in several European Tour events, where he experienced a notable playoff loss.

Overall, Vaughan's career reflects a strong performance on the Sunshine Tour and a commendable presence in European golf, underscoring his versatility and skill as a professional golfer.

VERNON, MRS A E (ORMSBY) UNION SOUTH AFRICA

Mrs. Vernon made a significant mark in South African and international golf with her impressive achievements.

A report from the SA Ladies Championship, 1934 went as follows: The further victory of Mrs Vernon in the SA Championship, in which she defeated Mrs Witherow (O.F.S. Champion) at Maccauvlei, must remind every golfer in the land of her splendid record. Mrs. Vernon had what was probably her first big success in the Irish Championship of 1909 at Lahinch, Co. Clare, when she beat Miss V. Hezlet in the final. The two Hezlet girls were at the top of their cycle of successes at the time, and Miss Ormsby's (Mrs. Vernon's maiden name) victory brought her into the forefront of golfers immediately.

Mrs. Vernon had not been in South Africa very long before she won the W. P. Championship, her victories in all totaling three, in 1920, 1921, 1922. Her first S.A. title was won at Wynberg in 1921, the other wins coming in 1925 (Rapenburg), 1926 (Durban C.C.), and now in 1934 at Maccauvlei. Her five Transvaal Championship victories were scored in 1927 and three following years, and again in 1930 at E.R.P.M.

And now, Sid Brews having set the fashion for golf "doubles", Mrs. Vernon, redoubtable member of the Royal Johannesburg Club, has brought off one of the best. In March 1934 at E.R.P.M. she won the Transvaal Championship for the fifth time and at Maccaudei at the beginning of this month she crowned herself national champion for the fourth time.

The previous year Miss Angela Burwell held the South African, Western Province and Royal Cape Championships at the same time so that "Vernie's" success is hardly a record, but everyone will "joy" with her on a very fine performance. No doubt permission will have to be obtained to say that Mrs. Vernon is - well, in the semi-final against Miss Betty Frost, the brilliant young player of Port Elizabeth, there was 34 years difference between the ages of the contestants.

Her success in both the South African and international circuits, including her impressive double victories, solidified her legacy in the sport. Mrs. Vernon was recognized for her contributions to golf by being inducted into the Southern Africa Golf Hall of Fame.

VERWEY, BOBBY (1941) SOUTH AFRICA

Frank Robert Verwey is notable for his impressive golf career and contributions to the sport: He is the son of former South African PGA champion Jock Verwey, and Gary Player's brother-in-law. As a junior, he won the Prentice Memorial three times in the 1950's, and as a junior never lost a stroke play tournament, whilst he won the Transvaal Amateur 1959, 2nd 1959, and 2nd in the German Amateur.

He won the 1962 German Open and the 1965 Almaden Open Invitational on the PGA Tour. He was a member of the European Tour from 1978 - 1980, and he won several professional tournaments in his home country and represented South Africa in the World Cup in 1978 and 1980.

On the PGA Tour he only had 1 win, the 1965 Almaden Open Invitational, but plenty of top-10 finishes including: Canadian Open 3^{rrd} 1962 (4th major at that time); Oklahoma Open 2nd 1964; San Jose Alma Den Classic 1965; Minnestota Classic 2nd 1967; Transkei Independence Invitational 1976; Sun City Classic 2nd 1980; 3rd European Open, Martini Open; Finished Top 4 in two Dutch Opens; 1st Engadine Open, Switzerland '60's; 1st Ramstine Airforce Base, Germany; and 3rd British Masters, Little Aston.

Other victories include the Natal Open 1963, 1964, 2nd; Cock 'o North 2nd 1963, Transvaal Open 1965, 1968, 2nd 1961, 1965, 1969; Western Province (3) 1963, 1968, 2nd 1961; Pepsi Open 1968; Transkei Open 1975; and the SA Open 2nd 1976

On the European Senior Tour he had 6 wins including the 1991 Senior British Open Championship. In 2018 he was selected for induction into the Southern Africa Golf Hall of Fame.

He was a regular on the European Seniors Tour for the first few years after its establishment in 1992, and finished in the top ten on the Order of Merit four times. Achievements include representing South Africa in the World Cup 1978, 1980, Captained the PGA, Nominated for induction into the Southern Africa Golf Hall of Fame Inductee.

Bobby Verwey's career is distinguished by his successes both in South Africa and internationally, with significant achievements on both the regular and senior tours.

VERWEY, JOCK UNION SOUTH AFRICA

Jock Verwey was a prominent South African golfer whose career spanned both amateur and professional achievements. In the early 1930s, Verwey made his mark by finishing as the runner-up in the South African Open in consecutive years, 1934 and 1935. His impressive performances in these tournaments earned him the Freddie Tait Trophy in both years, which is awarded to the leading amateur golfer in the South African Open.

Transitioning to professional golf, Verwey continued to showcase his talent. He enjoyed considerable success in the Lexington PGA, securing victories in 1948, 1949, and 1954. These wins highlighted his skill and consistency in the professional ranks.

Jock Verwey remains a significant figure in South African golf history, remembered for his achievements both as an amateur and a professional. His contributions to the sport have left a lasting legacy.

VINCENT, KIERAN (1997) ZIMBABWE

Kieran Vincent (Scott's younger brother) played college golf at Liberty University in Virginia, where he was Big South Conference Rookie of the Year in 2017. He currently plays on the Asian Tour and the LIV Golf. He wonthe 2023 International Series Vietnam from four shots back to overtake overnight leader Takumi Kanaya. He carded a six-under 66 to finish on 19-under overall, one shot ahead of Anirban Lahiri and Kevin Yuan. He also won the 2024 Kit Kat Cash & Carry Pro-Am by 4 strokes on the Sunshine Tour.

VINCENT, SCOTT NICHOLAS (1992) ZIMBABWE

Scott Nicholas Vincent, nicknamed Mhondoro (lion), plays on the LIV Golf Series. He has won three times on the Japan Golf Tour. In 2022 he won the International Series England on the Asian Tour, as well as the International Series Order of Merit. He represented Zimbabwe in the 2018 World Cup of Golf and the 2020 Tokyo Summer Olympics, being the first Zimbabwean golfer to do so, and presently has a Wold Ranking of 78, and (5) Professional wins.

Vincent turned professional in 2015. After five runner-up finishes on the Asian Tour between 2016 and 2018, he finally got his first major tour victory at the 2021 Sansan KBC Augusta on the Japan Golf Tour. He also won the ANA Open three weeks later shooting a 65 in the final round. In May 2022, Vincent won the Gateway to The Open Mizuno Open, beating Anthony Quayle in a playoff. A week later, Vincent won the International Series England at Slaley Hall in Northumberland, England carding a final-round 66 to win by one shot over Travis Smyth and claimed his first Asian Tour victory.

Vincent's International Series England win gave him the status to play in the 2022 LIV Golf Invitational Series. He played on three different teams before becoming a regular on Joaquín Niemann's Torque GC. In December 2022, Vincent won the Asian Tour's International Series Order of Merit. In 2023 LIV Golf League, Vincent finished in the top-24 in the individual standings to earn a spot for 2024. His younger brother; Kieran, is also a professional golfer.

VINCENT, DR VANE MOZAMBIQUE

Dr. Vane Vincent was a renowned figure in golf course design, leaving a lasting impact with his work both in South Africa and internationally. His collaboration with Gary Player on numerous projects helped shape the design of several notable golf courses around the world.

In South Africa, Dr. Vincent's influence can be seen in a range of courses, including Rand Mines, White River, Fourways, and Middleburg. He also made his mark on Muizenburg, Boksburg, Pretoria, Pretoria West, Steelpoort, Richards Bay, Port Elizabeth, and Mdantsane, each reflecting his commitment to creating challenging and aesthetically pleasing golf experiences.

Beyond South Africa, Dr. Vincent's design expertise extended to international courses such as Elephant Hills in Zimbabwe, Noto Fuji Challenge and Hiroshima in Japan, St. Geran in Mauritius, Nossi Be in Madagascar, and Orapa in Botswana. These projects showcase his global influence and dedication to enhancing the game of golf through thoughtful and innovative course design.

VON RUBEN, TANDI (MCCULLUM) (1986) SOUTH AFRICA

Tandi McCallum turned professional in 2008 after winning six national amateur tournaments. She secured her first professional victory at the 2009 South African Women's Open. McCallum was the runner-up at the 2010 Women's Indian Open and the 2012 Lalla Meryem Cup. At the Hero Honda Women's Indian Open in 2010, she was part of a 4-way playoff, ultimately losing to Laura Davies. In 2012, she tied for second at the Lalla Meryem Cup alongside Marianne Skarpnord, three strokes behind Karen Lunn. That same year, she finished tied fourth at the South African Women's Open, just two strokes behind Caroline Masson, and ended the season ranked 50th in the LET Order of Merit, her career best.

In 2014, McCallum left the LET to join the Sunshine Ladies Tour, where she won the Sun International Ladies Challenge and finished third in the inaugural Order of Merit, behind Lee-Anne Pace and Monique Smit. She was the runner-up at the 2017 Dimension Data Ladies Challenge, 2018 and 2019 Investec Royal Swazi (Ladies), 2019 Joburg Ladies Open, and 2020 SuperSport Ladies Challenge. She has three professional wins to date.

W

WALKER, ARTHUR "KING" UNION SOUTH AFRICA

'King' Arthur Walker was a dominant figure in South African amateur golf during the late 1950s. Representing South Africa from 1957 to 1959, Walker was renowned as the best bunker player of his era. His remarkable tournament record solidified his legacy, earning him the Springbok title in 1957, 1958, and 1960. He was also nominated for the 1958 Sportsman of the Year and served as President of the Southern Transvaal Golf Union from 1970 to 1971.

Walker's most significant achievements include winning the South African Amateur Championship in 1959, with runner-up finishes in 1956 and 1958. He also claimed the Proudfoot Trophy in 1958 as the leading qualifier. Internationally, Walker was part of the South African team that won the Commonwealth Tournament and made headlines by winning the English Amateur in 1957, despite some adverse comments due to his South African accent. His English parentage qualified him for the tournament, where he also reached the semi-finals of the British Amateur that same year.

His other notable victories include the Free State Amateur in 1950, the Transvaal Amateur in 1957 and 1958, the Natal Amateur in 1954, 1956, and 1958, the Transvaal Stroke Play in 1956, the Orange Free State Amateur in 1956 and 1957, the Silver Vase in 1956, 1957, and 1958, the Eastern Transvaal Amateur from 1955 to 1958, the Western Transvaal in 1956 and 1958, the Maccauvlei Open Match Play in 1956 and 1957, and the Vaal Amateur in 1962 and 1963. He was also the leading amateur in three professional tournaments from 1957 to 1962.

Walker had several runner-up finishes, including in the Mills 1000 Guineas Amateur (1952), Mozambique Amateur (1955), Swaziland Amateur (1955), Mashonaland Amateur (1956), and Vaal Amateur (1959). Later in his career, he won the South African Senior Amateur in 1977, 1978, and 1980, further cementing his legacy in South African golf.

WALTMAN, RETIEF (1939) SOUTH AFRICA

Retief Waltman was a brilliant young South African golfer who, at the peak of his career, made the extraordinary decision to walk away from the sport. Known as the heir apparent to Gary Player, Waltman's story is one of faith over fame. Despite his remarkable talent and potential to become a superstar, Waltman chose a path of spiritual fulfillment, finding meaning in the Bible rather than in birdies.

In 1964, after narrowly missing the cut at his first Masters with rounds of 72 and 78, Waltman decided he had had enough. At just 25 years old, he packed up his bags, handed ovr his clubs to fellow golfer Dave Thomas, and left the game behind. His decision shocked the golf world, as he had already won the South African Open twice, an impressive feat considering legends like Bobby Locke and Gary Player had dominated the tournament during that era.

Waltman was a hero in his homeland, and his impact was so profound that a young boy from Pietersburg was named in his honor—Retief Goosen, who would go on to become a golfing great himself. Waltman idolized Ben Hogan, often wearing a flat white cap as a tribute to Hogan, who he considered the greatest golfer of all time. Waltman fondly remembered playing alongside Hogan at the Dallas Open, where Hogan shot a 67 to Waltman's 72.

Henry Longhurst, a noted golf writer, once commented on Waltman's deep faith, saying that Waltman sincerely believed he received divine help and guidance in winning, particularly in his victories at the South African Open. However, the materialism and relentless focus on money in professional golf eventually disillusioned him. Unlike many who threatened to quit, Waltman quietly and resolutely walked away from the game.

As a professional, Waltman represented South Africa in the Canada Cup in 1961 and 1963. His notable victories included winning the Cock o' the North in 1958 and 1961, the South African Open in 1961 and 1963, and the Dutch Open in 1963. He also had several runner-up finishes, including in the South African Dunlop (1960, 1963), the South African Masters, and the Woodlawn International in 1963. Waltman retired from professional golf in 1964, dedicating his life to missionary work, during which he survived three knife attacks.

Retief Waltman's story is a testament to his unwavering faith and his belief in living a life with purpose beyond the fairways.

WARRINGTON, WENDY SOUTH AFRICA

Warrington's journey in golf began with her representing the Junior Springboks in 1976, and she went on to earn Springbok and Protea colors, showcasing her prowess in various prestigious tournaments from 1985 to 2012. Her impressive international career took her across Europe and beyond, playing in countries such as France, Switzerland, Belgium, Austria, Scotland, Ireland, Wales, Nigeria, Kenya, Hong Kong, Taiwan, and Canada. She also competed in significant events like the World Cup in Chile and the Commonwealth Games in Australia.

Wendy Warrington and Bobby Cole

Her golfing achievements are numerous. She clinched the South African Women's Stroke Play Championship in 1988 and won the South African Women's Championship four times— in 1985, 1986, 1998, and 1999. Notably, she was the runner-up in the 1982 edition of the South African Women's Championship. Warrington's success extended to winning the All Africa individual title, numerous Provincial Championships, and the Clovelly Club Championships an impressive 30 times.

Moreover, her legacy was further solidified when she was part of the triumphant team at the All Africa Challenge Trophy in 1994, marking her as one of South Africa's top female golfers. Her career, distinguished by her skill, consistency, and sportsmanship, remains an inspiring chapter in the history of South African golf, recognised by being inducted into the Southern Africa Golf Hall of Fame.

WATERMEYER, CHRISTIAN UNION SOUTH AFRICA

Christian Watermeyer had a commendable amateur golf career, marked by several significant achievements. He won the South African Amateur Championship in 1947 and finished as the runner-up in 1948. His success extended to regional competitions as well, where he claimed victory in the Western Province Amateur Championship multiple times, winning in 1933, 1934, 1935, and 1939. Additionally, Watermeyer was part of the

Transvaal B team that competed in the Inter-Centre team events in 1949 and 1953, further demonstrating his consistent performance in the sport.

WATERMEYER, (CHIEF JUSTICE) H.E. JACK

Chief Justice H.E. Jack Watermeyer was a highly influential figure in South African golf, both as an administrator and a player. His contributions to the sport earned him induction into the Southern Africa Golf Hall of Fame. Watermeyer made a significant impact as an administrator, serving as the Vice-President of the South African Golf Union (SAGU) from 1959 to 1960, President from 1962 to 1963, and as the Honorary President of the South African Professional Golfers' Association (SAPGA) in 1962. He also held the position of President of the Western Province Golf Union (WPGU), was a Springbok team member and manager in 1947, and served on the SAGU Executive and as a selector in 1958.

In addition to his administrative achievements, Watermeyer had an impressive amateur golf career. He won the South African Amateur Championship in 1940 and was the runner-up in 1934. His success in regional tournaments included victories in the Western Province Amateur Championship in 1946 and 1949, with second-place finishes in 1934, 1935, and 1939. He also finished second in the South Western Districts (SWD) Amateur Championship in 1939 and the Western Province Open in 1938. Watermeyer's legacy in South African golf is marked by both his on-course accomplishments and his leadership in advancing the sport.

WATERS, LAURIE TRANSVAAL REPUBLIC, UNION SOUTH AFRICA, RHODESIA

Laurence Buddo Waters played a key role in shaping the development of golf in Southern Africa, blending his skills as a golfer, club maker, and course designer into a pioneering career that spanned more than four decades. Starting as a schoolboy caddie for Hugh Kirkaldy at St Andrews in Scotland, Waters was apprenticed under Old Tom Morris, a legendary figure in golf. However, health concerns prompted his move to warmer climates, ultimately leading him to South Africa, where his influence on the game became profound.

In 1898, Waters was appointed the professional at Johannesburg Golf Club, a role he held for over 20 years. With a modest salary of 15 pounds per month, he undertook a wide range of duties, from making and repairing clubs to tending the bar, giving lessons, maintaining the course, and even introducing innovative features like the first grass tee used in the Transvaal. His design of the new course at Orange Grove laid the groundwork for what would later become the West Course at the Royal Johannesburg & Kensington Golf Club, a testament to his lasting impact on the region's golfing landscape.

Waters' talents were not confined to the workshop or course maintenance—he was also a highly skilled golfer. His achievements include winning the South African Open four times (in 1903, 1904, 1907, and 1920) and securing three Transvaal Open titles. Waters also consulted on the design of other courses as golf grew in popularity across Southern Africa.

After leaving Johannesburg, he spent 17 years as the professional at Royal Salisbury Golf Club in Rhodesia, where he continued to influence the game. His dedication to golf, both as a player and a professional, cemented his legacy as a foundational figure in the sport's development in the region.

WATSON, DENIS (1955) RHODESIA, SOUTH AFRICA

Denis Leslie Watson, a prominent figure in golf, began his career in the early 1970s amidst a tumultuous period in Rhodesian history, serving in the Rhodesian military during what he described as a "terrorist war." Despite the challenges, Watson excelled in golf, representing Rhodesia at the 1974 Eisenhower Trophy in the Dominican Republic alongside Mark McNulty, George Harvey, and Teddy Webber. The team finished 14th, with Watson emerging as the best scoring Rhodesian player.

In August 1975, Watson and George Harvey represented Rhodesia at the Coupa El Rincon in Bogotá, Colombia, among 18 two-man nation teams. The Rhodesian team triumphed, finishing ten strokes ahead of Sweden, with Watson winning individually, posting a 7-under-par 281, five strokes ahead of Jan Rube of Sweden. For his outstanding achievements, Watson was awarded Rhodesian Sportsman of the Year in 1975. He later immigrated to South Africa to further his golf career and represented the

country at the World Series of Golf in 1980 and 1982.

Watson's international career took off when he successfully qualified for the PGA Tour at the 1981 PGA Tour Qualifying School, finishing in fourth place. In 1982, he quickly became a tournament contender in the U.S., finishing joint second in the Tallahassee Open and narrowly missing victory in a playoff with Jack Nicklaus and Tom Kite at the Bay Hill Classic. Despite being nearest on the first extra hole, it was Kite who holed from off the green to win. Watson continued to perform well, finishing second at the 1982 and 1984 Tallahassee Opens, and second at the 1983 Greater Greensboro Open.

The pinnacle of Watson's career came in 1984, a year in which he recorded victories at the Buick Open, NEC World Series of Golf, and the Panasonic Las Vegas Invitational, tying for the most wins on the PGA Tour that season and finishing fourth on the money list. He was also nominated for South African Sportsman of the Year. However, Watson's career was marred by a controversial ruling at the 1985 U.S. Open, where he finished tied for second. A two-stroke penalty, assessed after Watson waited too long for a putt to drop, 35 seconds instead of 10 seconds, ultimately cost him a chance to force a playoff. The rules were clear, even if the ball was moving. The ruling was later amended, but the decision prevented Watson from claiming the title, with Andy North eventually winning by one shot.

Tragedy struck later that year during the Goodyear Classic in South Africa when Watson, while hitting his ball out of the rough, struck a hidden tree stump, causing severe damage to his wrist, elbow, and neck. Despite winning the tournament, the injury required surgery, and he was initially told he might never play again. Although Watson made a comeback, he struggled to regain his previous form, managing a few notable finishes, including second place at the 1987 St. Jude Classic and the 1993 BC Open, before retiring towards the end of the 1990s.

After turning fifty, Watson joined the Champions Tour, where he began to rediscover his competitive form. In 2007, he won the Senior PGA Championship at Kiawah Island, a senior major, by two strokes over Argentina's Eduardo Romero. This victory marked his first win in 21 years, and he was subsequently voted the 2007 Champions Tour Rookie of the Year. Watson's resilience and determination throughout his career left an indelible mark on the world of golf.

WEBBER, TEDDY (1951) RHODESIA

Edward Arthur 'Teddy' Webber, a remarkable golfer from Umtali, Rhodesia, is renowned for his exceptional temperament and impressive achievements in the world of golf. His ability to remain calm under pressure complemented his golfing talent, marking him as a standout sportsman.

Webber's significant achievements began in earnest with his victory in the South African Amateur Match Play Championship in 1977. This win, notable as he was the first Rhodesian to secure the title, followed a standout year on the local circuit. He won the Rhodesian Amateur by an impressive eleven strokes and also claimed victories in the Mashonaland, Manicaland, and Midlands championships, as well as the Follow-the-Sun tournament at Triangle.

In 1978, Webber cemented his status as one of Southern Africa's premier golfers by winning the South African Amateur Match Play title for the second time, becoming the first player to achieve this feat. His performance at the Durban Country Club, where he defeated Etienne Groenewald 3 & 2, was particularly noteworthy given that he had recently completed an army call-up and was not in peak condition. George Blumberg, a respected figure in South African golf, praised Webber as "the most professional amateur in the business."

Webber's early career saw him winning the Rhodesian Junior Championship in 1968 and finishing as the runner-up to Mark McNulty in the Rhodesian Senior Championship in 1974. His representation of Rhodesia in the Eisenhower Trophy was significant, with the team finishing 13th in the Dominican Republic in 1974 and 5th in the world individual placings at Penina Golf Club, Portugal in 1976. His 1977 season was remarkable, with multiple titles and his first South African victory, beating Richter van Niekerk on the 37th hole at Bryanston Country Club.

In recognition of his outstanding achievements, Webber was named Rhodesian Sportsman of the Year in 1978, following his successful defense of the South African title. He was also a finalist for Golfer of the Year in 1977.

Later in 1978, Webber made the pivotal decision to turn professional. His debut on the Sunshine Circuit saw him finish 19th in the South African Professional Golf Association's Order of Merit. By March 1979, he had taken up the position of professional at Royal Salisbury Golf Club, where he applied his expertise and experience to benefit the club's members.

Webber's legacy is marked by his exceptional amateur career, professional success, and contributions to the sport, demonstrating both his golfing prowess and his admirable sportsmanship.

WESSELS, ROGER MARK (1961) SOUTH AFRICA

Roger Mark Wessels is a distinguished South African golfer whose career spanned several notable tours and achievements.

Wessels made his mark on the Southern Africa Tour, where he enjoyed considerable success. One of his most significant achievements was winning the South African PGA Championship in 1991, a testament to his skill and competitiveness in the region.

His talent extended beyond South Africa to the international stage. In 1994, he claimed the Canadian Masters title on the Canadian Tour, showcasing his ability to compete effectively on the North American circuit. That same year, he represented South Africa in the World Cup, further enhancing his international golfing credentials.

Wessels competed on the European Tour from 1995 to 2003. His standout performance came in 2000 when he finished 35th on the Order of Merit, reflecting his consistent and high-level play throughout the season.

In total, Wessels amassed 12 professional wins over the course of his career. After retiring from tournament golf at the end of 2003, he transitioned to a role as a teaching professional. In this capacity, he continues to share his expertise and passion for the game, contributing to the sport's development by mentoring and guiding aspiring golfers.

WESTBROOK, TERRY (1939) RHODESIA, SOUTH AFRICA

Terrence E. Westbrook lost his left hand's middle finger and a large portion of his left thumb in a childhood accident. Despite this he managed to become a professional golfer.

One of his earliest successes was at the 1963 Dunlop South African Masters where he finished joint runner-up, three behind Bruce Keyter. His first professional victories were at the Cock of the North tournament in Zambia where he won the event in 1966 and successfully defended the championship twice.

His best years were in the early 1970s. In February 1970, Westbrook finished runner-up at the South African Open, three behind England's

Tommy Horton. In January 1971, at the beginning of the 1970-71 season, Westbrook started the final round of the Natal Open tied with fellow South Africa golfers Bobby Cole and Simon Hobday. With a final round 68 (-4) he finished at 283 (-5) and defeated Cole by one. Later in the year, at the beginning of the 1971-72 season, Westbrook again won. Three back of England's Peter Oosterhuis at the beginning of the final round, Westbrook overcame him with a final round 69 (-3) to win the Schoeman Park Open by two.

In 1973 he recorded his highest finish on the European Tour, reaching the finals of the Piccadilly Medal, a medal match play event. He won his first four matches of the event then defeated compatriot Hugh Baiocchi on the 20th hole of the quarterfinals and Scottish club professional Alistair Thomson in the semi-final. Two years after defeating Peter Oosterhuis in South Africa, he would compete against the English star again in the final round, but he would not have as much luck in the final match, as Oosterhuis played excellently against Westbrook, shooting 67 (-6) to win easily by six strokes.

Westbrook accumulated a total of 5 professional victories over his career. His ability to succeed despite physical limitations remains an inspiring story in the world of golf.

WESTNER, WAYNE (1961-2017) SOUTH AFRICA

Wayne Brett Westner was a prominent figure in Southern African golf whose career was marked by notable achievements and a tragic end.

Westner's golfing prowess was evident through his significant victories on both the Southern Africa and European Tours. He claimed the South African Open title twice, in 1988 and 1991, and enjoyed additional success on the European Tour  with two wins. His most memorable triumph came in 1996 when he and Ernie Els won the World Cup of Golf held near Cape Town. The pair's performance was dominant, with Els winning the individual event and Westner finishing second, while their combined effort secured a resounding victory in the team event by 18 shots against the USA team of Steve Jones and Tom Lehman.

Westner also had notable successes in individual tournaments. In 1992, he reached the fourth hole of a sudden-death playoff at the Carroll's Irish Open, where he narrowly lost to Nick Faldo in a playoff. He bounced back from this defeat with a win at the 1993 Dubai Desert Classic. The following year, he secured the 1996 FNB Players Championship and was crowned the Sunshine Tour Order of Merit winner for the 1995/96 season. He had a world ranking of 40.

However, Westner's career faced a setback in 1998 during the Madeira Island Open. In a pre-tournament Pro-Am, he sustained a serious injury after falling from a height when a railway sleeper gave way. This injury, which involved torn ankle ligaments, limited his play for the rest of the season and ultimately hindered his recovery. Despite this, he continued to contribute to the sport when he relocated to Ireland in 1998 where he set up his own Wayne Westner Golf Academy in Celbridge, Co Kildare. Some 1100 students received lessons there before he returned to Durban in 2006.

In team golf, Westner represented South Africa in seven prestigious events. He competed in the Dunhill Cup in 1994 and 1996, and the World Cup in 1994, 1996 (where he and Els won), and 1997. He was also part of the Southern African team that won the Alfred Dunhill Challenge in 1995.

Westner's career was distinguished by 14 professional wins and significant contributions to golf education. Tragically, in 2017, Wayne Westner took his own life, a loss that deeply impacted the golfing community. His legacy is remembered for his competitive successes, contributions to the sport, and his lasting influence on aspiring golfers through his golf academy.

WHARTON-HOOD, DORIAN SOUTH AFRICA

Dorian Wharton-Hood was a highly accomplished amateur golfer and a significant contributor to golf administration in South Africa, leaving a lasting legacy in both areas.

In his golfing career, Wharton-Hood achieved notable success. In 1963, he won the Royal Johannesburg Silver Vase, defeating Dave Symons by a remarkable 11 shots and setting a record score of 68, 68 = 136. That same year, he showcased his prowess at the Richelieu Grand Prix, where he finished as the leading amateur with a score of 277 (65, 70, 71, 71), tying Bobby Locke's lowest amateur score from 1938.

Wharton-Hood's performance in the South African Amateur was impressive, particularly in 1964, when he was the runner-up after defeating three Springboks in successive rounds. He also reached the quarter-finals in 1965 and 1967. His victory at the 1964 WP Amateur Match Play further solidified his reputation. In the 1965 Inter-Club League, he played No. 1 for Royal Johannesburg in Southern Transvaal/ Transvaal, winning all 10 of his matches and defeating four Springboks.

In 1966, Wharton-Hood excelled in both match play and stroke play at the E.P. Amateur, setting a record score of 134 (69, 65). He continued his success in 1968 by winning the Natal Amateur Match Play. Despite being runner-up in the Natal Amateur in 1970 and 1974, he remained a prominent figure in South African amateur golf, also achieving notable finishes in the Natal Open.

Wharton-Hood's contributions extended beyond his personal achievements as he played on more teams than any other South African golfer from 1957 to 1993. His involvement in golf administration was equally impactful. From 1967 to 1974, he served on the Natal Nomads Committee, where he was Vice-Captain in 1968 and Captain in 1969. Later, from 1997 to 2000, he was actively involved with The River Club, serving as Vice-President in 1997, President from 1998 to 2000, and Director from 1998 onwards.

Dorian Wharton-Hood's legacy in golf is marked by his impressive amateur career and his extensive involvement in golf administration, contributing significantly to the growth and development of the sport in South Africa.

WILTSHIRE, MARK SOUTH AFRICA

Mark Wiltshire is a PGA Fellow Professional with over 40 years of involvement in the golfing world. His career includes an 11-year stint as a full-time touring professional, followed by roles as the Tournament & Operations Director for the Sunshine Tour in South Africa, where he coordinated major events like the 1995 World Cup of Golf at Erinvale. He also served as General Manager of the World of Golf, a pioneering golf theme park, where he introduced the first Gary Player Golf Academy in South Africa.

Following this, Wiltshire became the Director of Golf at Fancourt, overseeing The Links, Bramble Hill, and the Golf Teaching Academy. During his tenure, he helped organize key tournaments such as the 2003 Presidents Cup, the 2005 inaugural Women's World Cup of Golf, and the 2006 South African Airways Open. His initiatives at Fancourt included the formation of a junior program and a position on the board of the Ernie Els and Fancourt Foundation.

Wiltshire later founded MWG (Pty) Ltd., a company specializing in golf operations, course maintenance, design, and estate management, working on projects throughout Africa and as far as the Fiji Islands. MWG provides comprehensive management solutions for golf courses, including business plans, golf course design and construction, and golf estate management.

Notable projects include:

- Mont Choisy Golf Course (Mauritius): MWG was tasked with preparing the golf operations setup and business plan for this residential and commercial development.
- Humewood Golf Club (Port Elizabeth, South Africa): Wiltshire was responsible for turning around the club's financial health through strategic marketing and golf course management.
- Pecanwood Golf & Country Club (Gauteng, South Africa): MWG implemented a turnaround strategy aimed at restoring the club's facilities and sustainability.
- Nkana & Mufulira Golf Clubs (Zambia): Wiltshire managed the installation of new irrigation systems and prepared Nkana Golf Course for the Zambian Open.
- Mumi Golf Club (Democratic Republic of Congo): MWG was appointed to build and manage a 9-hole course for the Mumi Mine plc.

Wiltshire's international experience spans across several countries, including Uganda, Madagascar, Nigeria, and Mauritius. His company, MWG, continues to offer golf management and consultation services, aiding golf course developments globally.

WHITE, BOB RHODESIA

Bob White had a distinguished career in Rhodesian golf, marked by impressive performances and recognition despite the challenges of serving in the Rhodesian bush war. Here's a summary of his career achievements:Another excellent career during Rhodesia's golden 70s, despite call-ups to fight in the Rhodesian bush war. Bob White was the 1972 Rhodesian Golfer Year; S Rhodesia 1964 – many caps; Rhodesia 1969 – many caps; 1967 nominated Rhodesian Sportsman of the Year.

His career Record included S. Rhodesia Amateur 2nd 1967; S. Rhodesia Open 1965, 2nd 1963; Mashonaland Amateur 1966, 72; Mashonaland Open 2nd 1966; Manicaland 1963; Eisenhower Individual 10th Bob White's contributions to Rhodesian golf during a challenging period are notable for his consistent performances and significant achievements.

WHITELAW, CLINTON JOHN (1970) SOUTH AFRICA

Clinton John Whitelaw had a noteworthy golf career with several significant achievements: Whitelaw won three tournaments on the Sunshine Tour, including the 1993 South African Open, while he won the 1993 California State Open. On the European Tour he won the 1997 Moroccan Open. However he was unable to repeat that performance in the following seasons due to a recurring lumbar spine injury.

In 2000, Whitelaw, with (5) professional wins effectively retired from tournament golf, playing only a few events on the Sunshine Tour each year through 2011. He is now an instructor and works as a head teaching professional in Sarasota, Florida.

Whitelaw's career was marked by notable victories and a strong presence on multiple tours, despite challenges from injury.

WILKES, BRIAN UNION SOUTH AFRICA

Brian Wilkes, the older brother of Trevor Wilkes, made a notable impact in professional golf, particularly on the European circuit.

One of the highlights of his career came in 1952 when he finished as the runner-up at the Belgium Open, just four strokes behind the winner,

Antonio Cerda. This performance established him as a competitive golfer in the European scene.

In 1966, Wilkes achieved a significant victory at the Dutch Open. He secured the win with a score of 279, finishing two strokes ahead of Brian Huggett. This win was a standout moment in his career and showcased his talent and skill on the European Tour.

Despite these notable achievements, detailed information about the rest of his career is less documented. Nonetheless, Wilkes' victories and competitive performances in key tournaments reflect a successful period in his professional golf career.

WILKES, TREVOR SOUTH AFRICA

Trevor Wilkes's golfing journey unfolded with remarkable achievements on the course and a commendable transition into golf administration. His career as a professional golfer began in the mid-1950s and was marked by an impressive string of successes across various tournaments.

During the years spanning from 1956 to 1968, Wilkes established himself as a formidable player. His victories included four notable tournament wins, with each triumph adding to his growing reputation. His consistency was evident through four runner-up finishes and twelve third-place spots, underscoring his ability to stay competitive across different events. Among his achievements, the Daks Tournament in 1956 and the Singapore Open in 1962 stood out, reflecting his versatility and skill. He also claimed victories at the Anglo-Africa Glass in 1958 and the Metropolitan Open in 1964. Despite his successes, he often found himself finishing just shy of the top spot, with second-place finishes at prestigious events such as the French Open, the Swiss Open, and the South African Open.

Wilkes's career was characterized by his resilience and competitive spirit, as evidenced by his twenty-seven top-five finishes in various tournaments. His performance in the South African Tour was particularly notable as he topped the Order of Merit, a testament to his consistent excellence throughout the season. His global presence was also significant, with representations at three World Cups, where he showcased his talent on an international stage.

Following his competitive playing career, Wilkes transitioned to a prominent role as a club professional. Starting at the Circle Golf Club from 1966 to 1970, he began shaping his post-competitive career. His expertise was further demonstrated at Randpark, Selbourne Park, and later at Linton Hall, where he served as Head Professional from 1998 to 2014. His role at Selbourne, continuing until 2014, highlighted his enduring commitment to the sport.

In addition to his roles in golf clubs, Wilkes also ventured into the retail sector from 1970 to 1986 before returning to golf. His contributions extended beyond the course as he produced an instructional video on golf, sharing his knowledge with a broader audience. His dedication to the sport was recognized with awards such as the KZN Golf Teacher of the Year in 2001 and honorary life membership of the PGA.

Trevor Wilkes's legacy is marked by his significant achievements on the golf course and his lasting impact on the sport through his roles in golf administration and instruction. His career reflects a deep passion for golf and a commitment to advancing the game.

WILLIAMS, ANNE UNION SOUTH AFRICA

Anne Williams was a prominent figure in South African golf during the late 1920s, distinguished by her remarkable achievements in a relatively short competitive career. Her standout performances left a significant mark on the sport.

Williams's career was highlighted by her success in the South African Ladies Championship, where she secured victories in both 1928 and 1929. These triumphs were particularly notable as they occurred during the early stages of her golfing journey and were the only times she competed in the championship. Her victories established her as a leading player of her time.

In addition to her successes at the national level, Williams also excelled in regional tournaments. She won the Eastern Province Ladies Championship in 1929 and added two more victories in the same championship in subsequent years. These achievements further cemented her reputation as a top golfer in the Eastern Province.

Anne Williams's exceptional talent and dominance in these key tournaments underscore her significant contributions to South African golf during her active years. Her legacy remains a testament to her skill and dedication to the sport.

WILLIAMS, BOB SOUTH AFRICA

Bob Williams made a significant impact on amateur golf through a career marked by notable achievements both domestically and internationally. His career was distinguished by multiple wins and competitive performances across various tournaments.

Williams's prominence in South African golf was cemented with victories at the South African Amateur Championship in 1961 and again in 1968, where he defeated Reg Taylor in the final. These wins were pivotal moments in his career, showcasing his skill and consistency.

In 1959, Williams was a key member of the winning South African team at the Commonwealth Tournament, further establishing his status in the amateur golf community. His contributions were not limited to individual successes; he also represented the Springbok team in 1959 and 1968, highlighting his role in South African golf at an international level.

His domestic achievements included triumphs at the Transvaal Amateur Championship, where he won in 1965 by defeating Hugh Baiocchi in the final. He was also the champion at the Transvaal Stroke-Play Championship in 1963 and 1965, and claimed victories at the East Rand Open Amateur in 1961 and 1966. His performance at the Transvaal Open Championship was noteworthy, as he was recognized as the leading amateur in 1959 and 1961.

Williams's accomplishments extended to other notable events. He was the leading amateur at the Dunlop Masters in 1960 and participated in the Inter-Cetre Team (Transvaal A) in 1960, 1961, and 1966. His competitive spirit was evident as he also finished as runner-up in several tournaments, including the Silver Vase in 1959, the Christmas Open in 1962, and the South Transvaal Closed Championship in 1971. He also had strong finishes in the Mozambique Open in 1963 and the Swaziland Open in 1969.

Bob Williams's career reflects a period of strong performance and dedication to amateur golf, marked by his significant achievements across various championships and tournaments.

WILLIAMS, CHRIS (1959) SOUTH AFRICA

Christopher Gary Williams has crafted an impressive and versatile career in professional golf, marked by significant achievements across various tours. His journey began on the Sunshine Tour, where he made a notable debut with a win at the Lexington PGA Championship in 1985. This victory set the stage for a successful run, as Williams went on to secure seven more wins on the Sunshine Tour, demonstrating his prowess on home soil.

One of his standout victories came in 1998 when he won the Masters of Malaysia and the PGA Championship, adding to his growing reputation. These wins were crucial highlights in his career, showcasing his ability to compete at a high level internationally.

Williams's career took an exciting turn when he transitioned to the Asian Tour, where he continued to build on his success. He secured victories in both the 1998 Masters of Malaysia and the PGA Championship, underscoring his adaptability and skill across different circuits.

Upon turning 50, Williams joined the European Senior Tour, where he found continued success. He claimed victories at the Aberdeen Brunei Senior Masters in March 2011 and the Shariah Senior Golf Masters in 2017. These achievements demonstrated his enduring talent and ability to compete effectively in the senior ranks.

Throughout his career, Williams accumulated a total of 17 professional wins, marking a distinguished journey across various tours. Despite a notable playoff loss to Tony Johnstone in 1989 at the Lexington PGA Championship, Williams's career remains a testament to his skill, adaptability, and longevity in the sport. His success across different tours and age groups highlights his remarkable versatility and enduring impact on the world of golf.

WULFF, GRAHAM UNION SOUTH AFRICA

Papwa Sewgolum and Graham Wulff 1959

Graham Wulff's journey with Papwa Sewgolum is indeed an extraordinary tale of compassion, equality, and breaking racial barriers during apartheid-era South Africa. Wulff's unwavering support for Papwa, a talented golfer of Indian descent, during a period of systemic racism speaks volumes about his character and belief in fairness.

Wulff, the man behind the creation of Oil of Olay, was one of the wealthiest and most open-minded men in Natal at the time. After witnessing Papwa's exceptional skill while caddying in his fourball, Wulff became a key figure in Papwa's career, encouraging him to pursue professional golf. He went far beyond mere words of encouragement—he provided Papwa with equipment, bought him a house, and even funded his international travel for competitions. Despite these efforts, Papwa faced relentless racial discrimination, being barred from playing in white professional tournaments.

In a bold move to break this racial stranglehold, Wulff arranged for a film to be made of Papwa demonstrating his reverse grip, sending it to the Australian PGA. Even with this display of undeniable talent, Australian authorities refused to grant Papwa a visa due to their own racial policies, which mirrored the apartheid system. Undeterred, Wulff continued his efforts to propel Papwa to the global stage.

One of the greatest challenges came when Wulff raised funds for Papwa to compete in The Open Championship at Muirfield. Though Papwa obtained a passport, South African Airways refused to sell tickets to black passengers. This did not stop Wulff. As the chairperson of the South African Aero Club, he purchased a Piper Comanche and personally flew Papwa across Africa to London. Despite an adventurous and at times challenging journey, they arrived, and Papwa competed at Muirfield, making the cut but unable to make a lasting impact.

The Dutch Open, however, was different. Papwa not only competed but won the tournament against a top field of players. This victory became a defining moment in South African golf, signaling that no racial barrier could suppress true talent. Upon his return to South Africa, Papwa was greeted by 100,000 people, a celebration that even the apartheid government could not ignore.

Wulff's generosity and commitment to Papwa were not driven by personal gain. When questioned, he consistently responded that his actions were born out of the belief that anyone with great skill, regardless of color, deserved an opportunity. His efforts gained international recognition, and he was later invited by the government of Indian Prime Minister Indira Gandhi to receive an honor for his support of Papwa.

This story exemplifies how individual actions, rooted in fairness and equality, can make an indelible mark on history, challenge societal norms, and inspire future generations. Wulff's unwavering support for Papwa not only helped a gifted golfer overcome significant obstacles but also contributed to changing perceptions during one of the darkest periods in South Africa's history.

WYNNE, BERNARD UNION SOUTH AFRICA

Bernard Wynne's career is a testament to his remarkable skill and influence in South African golf. Known for his flawless swing and precise hitting, Wynne made an indelible mark on the sport. His dominance began with the South African Amateur Championships, where he claimed victory in 1928, 1930, 1933, and 1938. Winning the South African Amateur four times, Wynne joined an elite group of golfers who have achieved such a feat.

In addition to his success in the South African Amateur, Wynne earned the Freddie Tait Trophy in 1929 and 1931. This accolade, awarded to the lowest-placed amateur in the South African Open, highlighted his exceptional performance in national competitions. His prowess extended to the Western Province title, which he won in 1932, further showcasing his competitive edge.

Wynne's achievements also included multiple victories in the E.P. Amateur from 1927 to 1929, with additional runner-up finishes in 1931 and 1934. He demonstrated his versatility and dominance by securing the E.P. & Border Amateur title in 1937, along with another runner-up spot that same year.

His exceptional skill and consistency set him apart from his peers, earning him accolades that stand alongside the greatest golfers of his era and he was inducted into the 2009 Southern Africa Golf Hall of Fame. His contributions to South African golf remain highly respected and celebrated.

Z

ZERMAN, MANNY SOUTH AFRICA

Manny Zerman's golf journey is marked by both exceptional achievements and profound personal reflections. He began his rise in the sport with a series of impressive performances in amateur golf. Notably, Zerman made history by being the only male golfer to finish runner-up at the U.S. Amateur in consecutive years, with a memorable encounter against his high school teammate, Phil Mickelson, in the 1990 championship match. His college years at the University of Arizona were equally distinguished, where he secured a third-place finish in the 1990 NCAA tournament behind Mickelson.

Zerman's amateur success continued to shine when he became the low amateur at the 1992 Masters. His performance at Augusta, where he shot rounds of 70 and 71, made him the first foreign-born player to achieve this honor. His ability to make the cut as the only amateur further demonstrated his talent and promise.

Turning professional, Zerman found success on the Asian and Canadian Tours, winning multiple tournaments and establishing himself as a formidable competitor. However, a pivotal moment in his career came at the 2000 Open Championship at St. Andrews. During this event, Zerman experienced a profound epiphany that led him to reassess his approach to professional golf. This moment of clarity prompted him to step away from competitive play, seeking a renewed relationship with the sport.

Today, Zerman channels his passion for golf into teaching at Miami Shores Country Club. He enjoys a more relaxed approach to the game, living on the same street and sharing his extensive knowledge with others. His story is a compelling blend of competitive excellence, personal growth, and enduring love for golf, reflecting his resilience and adaptability throughout his career.

YOUNG GUNS TO WATCH……………..

JARVIS, CASEY (2003) SOUTH AFRICA

Casey Jarvis has rapidly established himself as a formidable talent in professional golf with a string of notable achievements.

In 2023, Jarvis made headlines by shooting a remarkable 59 in the third round of the Stella Artois Players Championship. At just 19 years old, he became the second youngest golfer to achieve this impressive feat, underscoring his exceptional skill and promising future.

His success on the Sunshine Tour has been equally notable. Jarvis was named Rookie of the Year, a testament to his standout performance in his debut season. He further cemented his reputation by winning the Euram Bank Open in Austria, a victory that propelled him to the top of the Race to Mallorca season ranking and highlighted his ability to compete at a high level on an international stage.

Jarvis's amateur career was marked by significant accomplishments as well. In 2019, he was part of the South African team that won the Junior Golf World Cup in Japan, alongside notable teammates Samuel Simpson, Martin Vorster, and Christo Lamprecht. At just 16 years old in 2020, Jarvis clinched both the South African Stroke Play Championship and the South African Amateur Championship, showcasing his burgeoning talent early on. He continued his dominance with back-to-back wins at the African Amateur Stroke Play Championship in 2021 and 2022.

Before turning professional, Jarvis also made his mark on the Development Tour, winning on the Big Easy Tour, which set the stage for his professional career.

Turning professional brought new opportunities for Jarvis, and his performance in 2022 was impressive. He finished as a runner-up at both the South African PGA Championship and The Tour Championship, earning him the Rookie of the Year award. His achievements continued on the Challenge Tour, where he secured a second-place finish at the SDC Open, followed by runner-up positions at the Copenhagen Challenge and the D+D Real Czech Challenge, before eventually winning the Euram Bank Open.

Jarvis's early career achievements reflect his exceptional talent and potential, positioning him as a rising star in the world of golf.

LAMPRECHT, CHRISTO (2001) SOUTH AFRICA

Christo Lamprecht's career has been a story of notable achievements and impressive performances, both as an amateur and a professional.

In 2023, Lamprecht made headlines by becoming the third South African in six years to win The Amateur Championship. This significant victory not only showcased his talent but also earned him exemptions to the 2023 Open Championship, where he won the Silver Medal as the low amateur. His achievements in 2023 culminated with him rising to the top of the World Amateur Golf Ranking in September, further solidifying his place among the world's elite amateur golfers.

Standing tall at 6 feet 8 inches, Lamprecht has leveraged his physical advantage to excel on the golf course, making a significant impact with his powerful game.

Lamprecht's amateur career has been distinguished by several notable successes. In 2017, he became the youngest player ever to win the South African Amateur Championship, setting the stage for a series of impressive performances. The following year, he made his mark internationally by winning the East of Ireland Amateur, tying for eighth at the St Andrews Links Trophy, and placing 11th at the Junior Players Championship.

In 2019, Lamprecht demonstrated his competitive edge by finishing as the runner-up at both the Southern Cape Amateur Open and the All Africa Juniors Challenge. His prowess on the international stage was further highlighted when he led the South African team to victory in the Junior Golf World Cup.

The year 2021 saw Lamprecht as a key player in the Spirit International Amateur Golf Championship, where he tied for fourth place and captained the South African team to an eighth-place finish. His performance in 2022 included competing in the Arnold Palmer Cup, tying for sixth at the U.S. Amateur, and tying for ninth at the European Amateur Championship.

Lamprecht's college career at Georgia Tech, spanning from 2020 to 2024, was marked by significant achievements. He earned All-American honors and was a finalist for prestigious awards such as the Ben Hogan Award, Fred Haskins Award, and Jack Nicklaus Award. He won the Byron Nelson Award in 2023 and was named the GTAA Male Athlete of the Year and ACC Player of the Year.

Turning professional in May 2024, Lamprecht joined the Korn Ferry Tour, where he quickly made an impact by tying for fifth place in his fourth start. His transition to professional golf has been promising, building on the strong foundation of his amateur success.

Throughout his career, Lamprecht has represented South Africa and the International team in various team events, including the Junior Golf World Cup, Junior Presidents Cup, Spirit International, Eisenhower Trophy, and the Arnold Palmer Cup. His exceptional skill and leadership in amateur golf have set a strong precedent for his burgeoning professional career.

NIENABER, WILCO (2000) SOUTH AFRICA

Wilco Nienaber is known for his impressive distance off the tee and has made significant strides in professional golf. He won the 2021 Dimension Data Pro-Am, securing his first professional victory in a playoff against Henric Sturehed. This win advanced him to 135th in the Official World Golf Ranking.

Nienaber, who turned professional in mid-2019, has had a notable career. He represented South Africa at the 2018 Eisenhower Trophy in Ireland, finishing 3 under par individually. His European Tour debut came in December 2018 at the South African Open, where he made the cut with rounds of 69.

In early 2020, he finished as runner-up in the Limpopo Championship on the Challenge Tour and recorded his first top-10 on the European Tour with a 4th place finish at the Hero Open in August 2020.

Nienaber also made headlines in November 2020 at the Joburg Open, where he hit a record-setting 439-yard drive on the 4th hole, surpassing the PGA Tour season record at the time. He finished the tournament in second place, just two shots behind Joachim B. Hansen.

JOVAN REBULA (1997) SOUTH AFRICA

Jovan Rebula, Ernie Els's nephew, made significant strides in amateur golf before turning professional in June 2021. He became the second South African to win The Amateur Championship in 2018, which earned him exemptions to the 2018 Open Championship, 2019 Masters Tournament, and 2019 U.S. Open.

Rebula also showcased his leadership and competitive spirit in team events, serving as the captain of the South African team at the 2016 Eisenhower Trophy and playing as captain in the 2018 edition.

During his college years at Auburn University, he joined the Auburn Tigers men's golf team in 2016. His performance was impressive, consistently finishing in the top-10 at numerous tournaments across multiple seasons. Notably, he contributed to Auburn's SEC championship win in 2018 and represented the International team in the Arnold Palmer

Cup in 2018. Rebula also claimed victory over U.S. Amateur champion Viktor Hovland in the 2019 Georgia Cup.

POTGIETER, ALDRICH (2004) SOUTH AFRICA, AUSTRALIA

Aldrich Potgieter's golf career has been nothing short of extraordinary, characterized by impressive achievements and a swift ascent through the sport's ranks.

Potgieter's early exposure to golf began at the Louis Oosthuizen Junior Golf Academy, and his journey took him to Perth, Western Australia, where he joined Kingsway Christian College's Golf Program. His junior career was distinguished by a series of notable victories. In 2020, he dominated the South Australian Junior Masters, winning by an impressive nine shots. The following year, Potgieter continued his ascent by claiming victory at the Western Australian Amateur and finishing as the runner-up in the Australian Boys' Amateur.

2022 marked a particularly stellar year for Potgieter. He triumphed at the Nomads South African Juniors International, the Nomads SA Boys U19 Championship, and the Western Province Amateur. His most remarkable achievement came when he won The Amateur Championship at just 17 years old, making him the second youngest winner in the tournament's history.

In 2023, Potgieter continued to build on his success. He won the African Amateur Stroke Play Championship and competed in the Junior Invitational at Sage Valley. He also participated in the Georgia Cup, a match between the reigning U.S. Amateur champion and the British Amateur champion, further showcasing his burgeoning talent.

Turning professional in June 2023, Potgieter quickly made headlines on the Korn Ferry Tour. In January 2024, he became the youngest winner in Korn Ferry Tour history by securing victory at The Bahamas Great Abaco Classic. His triumph, with a two-stroke lead over Quade Cummins, highlighted his exceptional skill and promise as a rising star in professional golf who now qualifies for the PGA Tour.

Potgieter's rapid progression from a standout junior to a professional champion underscores his exceptional talent and suggests a bright future ahead in the world of golf.

VAN VELZEN, RYAN (2002) SOUTH AFRICA

Ryan van Velzen, a promising young South African golfer, earned his debut in "Africa's Major" by winning the Sunshine Tour Order of Merit delivered by The Courier Guy for the 2023/24 season. At just 22 years old, Van Velzen has already claimed three victories on the Sunshine Tour, including the 2023 Limpopo Championship, the 2023 Bain's Whisky Teams Challenge alongside Luca Filippi, and the 2024 Mediclinic Invitational.

The son of former touring professional Rob van Velzen, Ryan enjoyed a breakout 2023/24 season, highlighted by 11 top-10 finishes. Among these was a fifth-place finish in the FBC Zimbabwe Open, a tie for third in the South African PGA Championship, a tie for second in the DP World Tour co-sanctioned Investec South African Open, and seventh and second-place finishes in the European Challenge Tour co-sanctioned SDC Open and Bain's Whisky Cape Town Open, respectively. His exceptional consistency and performance throughout the season earned him the Sunshine Tour Order of Merit title and a DP World Tour card for the 2025 season.

This milestone year also marked his debut in the Major Championships, as he successfully qualified for both The PGA Championship and The Open, further establishing himself as one of South Africa's brightest young golfing talents.

WILLIAMS, ROBIN (2001) SOUTH AFRICA, ENGLAND

Robin Tiger Williams has quickly established himself as a rising star in professional golf, showcasing a remarkable blend of talent and early success. His career began with notable achievements in amateur golf, where he made significant strides on the international stage. Williams excelled in amateur competitions, winning the Jacques Léglise Trophy in both 2017 and 2018 while representing Great Britain & Ireland. His impressive performance continued with his participation in the Junior Ryder Cup in 2018, representing Europe. His amateur career also included a notable runner-up finish at the St Andrews Links Trophy in 2021, where he lost in a playoff to Jack Cope.

Turning professional in July 2021, Williams quickly made his mark on the golf scene. His professional career gained momentum with a win at the Altron Vusi Ngubeni Tournament in April 2023. This success was followed by a victory on the Big Easy Tour in August 2023. His achievements on the Sunshine Tour further highlighted his growing prowess, as he claimed victory at the Fortress Invitational in October 2023. Williams also demonstrated his competitive edge with a runner-up finish at the SDC Championship in March 2024, where he lost in a sudden-death playoff to Jordan Gumberg.

His impressive performance and consistent success earned him the Sunshine Tour Rookie of the Year title for the 2023-24 season. Williams' early achievements reflect his potential for a bright future in professional golf, showcasing his ability to compete at a high level across various tours.

Author's Notes

This golfing list highlights those who have made significant contributions to the sport and have had a major impact on African and global golf. Including a diverse range of players reflects the richness of African golf history and acknowledges the achievements of golfers from various backgrounds.

I trust my work through organizations such as *Finding the Fair Way Trust* and *The Little Golf Trust* to both uplift caddies and young girls, hopefully highlights my commitment to using golf as a vehicle for social change. Additionally, while my co-founding the South African Golf Museum and the Southern Africa Golf Hall of Fame was intended to preserve the game's history.

Recognition followed by Compleat Golfer with the 'Greatest Contribution to the Golf Industry' award, and my books, including When We Were Champions, PAPWA, and Africa Golf Who's Who, demonstrate my understanding of the sport's rich history and the importance of shining a light on those whose contributions have often been overlooked.

Finally, I would like to list my selection in the following categories, especially including those of colour as they are never included in such list.

AFRICA'S GREATEST GOLFERS[1]

Gary Player (ranked 2 – 9 majors)
Bobby Locke (ranked 1 – 4 majors)
Ernie Els (ranked 1 – 4 majors)
Nick Price *Zimbabwe* (ranked 1 – 3 majors)
Retief Goosen (ranked 3 – 2 majors)
Louis Oosthuizen (ranked 3 – 1 major)
David Frost (ranked 6 – 1 senior major)
Sid Brews (8 SA Opens)
Harold Henning (54 victories – Canada Cup)
Mark McNulty *Zimbabwe* (ranked 3 – 1 senior major)
Dale Hayes (ranked top 10 – World Cup – retired 28)
Charl Schwartzel (ranked 5 - 1 major)
Trevor Immelman (ranked 12 - 1 major)
Sewsunker 'Papwa' Sewgolum (77 victories)
Denis Watson *Zimbabwe* (1 senior major),
Rory Sabbatini (ranked 8),
Tim Clark (ranked 15),
Lewis Chitengwa *Zimbabwe* (World Junior, SA Amateur)
Branden Grace (ranked 10),
Cobie le Grange (ranked 15)

Other notable golfers:

Fulton Allem, Hugh Baiocchi, John Bland, Jock Brews, Bobby Cole, George Fotheringham, Hassan Hassanein *Egypt*, Simon Hobday *Zambia*, Denis Hutchingson *Southern Rhodesia*, Tony Johnstone *Zimbabwe*, Retief Waltman, Wayne Westner.

---

1   Sally Little (ranked 2, LPGA, 2-majors) is not included in this list as I only focused on male golfers.

AFRICA'S GREATEST WOMEN GOLFERS

Sally Little (ranked 2 – 2 majors)
Ashleigh (Simon) Buhai (ranked 18 - 1 major)
Maud (Titterton) Gibb *England, Scotland* (1 major)
Lee-Anne Pace
Alison Sheard (1 pre-major)
Rita (Levetan) Easton
Mrs E. Vernon
Jeanette Burd
Jacqui (Smith) Mercer
Gillian (Whitfield) Tebbutt

This list reflects the diverse achievements and contributions of women golfers from Africa, acknowledging their significant impact on the sport.

AFRICA'S GREATEST 'BLACK' GOLFERS

Sewsunker 'Papwa' Sewgolum
Hassan Hassanein *Egypt*
Lewis Chitengwa *Zimbabwe*
Vincent Tshabalala
James Lebbie *Sierra Leone*
Joe Dlamini *Swaziland*
Heinrich Bruiners
Sadi Onita *Uganda*
Ismail Chowglay
Robin Williams

This list acknowledges the significant contributions and achievements of Black golfers across Africa, highlighting their impact on the sport and their pioneering roles.

AFRICAN WORLD RANKINGS

Ernie Els - 1
Nick Price *Zimbabwe* - 1
Bobby Locke - 1 (unofficial)
Gary Player - 1 (unofficial)
Sally Little - 2
Retief Goosen - 3
Mark McNulty *Zimbabwe* - 3
Louis Oosthuizen - 3
Charl Schwartzel - 5
Sid Brews - 5 (unofficial)
David Frost - 6

AFRICAN MAJOR WINNERS

Gary Player - 9
Bobby Locke - 4
Ernie Els - 4
Nick Price *Zimbabwe* - 3
Sally Little - 2
Retief Goosen - 2
Louis Oosthuizen - 1
Charl Schwartzel - 1
Trevor Immelman - 1
Ashleigh (Simon) Buhai - 1
Maud (Titterton) Gibb *England* - 1

AFRICA SENIOR MAJOR WINNERS

Gary Player - 9
Bobby Verwey - 1
Denis Watson *Zimbabwe* - 1
John Fourie - 1
Mark McNulty *Zimbabwe* - 1
David Frost - 1
Simon Hobday *Northern Rhodesia* - 1
Ernie Els - 1
Retief Goosen - 1